LearningExpress®'s
GRE® TEST SUCCESS
In Only 5 Steps!

LEARNINGEXPRESS®'S

GRE® TEST
SUCCESS
In Only 5 Steps!

LEARNINGEXPRESS®

NEW YORK

Library of Congress Cataloging-in-Publication Data:
Reed, C. Roebuck (Celia Roebuck)
    LearningExpress's GRE test success in only 5 steps! / C. Roebuck Reed, Margaret Piskitel,
    and Maxwell Antor.—1st ed.
        p. cm.
        ISBN 1-57685-471-X
    1. Greaduate Record Examination—Study guides. I. Title: GRE test success in only 5 steps!. II.
    Piskitel, Margaret. III. Antor, Maxwell. IV. LearningExpress (Organization) V. Title.
    LB2367.4.R44 2003
378.1'622 — dc21   2003007667

Printed in the United States of America
9 8 7 6 5 4 3 2 1
First Edition

ISBN 1-57685-471-X

For more information or to place an order, contact LearningExpress at:
    55 Broadway
    8th Floor
    New York, NY 10006

Or visit us at:
    www.learnatest.com

About the Authors

C. Roebuck Reed is a CSET test preparation instructor and trainer from Burbank, California, as well as a writer and documentarian of educational and entertainment projects. She is the coauthor of *SAT Exam Success*.

Margaret Piskitel is an education specialist from New York, New York.

Maxwell Antor is a high school math teacher and math writer for *SAT Exam Success* and *GED Exam Success*. He is from Oakland, California.

Contents

Chapter 1   **About the GRE General Test**   1

Chapter 2   **Studying for the GRE Test**   13

Where Do I Start?   13

I Need a Plan   14

I Need a Place   16

Study Strategies   20

You Are Worth It: Motivational Techniques That Work   23

Learning Strategies and Test-Taking Strategies   26

Testing Psychology   29

Multiple-Choice Strategies   33

The Endgame   34

In a Nutshell   37

Chapter 3   **The GRE Analytical Writing Section**   39

Pretest   39

Introduction to the GRE Analytical Writing Section   43

About the Analytical Writing Section   44

The Analytical Writing Process   47

Present Your Perspective on an Issue—Attack Mode   47

Analyze an Argument—Attack Mode   59

Tips and Strategies for the Official Test   67

Practice   69

CONTENTS

Chapter 4   **The GRE Verbal Section**   **85**

Pretest   85

Introduction to the Verbal Section   92

What to Expect on the GRE Verbal Section   92

The Four Types of Verbal Section Questions   93

A Lesson a Day Makes the Test Go Your Way   96

How to Approach Analogies   97

How to Approach Antonyms   101

How to Approach Sentence Completion Questions   104

The Top Seven Steps for Answering Sentence Completion Questions   110

How to Approach Reading Comprehension Questions   112

Tips and Strategies for the Official Test   119

Practice   122

Chapter 5   **The GRE Quantitative Section**   **149**

Introduction to the Quantitative Section   149

The Two Types of Quantitative Section Questions   152

About the Pretest   152

Pretest   153

Arithmetic Review   159

Algebra Review   171

Geometry Review   184

Data Analysis Review   209

Tips and Strategies for the Official Test   216

Practice   219

Appendix   **Additional Resources**   **245**

About the GRE General Test

The Five Ws of the GRE General Test

Q: *Who takes the GRE General Test?*

A. Most applicants to graduate programs take the GRE General Test.

Q: *What is on the GRE General Test?*

A: There are three sections: Analytical Writing, Verbal, and Quantitative.

Q: *When is the GRE General Test offered?*

A: The test is offered year-round.

Q: *Where can I take the GRE General Test?*

A: The exam is offered at testing centers throughout the United States and the world.

Q: *Why do I have to take the GRE General Test?*

A: Graduate programs require you to take the GRE General Test in order to assess your logical and critical reasoning skills.

Why the GRE General Test?

Before you went to college, you may have taken the SAT exam or another college admissions test. Those exams are designed to help colleges determine whether or not prospective students can do the type and level of work they will encounter in postsecondary school. The Graduate Record Exam, or GRE test, like the SAT exam, is designed by Educational Testing Service® (ETS®), and if you took the SAT exam, the basic format of the GRE test will seem familiar to you. Instead of testing college-level skills as the SAT exam does, the GRE test assesses abilities required for success in graduate school—the ability to understand and convey ideas using language and the ability to apply basic math concepts to solve problems and analyze data. This is why many graduate programs want prospective students to take the exam. They want you to show that you can correctly analyze complex material, that you can think logically, and that you can clearly communicate your thoughts in written form.

Who Takes the GRE General Test?

Just as most colleges require prospective students to submit standardized test scores, so do many graduate programs want to see GRE test results. If you are applying to a master's or doctoral program, you may need to take the exam. Of course, test results are only a part of the information that schools use to make admissions decisions. Factors such as grades, recommendations, and professional experience are also considered. Universities know that some students who struggle with standardized tests perform very well in their graduate course work, and vice versa. Still, the GRE test is a crucial part of the admission process and one on which you naturally want to perform well.

Maybe you are thinking, "But I'm not applying to study English, and I don't plan to use math in my work; why do I have to take this kind of test?" Still, no matter what field of study you plan to undertake in graduate school, you must be able to think clearly and logically and to express your thoughts in writing. You must be able to read and comprehend complex, densely written works, because that is the sort of material you will encounter in graduate school. And, you must be comfortable manipulating numbers and using them to represent concrete objects or abstract ideas. For example, if you want to attain a master's degree in Urban Planning, you may need to perform tasks such as statistical analysis of traffic flow and projections of population trends. Social workers will need to use demographic numbers regarding the needs of underserved groups. Even aspiring filmmakers must confidently manipulate budget numbers. Just as college-level studies were a step up from the kind of work you did in high school, graduate school requires you to think in even more sophisticated ways. That is why graduate programs ask you to take the GRE test.

When Is the GRE General Test Offered?

In the United States and in most countries of the world, the GRE test is now administered as a computer-based test (CBT), also called a computer-adaptive test (CAT). You make an appointment to go to a testing center, where you take the exam. You may either choose a center from the list in the *GRE Registration Bulletin*, or ETS will assign you to the nearest location. The exam is offered during the first three weeks of every month, year-round.

You may want to avoid the November-through-January test-taking season when most exam takers sign up for testing. It is the busiest time of year for the test centers. However, if that is when you need to take the exam, you should sign up as early as possible to make sure you get the date and time you want. Remember, you want to leave ample time for ETS, the creators of the test, to report your scores to your chosen institution(s) by the deadline. The *Bulletin* contains information on how long it will take ETS to score your exam.

How Do I Sign Up?

First, you need to obtain the official *GRE Registration Bulletin*. You can do this by calling 609-771-7670 or by downloading the information from www.GRE.org. The actual registration can be done by mail, using the Authorization Voucher Request Form found in the *Bulletin* and sending a check or money order as payment. When you receive your voucher, you can contact Prometric Candidate Services Call Center at 800-473-2255 to schedule an appointment. If you prefer, you can call that number or an individual test center near you (see list at www.GRE.org) and register without a voucher, using a credit card. Finally, you can also register online with a credit card at www.GRE.org.

What Is on the Test?

The GRE General Test has three sections: Analytical Writing, Verbal, and Quantitative. The Analytical Writing portion of the exam tests your ability to understand and convey complex ideas, to analyze arguments, and to present a cohesive discussion of those ideas and arguments. It is always presented first. Next, the Verbal section tests your comprehension of the logical relationships between words, as well as your vocabulary and your ability to understand and think critically about complex written material. Finally, the Quantitative section tests your competence in arithmetic, algebra, and geometry, and your ability to apply these subjects within verbal contexts (word problems). There may also be an experimental section, presented within either the Verbal or the Quantitative section. You will not be able to tell which section is experimental, however, so it is important to work equally hard on all parts of the test. One thing you can be sure of is that the experimental section is always multiple choice, never essay.

How Long Is the Exam?

You are allowed four hours for the CBT/CAT exam, though the timed portion is 2 hours and 50 minutes. There is a ten-minute break after the Analytical Writing section and a one-minute break between the two subsequent sections. You may take as long as you need, within the four-hour limit, to familiarize yourself with the CBT/CAT format. You will want to familiarize yourself with the computer and the procedure before you

Seven Skills for Analytical Writing

- Critical thinking
- Logical organization
- Strong development of ideas
- Support of ideas with examples and evidence
- Appropriate word choice
- Clear and effective sentences
- Command of standard written English conventions

begin the timed portion of the test, so plan to allow yourself the full four hours so you do not add time pressure to any other stress you might be feeling.

There is a Help menu, which can be accessed at will, but if you need it during the actual exam, you will be using your precious minutes while the clock ticks. Be sure you have answered all your questions *about* the test *before* you start answering the actual test questions. That's what test preparation material is for, so use it. Also, there is a clock that appears onscreen during the exam, so you can see how much time you have left in any given section. If the clock bothers you, you can hide it. It will still come back onscreen to alert you when you have five minutes left in the section.

What Is a CBT/CAT?

A CBT/CAT is a test administered at a computer. CBT stands for Computer-Based Test and CAT stands for Computer-Adaptive Test. Special software enables the computer to accurately determine your proficiency at a given task within a short time. In brief, every test taker gets a different set of questions. The computer uses your performance on the early questions to give either easier or more difficult subsequent questions. This is the *adaptive* part. The harder the questions you successfully answer, the higher your score. You will find more information and specific strategies for CBT/CATs on the following pages.

What Is the Format of the Test?

Aside from the Analytical Writing section, which is covered next, there are two types of questions on the GRE General Test. The Verbal and Quantitative sections consist of multiple-choice questions. These sections are administered solely on the computer. There are two questions (commonly known as essay questions) on the Analytical Writing section, which require constructed responses. You will be required to type your responses on the computer, using a word-processing program.

What Is in the Analytical Writing Section

The Analytical Writing section was added to the GRE General Test in 2002. There are always two tasks, one in which you are required to write about your perspective on a particular topic and one in which you need to critique a given argument. You will spend 75 minutes on this two-part task, the first section to be presented on the exam.

Neither of these tasks requires any specialized content knowledge. Both are designed to test your ability to think critically, to organize and analyze arguments, and to clearly present your ideas in writing. In the

1. Your Thoughts on an Issue

Time: 45 Minutes

What you must do: think; organize your thoughts; support your thoughts with examples and reasons; clearly express in writing your thoughts, reasons, and examples.

2. Your Critique of an Argument

Time: 30 Minutes

What you must do: read and understand an argument; assess for completeness and accuracy the evidence provided and the claims made in the argument; clearly express in writing your assessment, using examples and evidence from the argument to make your points.

Analytical Writing chapter of this book, you will find useful approaches to thinking through, organizing, and writing your responses. It is important to prepare for this section of the exam.

You have 45 minutes to finish your response to the perspective, or issue, task. The question is presented as an opinion on a topic of general interest. You are asked to respond to this presentation of the issue, taking any viewpoint you desire. Your response is scored from zero to six, depending on how persuasively you present your views, use supporting examples, and offer evidence.

The second task asks you to analyze an argument that is presented to you. You must discuss the logical soundness of the argument itself, not whether you agree with the position taken. You have 30 minutes for this task, and it too will be scored from zero to six. Chapter 3, the Analytical Writing section of this book, contains all the information and strategies you need in order to do well on this part of the exam.

What Is on the Verbal Test?

The GRE Verbal test is a 30-minute section consisting of 30 questions. The verbal questions are of four types: analogies, antonyms, sentence completions, and reading comprehension questions.

Analogies test your vocabulary and your ability to identify relationships between pairs of words and the concepts they represent. There are simple techniques that can help you divine the relationships, and they are easily mastered with practice. You can learn and practice these techniques in Chapter 4 of this book.

The relationship of all **antonyms** is one of *opposition*. Basically, you need to pick the answer choice (i.e., the word or concept) that is most nearly the opposite of the question word. Like the analogies section, this is also a test of vocabulary and reasoning skills.

Sentence completion questions test your ability to follow the logic of complicated, though incomplete, sentences. Often the sentences are long and difficult to follow, and each contains either one or two blanks. Though

The Four Types of Verbal Questions at a Glance

1. *Antonyms* are opposites. You are given a word and asked to pick the word most nearly opposite it from the answer choices.

2. *Analogies* involve relationships between pairs of words. You are given a pair of words and asked to select the answer choice that contains a pair of words with a parallel relationship to the given words.

3. *Sentence Completion Questions* have complex sentences that contain either one or two blanks. You must construct a sentence's probable meaning using the sentence fragments as clues and then pick the answer that, when plugged into the sentence, conveys the correct meaning.

4. *Reading Comprehension Questions* follow prose passages. You must correctly answer questions about the implications and shades of meaning in each passage.

the vocabulary used is sometimes challenging, these questions primarily test your ability to use sentence fragments as context clues from which to construct meaning. Chapter 4 of this book discusses these clues and how to identify and use them to make logical predictions and successfully complete the sentences.

Reading comprehension questions may be the most familiar type of question on the GRE test. You are presented with a passage taken from the humanities or the social or natural sciences. You are then asked questions that test your understanding of what is stated or implied in the passage. Often, successfully answering the questions hinges, in some way, on your knowledge of vocabulary in the passage.

If it seems as though vocabulary is the common thread running through these question types, that is because it is. There are specific strategies for each of the verbal question types, and those will be discussed in the upcoming Verbal chapter of this book—but no matter how extensive your vocabulary already is, now is the time to start expanding it.

What Is in the Quantitative Section?

The good news for most test takers is that the GRE test doesn't test you on college-level math. Most of the math skills tested come from arithmetic, algebra, and geometry—the subjects you studied in secondary school. If you don't remember those skills, you should start brushing up on them right away; don't leave Chapter 5 to the last minute. This exam's twist on ordinary math is that you are asked to apply the basic skills within a larger context—that is, to reason quantitatively. Graduate programs want to know that you are comfortable working with numbers and using them to analyze the kinds of logical problems you are likely to encounter in your studies. For example, you will need to apply your quantitative skills to the analysis of data, including information presented in charts and tables. You will need to rapidly and accurately estimate more often than you will need to perform extensive calculations. That's a good thing, because you are not allowed to bring a calculator, or anything else, into the testing area. You won't really need a calculator, though. This section of the exam tests your ability to think about numbers and the things they represent and your ability

- High school arithmetic
- High school geometry
- High school algebra
- High school data analysis (probability, frequency, measurement, data representation, and interpretation)

to work logically with numbers; it does not test your number-crunching skills. There are 28 questions in the Quantitative test, and you will have 45 minutes to answer them. In Chapter 5 of this book you will find a wealth of tips, strategies, and practice questions.

Are There Strategies for GRE Test Success?

The most important strategies for doing well on the GRE General Test can be summed up as follows: Learn about the test and prepare for it. You already know those strategies; after all, you are reading these words. This gives you a head start on successful completion of the exam. When it comes to the GRE test, knowledge truly is power.

There are other strategies, however, that may be less obvious to you. Many of these are discussed at length in the chapters that follow, including specific strategies that apply to individual sections of the test.

ELIMINATE

One strategy that cannot be overemphasized is the strategy of elimination. The wonderful thing about multiple-choice questions is that the answer is always right there in front of you. You have only to identify the correct one. Ah, but there's the problem—what if you are not sure which one is the right answer? Think about it this way: If you are given four answer choices and you guess randomly, you have a one-in-four chance of guessing correctly. If you realize that one of the answers is wrong, you have improved your chances to one-in-three. If you can eliminate two of the wrong answers, you have a 50% chance of answering correctly. Therefore, when you encounter a question to which you are not sure you know the answer, the first step is to read all the answer choices and eliminate the ones that are obviously incorrect. Even though this is not a pencil-and-paper test, you should use the scratch paper supplied by the test center to note when you have eliminated an answer. Sometimes seeing the elimination process in this way helps you realize which answer is correct.

GUESS

Once you have ruled out as many incorrect choices as you can, you will have to guess. There is no penalty for guessing on the GRE test. If you guess incorrectly, one point is deducted from your possible raw score. If you leave the question blank, one point is deducted from your possible raw score.

You can see that you should first eliminate and then guess on all questions you don't know. If you can rule out even one wrong answer, your odds of guessing correctly have improved. The more wrong answers you eliminate, the more points you rack up. In fact, on many GRE test questions you can fairly easily rule out all but two possible answers. That means you have a 50% chance of being right even if you don't know the correct answer. In short, elimination of wrong answers followed by guessing is an important strategy for the GRE test.

UNDERSTAND THE COMPUTER-ADAPTIVE NATURE OF THE EXAM

Because of the computer-adaptive nature of the exam, you must answer each question as it appears on the screen. As you answer each question, the computer assesses your answer and then presents you with your next question, either a more difficult or an easier one, depending on whether or not you correctly answered the last one. That means you cannot go back to a previous question. You must answer each question as it is presented.

DO NOT SKIP ANY QUESTIONS

On questions you do not know, first eliminate wrong answers, then guess. The computer gives you two chances to finalize your answer. After you choose an answer and click on it, you click on the **Next** button. The computer then shows you an **Answer Confirm** button. When you click on that button, it is, as they say, "your final answer." The computer will score the question and choose your next one.

It is vital that you work extremely carefully on the initial questions in each section. Those are the questions that place you within a general score range. Think of a CBT/CAT as a TV game show, with points instead of money. The question types are the categories, and each category has difficult questions, which are worth more points or money, and easy questions, which are worth less. Every contestant starts with the same amount of points; that is, the computer initially thinks of you as having an average score. If you answer a question correctly, your score goes up and your next question is more difficult, giving you the opportunity to earn more points (not money, unfortunately). Every time you answer incorrectly, the computer gives you an easier question, which is ultimately worth less than the previous one. Even if you answer the subsequent question correctly, you are in a lower range than you were before. It could take you several questions to work back up to your previous level of difficulty, where the questions are worth more. That means it pays to take your time and double-check the first ten or so questions in each section, so the computer will place you in a higher range before it starts fine-tuning your score.

ANSWER ALL THE QUESTIONS

In addition to not skipping any questions, it is important to answer all the questions in each section. Try not to get stuck on any one question. If you don't know an answer, eliminate as many wrong answers as you can, then guess and move on. When your onscreen clock says five minutes, it's time to answer the remaining questions as quickly as you need to in order to answer them all. That's why you need to know how many questions are in each section (30 verbal and 28 quantitative). You may wish to practice answering questions, such as the ones found in Chapters 4 and 5, under time constraints matching the official exam conditions.

How Does the Scoring Work?

At the end of your CBT/CAT GRE General Test, you will have the opportunity to block your scores. If you choose to do so, your exam will never be scored, but ETS will report that you took the exam and chose not to have your scores reported. If you decide you want to see your scores for the test, you will be able to immediately see your unofficial scores for the Verbal and Quantitative sections only. However, once you choose to look at your scores, they will become part of your official GRE test record. The Analytical Writing section will not be scored by the computer, so it takes longer to receive your scores. Within about two weeks, complete scores are mailed to you and to your chosen recipients.

For the Verbal and Quantitative sections you will receive both raw scores and scaled scores. The raw scores reflect the number and difficulty level of questions you answered correctly. ETS then converts them to scaled scores, the scale being from 200 (an indicator that you showed up for the test) to 800 (meaning that you answered all questions correctly), reported in increments of ten points. You may recognize this scoring scale from the SAT exam. Also on your score report is the percentage of test takers who scored below you. For example, you might receive a raw score of 60, a scaled score of 640, and a "percentage below" of 91. That would mean you answered approximately three-fourths of the questions correctly, your scaled score is 640, and 91% of other test takers scored below you. Following at the end of this section is a chart showing potential raw scores and how they translate into both scaled scores and percentages.

The Analytical Writing questions are scored differently. Two professionally trained, unbiased readers read each of your two responses. Each reader scores each response on a scale of zero to six. The two readers' scores for each response are then averaged, unless they differ by more than one point. If that is the case, a third reader will score the essay to resolve the differences. After each of your essays has been scored and averaged, your two essays' scores are averaged and rounded up to the nearest half-point. You then receive that score as a single Analytical Writing score.

How Many Times May I Take the GRE General Test?

You may retake the exam as often as five times in a 12-month period. All scores, other than those you choose to cancel before looking at them, will be retained for a five-year period, and all will be reported whenever you request your scores be sent out.

How to Use this Book

Congratulations on having the foresight and motivation to prepare for the GRE test. Those qualities are vital elements of success in any endeavor, including in graduate school. Throughout this book you will find strategies to help in your preparation for the exam. Chapter 2 is devoted to proven study methods and test-taking tips that will improve your scores.

The single most crucial thing you can do to prepare is to familiarize yourself thoroughly with the exam before the test day comes. This will enable you to accurately assess your strengths and address your weaknesses in all three sections of the test. When you register for the GRE test, ETS will send you a CD-ROM, which contains GRE test POWERPREP. This software simulates actual testing conditions and uses the word processing program ETS has written for those who choose to compose their Analytical Writing essays on the computer instead of on paper. POWERPREP can also be downloaded from www.GRE.org/pprepdwnld.html.

ETS also sells a book called *Practicing to Take the General Test, 10th Edition.* This book contains questions from actual past GRE General Test editions, as well as a review of the math concepts tested on the exam

Ranges of Raw-to-Scale Score Conversion and Percents Below

Raw Score	Verbal Scaled Score	Verbal % Below	Quantitative Scaled Score	Quantitative % Below
68–76	730–800	99		
59–67	630–720	89–98		
50–58	540–620	70–88	720–800	75–94
41–49	450–530	45–69	630–710	57–74
32–40	370–440	22–44	530–620	36–56
23–31	300–360	5–21	410–520	14–35
14–22	230–290	1–4	270–400	1–13
0–13	200–220	1	200–260	1

and sampling of Analytical Writing essays with reader comments, which yield insights into the way the essays are read and scored. It is a good idea to purchase and carefully study this book, using it for practice and looking for patterns of question types. You can purchase it online at www.GRE.org/book.html. It will be worthwhile, in fact, to go to www.GRE.org, the official website, and spend some time exploring and mining it for useful information. Among the gems you will find are two lists of topics, from which ETS selects the actual Analytical Writing prompts. Don't get too excited, though—there are hundreds of potential topics on the lists. You can't prepare for each one you might encounter. Still, it is smart thinking on your part to peruse the lists.

There are many other study guides and test-prep books on the market. For the most part, they contain practice tests, not lessons, as in this book. However, you may glean the occasional nugget of useful information from them. You can also purchase more specialized books to help you in preparing for specific sections of the test. Because vocabulary is one of the primary skill or knowledge sets tested on the GRE test, improving your vocabulary is one of the most productive things you can do to prepare for the exam. LearningExpress publishes several practice books specifically targeted to the GRE test:

Analytical Writing and Verbal
501 Vocabulary Questions
501 Word Analogy Questions
501 Synonym and Antonym Questions
501 Writing Prompts
Vocabulary and Spelling Success in 20 Minutes a Day, 3rd edition

Quantitative
501 Algebra Questions
501 Geometry Questions
501 Quantitative Comparison Questions
Algebra Success in 20 Minutes a Day
Geometry Success in 20 Minutes a Day

Practicing with these study aids is an excellent way to work on your word power and strengthen your math skills. There are more resources listed in Appendix A. If you have taken the GRE General Test before but were not satisfied with your scores, you can improve them with repeat testing, *but only if you prepare.* You have made a good start simply by reading this book. The next chapter of this book, Studying for the GRE Test, will help you stay on the right path.

The Big Picture

In summary, there are three sections of the GRE test: the Analytical Writing section, the Verbal section, and the Quantitative section. The Analytical Writing section, which is your first section, is designed to test your ability to think critically and to convey your thoughts in writing. The Verbal section tests your knowledge of words, your ability to recognize the relationship between words and concepts, and the ease with which you can work with the component parts of sentences. The Quantitative section assesses your knowledge of basic mathematical concepts and your ability to apply these concepts within verbal contexts.

Read on for specific lessons and practice on the type of questions encountered on the GRE General Test, and get started on the journey toward a top score and a bright academic future!

CHAPTER

2 ▶

Studying for the GRE Test

▶ Where Do I Start?

Chances are, you don't have an unlimited amount of time to prepare for the GRE General Test. You have a life outside your plans for graduate school that may include work and family obligations. Or you may already be in school. How can you maximize the study time you *do* have? *To study* means to give one's attention to learning a subject; to look at with careful attention. Notice that the word *attention* comes up twice in this definition. How you study is as important as how much time you spend studying.

To study effectively, you need to focus all your attention on the material, so the preparation time you have must be quality time. This section of the book will help you determine which study strategies are right for you. It also will provide you with techniques for overcoming the two most common roadblocks to successful studying: anxiety and distraction.

Visualize Your Future

You have likely researched the graduate programs that you are interested in. Perhaps you are attracted to the work of certain faculty members and have decided you want to study with them. Maybe you know the reputations of a particular program and want the career opportunities it can offer. You may desire to go to a

The actor and comedian Jim Carrey is reported to have written himself a check for a million dollars when he was still struggling and broke. He carried that check in his wallet for years. Whenever he felt discouraged, he would take out the check and look at it. He visualized receiving a million-dollar check for his work. Jim Carrey made that million-dollar paycheck part of his reality, and reality added a few zeros for him.

school close to where you live. If you have not investigated your options, now is the time to do that. You can search online for information, contact schools directly, and ask reference librarians to help you search.

As you narrow your options to one or a few schools, you will want to learn as much about these particular program(s) as you possibly can. Perform Internet searches for all faculty members in a program to learn more about their particular areas of interest. This can help you make your decision. If you have already decided on a school, having knowledge of faculty interests and publications will give you an edge when you submit application materials and go for interviews.

If at all possible, visit the campus(es). In addition to helping you choose wisely, the information you gather is valuable input to help you form a visual image of yourself in graduate school. Visualization is a powerful tool. It motivates you to work toward your dreams, and that helps make your dreams a reality.

Once you know where you want to be, spend a little time envisioning yourself there. What are you doing? Giving a presentation? Engaging in conversation with an admired professor? Listening to an inspired lecture? Once you have created an image of yourself, go over your vision, keep it in your mind, and use it to reinforce your resolution to study. It can be hard to stick to a study plan. There are often other things you would rather be doing. Obstacles present themselves. You may be overwhelmed at times with the size of the task or you may be anxious about your chances for success. These are all common problems and they can all be overcome. This book will show you how.

▶ I Need a Plan

You already know a great deal about studying. You couldn't have gotten this far—to the doorstep of graduate school—without effective study skills. The following pages will help you fine-tune your study methods so you can make efficient use of your time.

The key to success in this endeavor, as in so many, is to take things one step at a time. Break this giant task down into manageable pieces. Your first step in successful studying is to think about your study plan.

What Should I Study?
First, you must decide what you need to study. You may want to start with a practice test to help you assess your strengths and weaknesses. Then make a list of each type of question and how well you scored on it. Analyze your list. What kinds of questions did you miss? What are the patterns you see? Do you need to work on data analysis? Charts and graphs? Do analogies throw you for a loop? Are you organizing your thoughts well

and conveying them clearly in your practice analytical essays? In other words, are you saying what you are trying to say? It is hard to accurately judge your own writing. Get feedback from someone whose opinions you trust and respect. Most important, don't forget to give yourself credit for all the answers you got right.

Once you are aware of what you know and what you still need to work on, you can effectively prioritize whatever study time you have available. Remember, no matter how you scored, no matter what areas you need to work on, you will get better with practice. The more you study and the more effectively you work, the better you will score on the actual exam.

How Do I Find the Time to Study?

Now is the time to create a realistic study schedule. You might be thinking that your life is too full without adding study time, too. But maybe you have more time available than you think. Think about your typical daily and weekly activities and determine when you have free time to devote to studying. Don't forget the short stretches, the ten minutes here, the fifteen minutes there. Sometimes you can do your best studying in short bursts. Now ask yourself what is more important to you in the long run than achieving your goals. Your life may seem quite full, but there is bound to be some time you spend at less productive activities, such as watching TV, that could be better spent to make your dreams come true. Remember, your future hangs in the balance. That's what you are really deciding here, your future, not just your agenda for a few Sunday nights.

I Deserve a Reward

One way you can help yourself stay motivated is by setting up a system of rewards. Write down a list of things you enjoy; they will be your rewards. For example, if you keep your commitment to study for an hour in the evening, you get to watch your favorite television show. If you stay on track all week, you can indulge in a Sunday afternoon banana split. Only *you* know what will keep you on task.

What Is My Style?

Another way to make your study time more effective is to think about how you learn best. Everyone has certain modes that he or she employs to make it easy to learn and remember information. Is your mode visual, auditory, kinesthetic, or a combination of two or all three? Here are some questions to help you determine your dominant learning style(s).

1. *If you have to remember an unusual word, do you*

   a. "see" the word in your mind?

   b. repeat the word aloud several times?

   c. trace or write the letters with your finger?

2. *When you meet new people, do you remember them by*

   a. their actions and mannerisms?

   b. their names (faces are hard to remember)?

   c. their faces (names are hard to remember)?

3. *In class, do you like to*

   a. take notes, even if you do not reread them?

   b. listen intently to every word?

   c. sit close and watch the instructor?

A visual learner would answer **a, c,** and **c.** An auditory learner would answer **b, b,** and **b.** A kinesthetic learner would answer **c, a,** and **a.**

A visual learner may have the following additional characteristics: She likes to read and is often a good speller. She often finds it hard to follow oral instructions, or even to listen, unless there is something interesting to watch, too. When a visual learner studies, she can make good use of graphic organizers such as charts and graphs. Flashcards will appeal to her and help her learn, especially if she uses colored markers. It will help her to form images in her mind as she learns a word or concept.

An auditory learner, by contrast, likes oral directions. He may find written materials confusing or boring. He often talks to himself and may even whisper aloud when he reads. He likes being read aloud to. An auditory learner will want to say things aloud as he studies. He could even make tapes for himself and listen to them later. Oral repetition is an important study tool for him. Making up rhymes or other oral mnemonic devices will help him, and he may like to listen to music as he works.

A kinesthetic learner likes to stay on the move. She finds it difficult to sit still for a long time and will often tap her foot and wave her hands around while speaking. She learns best by doing rather than observing. A kinesthetic learner may want to walk around as she practices what she is learning. Using her body helps her remember things. Taking notes is an important way of reinforcing knowledge for the kinesthetic learner, as is making flashcards.

It is important to note that most people learn through a mixture of styles, although they may have a distinct preference for one style over the others.

▶ I Need a Place

So far, you have gathered information. You know what you need to learn. You have thought about techniques to help you absorb what you are learning. Now it's time to think about where you are going to work and what kinds of things will enhance your learning experience.

Visual Learner
- Form images in your mind.
- Use color codes.
- Use flashcards.

Auditory Learner
- Say things out loud.
- Record tapes for yourself.
- Explain things to others.

Kinesthetic Learner
- Write it down.
- Walk or move around as you study.
- Act it out.

You know that in order to do your best work, especially when you are studying, you need to be focused, alert, and calm. Your undivided attention must be on the task at hand. That means you have to set up your study time and study place with a lot of forethought.

Five Questions about the Setting

1. *Where do I like to work? Where do I feel comfortable and free from distractions?*

If you have a desk in your living space, you may be used to studying there. If it's set up for your comfort and convenience (with all your study materials at hand) and if it is well-lit, then it's an obvious choice for you.

Maybe you usually work at the dining room table or the kitchen counter. Sometimes it can be hard to avoid distractions in shared living areas. If you share a living space, you may find it best to study away from home, perhaps at the local library or coffee shop. If you are currently in school, remember that you are adding your GRE test preparation time to your usual study schedule. Try to anticipate if this might create any scheduling conflicts with your normal study space.

2. *What time of day is best for me to study? When am I most alert and focused? Are there potential conflicts with other duties or family members that need to be worked out?*

If you are a morning person, maybe it makes sense for you to get up an hour or so earlier while you are preparing for the GRE test. That is often a time of relative quiet, when you can work without interruptions.

If you can't think well in the early morning, there will be another time of day or night that you can schedule as your GRE test study time. Just be sure you don't push yourself to stay up extra late to study. Study time is only productive if you are focused. You are not focused when you are tired or sleepy.

It's a good idea to set a regular and consistent time for study if you can, and to make those around you aware that this is your study time. You can expect more support for your efforts if you let family

When Can I Study?

Use the following table to determine the times during the week that are available to you for studying. Be sure to respect your sleep time.

	SUNDAY	MONDAY	TUESDAY	WEDNESDAY	THURSDAY	FRIDAY	SATURDAY
6:00 A.M.							
7:00 A.M.							
8:00 A.M.							
9:00 A.M.							
10:00 A.M.							
11:00 A.M.							
12:00 P.M.							
1:00 P.M.							
2:00 P.M.							
3:00 P.M.							
4:00 P.M.							
5:00 P.M.							
6:00 P.M.							
7:00 P.M.							
8:00 P.M.							
9:00 P.M.							
10:00 P.M.							

members and friends know you are working to achieve a goal and that you need to stay focused. Be sure to let them know you appreciate their support when you receive it.

There is one time slot each week that is the very best time to prepare for the GRE test, especially in the weeks leading up to the test. That is the day of the week and time of day you have scheduled to take the exam. If you practice taking the test and you work on improving your skills on that day and at that time, your mind and your body will be ready to operate at peak efficiency when you really need them. For example, if you are scheduled to take the GRE test on Saturday morning, get into the habit of studying for the test during the actual testing hours.

3. *How do sounds affect my ability to concentrate? Do I prefer silence? Does music enhance my concentration?*

Some people need relative quiet in order to study. Noises distract them. If you are one of these people, you know it by now, and you have a repertoire of strategies that help you achieve the level of silence you need. You probably already know that earplugs can be a real blessing.

Maybe you don't mind a little noise. Lucky you. Perhaps you even like music playing in the background while you study. Research has shown that the classical music of Mozart enhances math performance. Similar results have not been shown for other kinds of music, but, again, you know best what works for you.

The important thing is to be aware of the effect sound has on your ability to concentrate. It doesn't do any good to sit in front of the books and sing along with your favorite CD. Any temporary sacrifices you make—musical or otherwise—for the GRE test will be more than worth it when you achieve your goals.

4. *Is the light right? Does my study space have adequate lighting?*

Study lighting needs to be bright enough to read by comfortably. Lighting that is too dim can cause eyestrain and headaches. It can also make you sleepy. Lighting that is too bright, though, can make you uncomfortable and make it difficult to relax and focus. You can't control the lighting in many situations, including in the exam room itself, but you can create a lighting situation that is right for you when you study.

Experts say the best light for reading comes from behind, falling over your shoulder onto your book. If that isn't a possibility for you, then at least make sure the light falls onto your books, not into your eyes.

5. *What about food? Should I snack while I study? If so, on what?*

Only you can answer these questions. Does food energize you, or does it slow you down while you digest? If you are not sure, pay some attention to how your brain and body feel after eating. After a big meal, many individuals feel sluggish and sleepy, as the blood from their brains and muscles goes to their stomachs to aid in digestion. If the only time you have to study is right after dinner, you may want to pass on the second helpings and especially on dessert.

On the other hand, it is hard to concentrate fully when you are hungry. If it has been awhile since dinner, you may want to snack. Generally speaking, snacks are fine. There are two categories of foods you may want to avoid, however. Those are sugary snacks (e.g., candy, cookies, and ice cream) and caffeinated drinks (e.g., coffee, colas, some teas).

Sugar surges into your bloodstream quickly, making you feel energized, but it leaves your bloodstream just as quickly and you experience a rebound effect of feeling more tired than ever. Try keeping track of this sometime. See if you can learn how long it takes you to crash after a dose of sugar.

Caffeine is another trickster. In moderation, it produces an effect of alertness, but it is easy to cross the line into being jittery, and that's not a good mode for productive studying. Also, if you consume caffeine in the evening, it can interfere with a good night's sleep, leaving you feeling unrested in the morning. It's best to stay away from caffeinated drinks past lunchtime.

A Solid Foundation

Okay, so now what? You have taken a pretest. You have a list of what you want to study. You know what times of the day and the week are available to you for studying. You have a good idea about where you will study and what kind of environment you want to create for yourself. You have some ideas for how to motivate yourself and keep yourself on track. That's a good beginning. Now it's time to get more specific.

▶ Study Strategies

You may be tempted to skip ahead to Chapter 3 in order to dive into the practice sections. Don't do it— the study strategies explained in this section are absolutely necessary to understand prior to moving ahead.

The Right Tools

You have this book, which will give you a solid foundation of knowledge about the GRE test. You may also want to use *GRE Practicing to Take the General Test,* the best source for retired GRE test questions. You will also want to assemble some other study tools and dedicate them to your GRE test preparations:

- a good dictionary, such as *Merriam-Webster's Collegiate Dictionary, 10th Edition*
- a notebook or legal pad dedicated to your GRE test work
- pencils (and a pencil sharpener) or pens
- one or more colors of highlighter
- index or other note cards
- paper clips or sticky note pads for marking pages
- a calendar or personal digital assistant (PDA)

Have fun selecting your tools. Buy the type of pens you like the most. Select your favorite colors. You want to look forward to your time with these materials. They can be a little reward for doing your work. Even the feel of a special pen in your hand will give you a motivational boost when you sit down to work.

Information Gathering

You are already working on this step. Remember that the GRE test is given throughout the year, not only on a few test dates. You can go online to www.GRE.org to obtain a copy of the official *GRE Registration Bulletin.*

You can look at the Bulletin online or order a copy. In the *Bulletin*, you will find answers to the following questions:

- Where can I take the GRE test?
- How do I register?
- When should I register?
- How much does it cost?
- What do I need to bring with me to the exam?
- What kinds of questions are on the GRE test?

You already know a bit about the kinds of questions on the GRE test, and subsequent sections of this book will discuss these questions in detail and give you more study tips and strategies for answering them correctly. Answers to the other questions come from the official *GRE Registration Bulletin* and from the testing centers listed in the *Bulletin*. Seek out that information right away—you will need it as you set up your study plan.

The Study Plan

You have thought about how, when, and where you will study. You have collected your tools and gathered essential information. Now, you are ready to flesh out your study plan. Here are the steps:

1. *If you have not done so already, take a practice test.* You can use the questions in Chapters 3, 4, and 5 of this book or take one or more of the tests in *GRE: Practicing to Take the General Test*. To create an effective study plan, you need to have a good sense of exactly what you need to study.

2. *Analyze your test results.* No matter what your results are, don't worry about them. You are committing to this study plan because you are going to improve your score. Fear and worry are your enemies here; let go of them. Just look at each question as you score it. Why did you answer that question correctly? Did you know the answer or were you guessing? Why did you miss that question? Was there something you needed to know that you didn't know? If so, what was it? Make a list of the things you need to know and how many questions you missed because you did not know them. Think of how your score will improve as you learn these things.

   Did you misunderstand any of the questions? This is actually a common problem with the reading comprehension portion of the GRE Verbal test. The test makers at ETS write complex, grammatically precise questions. The language and style can seem difficult and unfamiliar. It is easy to be confused, and if you don't understand a question, your chances of answering correctly aren't good. The good news is that, with practice, you will become much better at understanding these kinds of questions. If misreading was the reason you missed some of the questions, that's actually a good thing. Your preparation time is going to start paying off right away.

   Did you make a careless mistake on any of the questions? Careless mistakes include marking the wrong bubble and simply misreading or mistaking one word or number for another. If you are making careless mistakes, you need to work on focusing. Again, this gets easier with practice.

3. *Make a list of your strengths and weaknesses.* This will point you in the right direction. Use your analysis of why you missed the questions you missed. Now you know what specific math, verbal, and logic

skills you need to work on, and you know what test-taking skills you need to improve. Don't forget to congratulate yourself for the things you did well.

4. *Determine your time frame.* Decide how much time you can devote each day and each week to your GRE test preparations. Use the chart you filled out previously. How many weeks are there until the test? Be realistic about how much time you have available—life will go on, with all its other demands—but don't forget to note when you have a few extra minutes. You will learn how to make good use of small windows of opportunity. Once you know how much time you have, estimate how long you need to work on each specific task you have set for yourself. You may find it useful to break down the Verbal section by question type (antonyms, analogies, sentence completions, critical reading) and the Quantitative section by subjects (arithmetic, geometry, algebra, and data analysis). You may have to prioritize your work in various areas, depending on the amount of time you have to prepare and the areas in which you can most improve your score.

5. *Prioritize your study plan.* "Learn everything by April 1" is not a useful plan. The first priority on your study plan should be to thoroughly go through this book so you can absorb the study tips and strategies for the exam. "Know your enemy" is the first and most important strategy in warfare, and, in this case, your testing weaknesses are your enemies. Studying and strategizing are the weapons that will enable you to defeat them.

Spend a few days, or even a week or two, going through this book. It will help you flesh out your study plans. For instance, you will learn in the Verbal section that a good vocabulary is one of your most important assets on the GRE test. You may decide that spending twenty minutes every day with a copy of LearningExpress's *Vocabulary and Spelling Success in 20 Minutes a Day* is a top priority for you. (By the way, don't worry about spelling for the GRE test; it's the vocabulary that is crucial.)

Let's say, for example, you have seven weeks until your test date. The following table shows one way you could set up your study schedule.

WEEK	STUDY SCHEDULE
Week One	Learn about and practice antonyms and analogies. Work on vocabulary.
Week Two	Learn about and practice critical reading and sentence completion questions. Work on vocabulary!
Week Three	Review Analytical Writing topics (go to www.GRE.org/pracmats.html), and practice writing essays.
Week Four	Practice Analytical Writing essays.
Week Five	Review sample Quantitative test questions. Find the kinds of questions you miss and determine which skills and processes you need to study. Practice.
Week Six	Continue Quantitative review and practice.
Week Seven	Review any question types you don't understand. Practice Analytical Writing. Get lots of rest!

Six Steps to Successful Studying

1. Take a practice test.
2. Analyze your results.
3. List your strengths and weaknesses.
4. Determine your time frame.
5. Prioritize your study plan.
6. Study!

Naturally, if you have longer than seven weeks to prepare, your weekly schedule will be divided differently. (And good for you, for starting ahead of time!) You may want to work on all your skills each week, making progress simultaneously on all fronts. That's fine too. Adjust the schedule accordingly. Your schedule will also be different if you have less than seven weeks, or if you are a whiz with numbers but have trouble with analytical writing.

6. *Just Do It!* Stick to your plan: It's easy to say but hard to do. How can you stay motivated? How do you follow your schedule so that you don't fall behind? How do you keep from thinking about other things when you are supposed to be working? These are really big questions, and there are no easy answers. Here are some tried and true techniques for self-motivation. You have to see what works for you.

▶ You Are Worth It: Motivational Techniques That Work

Whenever you find yourself tempted to give up your hard work for an hour or two of entertainment, remind yourself that many people never reach their goals because they seem so far away and difficult to achieve. It is important that you break down your GRE test preparation into small, manageable steps. It's also important to keep in mind why you are working so hard.

Remember your visualization about graduate school? The more often you practice that visualization, the more real it becomes to you. The more real it is, the more clearly you will see that your goal is within your grasp. Just stick to your plan: one day at a time.

Sometimes your study plans are derailed for legitimate reasons: You get sick; a family member needs your help; your teacher or boss assigns a project that takes more time than you expected. Life happens. Don't let it discourage you. Just pick up where you left off. Maybe you can squeeze in a little extra study time later. Keep working toward your goal.

Break It Down
Many individuals get discouraged when the task seems too big. It seems they will never get to the end. That's why it's a good idea to break down all big undertakings, like this one, into smaller, manageable bits. Set small goals for yourself. For example, "This week I will work on mastering analogies." "Mastering analogies" is a

Motivation Technique

We all need positive feedback. When you could use some motivational help, say the following out loud:

- My goal is to _____ (be specific) _____ .
- I am working to achieve my goal.
- I will succeed because I am working toward my goal.

much more manageable task than "preparing for the GRE test." Establish positive momentum and maintain it, one step at a time. That's how you get where you want to go.

Because You Deserve It

Don't forget to reward yourself for your progress. Your daily reward can be a small one. "When I finish this chapter, I'll make myself some lemonade." Your weekly reward might be more grand. "If I keep to my study plan every day this week, I'll buy that CD I want." Your big reward, of course, is being able to live out your dreams, the ones in your visualization.

You Are Not Alone

Another way to motivate yourself is to get other people to help you. Everybody likes being asked for help—it makes them feel important, especially when they are being approached for their expertise in a particular area.

You may want to form a study group with one or more of your friends. Maybe analogies just come naturally to you, but you struggle with algebra. Chances are you have a friend who is a math whiz but who may need help with writing strategies. You could agree to get together once a week or so for a tutoring and drilling session. You take one subject to study and explain, and your friend explains a different subject to you. Now you are (a) benefiting from your friend's expertise, (b) consolidating what you know by explaining it to someone else, (c) having more fun than you would on your own, and (d) helping yourself (and your friend) stay motivated to study.

Maybe a family member or a roommate could help you, too. If you are working on vocabulary, why not make up some flashcards with tough vocabulary and ask your roommate or a family member to work with you?

Thought Police

Finally, as you struggle to stay motivated, it helps to check in periodically with your thoughts—the things you sometimes find yourself thinking when you should be focusing on your work. A good time to check your thoughts is when the time comes to study. If you are thinking, "Oh boy, I'll have that last piece of chocolate when I finish this!" or "Yale has never seen an art history student like me," you are in good shape. If you are thinking, "That TV show I really like is on now," or "I could get in a few hoops before dark," you could be headed for trouble. It's not that there's anything wrong with television or basketball; it's just that you promised yourself you would work right now. Often, just noticing those deviant thoughts is enough to keep them in check. "Good try," you think to yourself, "but you have other commitments!" If you are still tempted to blow a hole in your schedule, sit down and think for a moment about why you are working so hard. Use your visualization. Promise yourself a bigger reward when you finish your work. You can do it because you *want* to do it. This is the person you want to be—disciplined, focused, and successful.

Finally, you may need to "trick" yourself into a study mode. Start with something easy, such as, "I'll just do a few flashcards." Often, starting with a quick and easy task will ease you into the work and motivate you to continue with your self-assigned task of the day.

Take Care of Yourself

You may have noticed that the last thing on the sample weekly chart is "get lots of rest." During the last few days before the exam, you should ease up on your study schedule. The natural tendency is to cram. Maybe that strategy has worked for you with other exams, but it's not a good idea with the GRE test. First, the GRE General Test is basically a three-hour test (think marathon!), and you need to be well rested to do your best. Second, cramming tends to raise your anxiety level, and your brain doesn't do its best work when you are anxious. Anxiety produces a fight-or-flight response that sends blood away from the brain to the arms and legs, in case we need to defend ourselves or run away. Without a good supply of oxygen-carrying blood, your brain won't be able to think as well as it can. So it is important to reduce your anxiety about the GRE test by relaxing and changing your anxious attitude to one of calm self-assurance.

How to Relax

If you want to do productive work the night before the GRE test, spend the time working on your confidence ("I've worked hard and will do well"). Visualize your graduate environment—really see yourself there. Here are some other relaxation techniques you can use if you find yourself getting anxious at any time before or during the GRE test.

1. *Breathe.* When most people think about breathing, they think about breathing *in*. The fact is, when you want to relax, it's more important to focus on breathing out. You want to be sure you are exhaling completely. It's also important to breathe deeply and to use abdominal breathing rather than shallow chest breathing. Try this: Place one hand on your stomach and the other hand on your chest. Sit up straight. Now, inhale deeply through your nose. Try to move your stomach as much as possible and your chest as little as possible. Exhale, and feel your stomach deflate. Again, your chest should hardly move. Count slowly as you breathe to make sure you spend at least as much time breathing out as you do breathing in. This kind of breathing relaxes you. It gets rid of carbon dioxide that can otherwise get trapped in the bottom of your lungs. You can practice this deep breathing anytime, anywhere you need to relax.

2. *Tense and relax your muscles.* As your anxiety mounts, your muscles tense, just in case they are going to be called on to fight or to flee. Of course, in the case of the GRE test, you have to fight with your brain and running away would result in a very low score. So the best thing you can do is to relax. It can be hard to know which muscles are tensed. Many people hold tension in their shoulders or their jaws, and are never even aware it's there. It's helpful to start with your toes and work your way up through all the

1. Breathe deeply and completely.
2. Tense and relax your muscles.
3. Visualize your success.

muscle groups, first tensing (really tightly!) and then relaxing each group. (Tense your toes, and relax. Tense your feet, and relax. Tense your calves, and relax . . .) Don't forget your facial muscles, especially your jaw.

3. *Visualize!* This is a different exercise from your graduate school visualization. In this one, you imagine yourself in a favorite place, a place you find especially soothing and pleasant. It could be a real place or one found only in your imagination. Focus on the sensations of your special place—what does it feel like, look like, sound like? You want to feel like you are really there. Take a few minutes to just relax in this place. It's there for you any time you need it, and it will always help you be calm and focused.

▶ Learning Strategies and Test-Taking Strategies

Sometimes you just get lucky. This is one of those times. Why? Because the following study techniques are also strategies that will help you when you take the GRE test. The more you practice them before the exam, the more natural they will be on test day.

Get Active

You may be thinking to yourself, "What does 'get active' mean?" It means interact with what you read. Ask questions. Make notes. Mark up passages. Don't be a passive reader, just looking at words. Be a thinker and a doer. This is not only a study strategy; it's also an important technique for the GRE test's reading comprehension questions, as well as an essential skill in graduate school. Of course, for the computer-based GRE test, you won't be marking on the actual passage, which will be displayed onscreen. Therefore, you may want to practice making notes on a separate piece of paper as you read. You should jot down key words, main ideas, and your own reactions to what you read. On test day, you will write on the scratch paper provided by the test center. You are allowed as much of this paper as you need, so use it.

Ask Questions

When you read a passage, such as the ones on the GRE test, ask questions such as:

1. What is this passage about?
2. What is the main idea, the topic?
3. What is the author's point of view or purpose in writing this?

4. What is the meaning of this word, in this sentence?

5. What does "it" refer to in this sentence? What is its antecedent?

6. Is this sentence part of the main idea, or is it a detail?

The more difficult the passage is, the more crucial it is that you ask these questions (and even more questions) about anything you don't understand. Think about a question as a clue to the answer. When you have asked the right questions, you are halfway to the right answer. These are the kinds of questions you will need to ask in order to answer the exam questions correctly. In graduate school, you will use the same questioning technique to help you comprehend densely written material (of which you will see a lot). It's essential that you start to practice asking and answering these questions. Quickly: What's the main idea of this passage?

Until you become very skilled at asking and answering questions about what you have read, it's a good idea to actually write questions out for yourself. For one thing, the act of writing helps you remember what questions to ask, especially for kinesthetic and visual learners. If you are an auditory learner, you will want to repeat them aloud as you write.

Mark It Up

Assuming the book belongs to you, get in the habit of highlighting and underlining when you read. When you open your book, pick up your pen, pencil, or highlighter. When you see a main idea, mark it. If there's an unfamiliar word or a word used in an unfamiliar context, mark it. The trick, though, is to be selective. If you are marking too much of the passage, you need to practice finding where the author states his or her main idea. Often, although not always, the main idea will be in the first sentence of the passage.

You can practice asking questions and marking main ideas and supporting details by going through the sample test passages in this book and in *GRE: Practicing to Take the General Test*. Check yourself by looking at the questions about those passages. How well do your ideas match up with the questions about the passages? Check the answers. Were you correct? If not, why?

On the computer-based GRE test, you will write the key words and ideas on your scratch paper. You may want to prepare by practicing this technique as you study for the test. Of course, you will also want to practice it with any borrowed books you use, such as library books.

Make Notes

Don't just *take* notes; *make* them. Making notes requires you to think about what you are reading. Asking questions, such as the ones mentioned previously, is one way to make notes. Another kind of note-making consists of your reactions to what you are reading. For example, you may disagree with an author's opinion. Write your reaction. Be sure to say *why* you disagree or agree, or why you are confused, etc. When you read the kinds of challenging materials you will find on the GRE test (and in graduate school), it should be more like a conversation than like a monologue on the part of the author. So what if the author cannot hear you? You can still hold up your end of the conversation. It will be more interesting for you, and you will get more out of what you read.

Make Connections

Another way of being interactive with what you study is to relate it to what you already know. For example, if you are trying to learn the word *demographic,* you may know that *demo*cracy refers to government run by the *people,* while *graphic* refers to *information,* written or drawn. Then you can remember that *demographic* has to do with *information* about *people.*

Making connections is one thing that differentiates *remembering* from *memorizing.* In the short run, it may seem easier to just memorize a word or a fact, but unless you understand what you are learning—unless you have connected it to what you already know—you are likely to forget it again. Then you will have wasted your study time and failed to improve your test score. Memorized information gets stored in your short-term memory, and that means it's forgotten within a few days, or even a few hours. Your long-term memory has to file new information to fit in with your existing information. That means you have to create connections to what you already know.

Both the analogies and the antonym questions on the GRE test call upon you to make connections quickly and accurately. Even if you know the vocabulary, you may miss the question if you can't nail the connection. Get in the habit of making connections.

Find Patterns

Success on the Quantitative section of the GRE test does not depend on math skills more advanced than algebra. It depends on how well you use basic math as a logic tool. One way to start practicing math logic is to look for patterns in the questions on the practice tests you take. As you look for patterns, you will see that the same kinds of questions appear in different guises. You may realize, for example, that you will be asked about the properties of triangles or to draw conclusions from charted relationships. Then you can practice the kinds of questions with which you have had difficulty, and you can learn to master them.

Math is easily learned when you find patterns and make connections and when you make it meaningful for yourself. Then, when you encounter the same type of question on the GRE test, you will know how to tackle them and find the right answers.

Break It Up

Just as you don't train to run a marathon by waiting until the last minute and then running twenty miles a day for five days before the race, you cannot effectively prepare for the GRE test by waiting until the last minute to study. Your brain works best when you give it a relatively small chunk of information, let it rest and process, and then give it another small chunk.

When you are studying vocabulary, for example, you may have a list of twenty words you want to learn. The most efficient way to learn twenty words is to break your list into four lists of five words each and learn one list before tackling the next. Making some kind of connection among the words in each list will help you remember them. Can you relate five of the words in some way? If not, can you make up an amusing sentence that uses all five words? Doing this kind of creative work is more fun than rote memorization, and makes it easier to learn because you are actively engaged with the material you are studying.

Five Times to Use Flashcards

1. During commercial breaks
2. While working out on the stationary bike
3. Just before you go to sleep
4. Whenever someone else is willing to help you
5. Any time you have a minute or more!

Flashcards are a great study aid for the GRE test. The act of writing on the cards engages your kinesthetic learning ability; seeing the cards uses your visual learning; and reading the cards aloud sets up auditory learning. Flashcards are also extremely portable and flexible in the ways they can be used. For example, you can pull them out while you wait for the bus; you can go over one or two while stopped at a traffic light, or you can run through a few while eating breakfast. What other times can you think of to work with flashcards?

Remember, your brain works best when you give it small, frequent assignments and then allow it time to process each one. Recent scientific studies show that sleep especially helps the brain process what it has learned. In other words, if you study before bed, you will know more when you wake up than you did before going to sleep. It is just one more reason for getting a good night's rest.

On the actual exam, it is important to give yourself permission to take a mini-break whenever you need it. If you need to stretch briefly after every question, that's okay. A quick stretch or a deep breath and forceful exhalation can do wonders to keep you focused and relaxed.

▶ Testing Psychology

As you already know, it is important to improve your vocabulary, practice your writing skills, and brush up on your math as you prepare for the GRE test. However, it's not sufficient to do only these things. Like all standardized tests, the GRE test also measures your test-taking skills. In this section, you will learn some of the best test-taking strategies for success on the GRE test, including approaches to the Analytical Writing Section. Strategies for each type of question will be discussed in more detail in Chapters 3, 4, and 5 of this book.

Get Familiar with the Exam to Combat Fear

In the previous section you learned that fear (or anxiety) is your enemy on the GRE test. Fear keeps you in fight-or-flight mode and makes thinking more difficult. What happens when you are feeling fearful or anxious? Your heart starts pounding-sending blood away from your brain to your limbs. Maybe you start feeling a little light-headed, a little disconnected, or even a little woozy. Are you in good condition for test-taking then? Of course not!

There is much truth in the saying that you fear what you don't understand. So, the best way to overcome the anxiety that keeps you from doing your best on the GRE test is to learn as much as you can about the test. The more you know about what to expect and the more practice you have with the exam, the more relaxed you will be, and the better you will perform on test day.

Taking practice tests and working with the tips and strategies in this book will help you immensely. You will get used to the kinds of questions on the GRE test and learn how to maximize your chances of answering correctly. You will build on what you already know and enhance the skill sets you need for GRE test success. By the time you enter the testing center, you will be familiar with the format of the test, the length of the test, and a number of strategies to help you succeed.

How to De-Stress

It is one thing to be told not to worry and another thing to *actually* not worry. How can you stop yourself from worrying? You can begin by replacing worried and anxious thoughts with positive ones. Following are some techniques.

Nip It in the Bud

What are you worried about? Maybe you are worried that you don't have enough time to prepare for the test. You are afraid you won't do well on the exam. This leads to anxiety about not getting into the right graduate program. Pretty soon, you are convinced your life is basically ruined, so why not just turn on the TV and resign yourself to a low-pay, dead-end job? Sounds silly when you put it that way, doesn't it? Fear has a way of escalating when you don't control it.

The best way to beat test anxiety is to *prevent* it. Don't let it get a good grip on you. Whenever you catch yourself worrying or thinking anxious thoughts about the GRE test, firmly tell yourself that you have nothing to worry about because you are preparing for GRE test success. Of course, for that strategy to work, you have to establish and stick to your study plan. There are two components, then, to beating test anxiety: *thinking* and *doing*.

Think about It

Different people have different ways of exhibiting test anxiety. You may deal with anxiety by working yourself into a frenzy, by limiting yourself to six hours of sleep, and by refusing to engage in leisure activities so you can get more work done. Meanwhile, your anxiety mounts. Or you may take the opposite approach, putting off working because the task seems so large and the time available so short. Of course, the more you procrastinate, the shorter the time becomes. You end up feeling more anxious, so you avoid working, and your anxiety mounts. These two approaches are like two sides of the same coin, and the denomination of the coin is *fear*. Before you can be productive, you must deal with your fears.

Face Your Fears

Admitting that you are worried about the GRE test is the first step toward conquering your fears. It can be helpful to write about your anxiety—name and describe your fears to begin the process of overcoming them.

Rules of the GRE Test Game

1. During test preparation, pretend you are actually taking the test.

2. During the actual test, pretend you are just practicing.

Start with the basic fear. You are worried you don't have enough time to prepare. Once you have written that fear down, you can come up with a way to eliminate it. Prioritize what you want to study, so that you work on the most important skills first. Start by working your way through this book. Look again at your schedule. Where can you squeeze in more study time? Remember that flashcards can be studied any time you have *one* free minute!

Maybe you have already allowed your anxieties to roam out of bounds by speculating on what will happen if you don't do well on the GRE test. Now you can see that this is a mistake, so go ahead and write down your fears of failure. Then write what would happen if you didn't do as well as you hoped. Would low scores keep you out of graduate school? No. Perhaps you wouldn't get into your first choice program, but some things in life can't be predicted. If you think hard enough, you can surely remember a time when things didn't work out the way you wanted them to, but turned out for the best anyway. It's good to make plans and work to achieve your goals, but it's also important to put your goals and plans in perspective.

If you didn't get into your first choice school would you be a less worthy person? No. Would your family stop loving you? No. Would the world come crashing down around you? Of course not.

Thinking about your fears in this way helps keep them in perspective. You know the GRE test is serious business. That's why you are preparing for it. But if you can persuade yourself to think about it as a game you want to play, you can control your fear and replace it with a simple, burning desire to win. There's nothing to be afraid of now. You just practice and prepare so that you will succeed on the test.

THINK POSITIVE

Half the battle with test anxiety is what and how you *think* about the test—what kinds of messages you are giving yourself about the exam. The other half is what you *do* to prepare. These two halves are interrelated: If you are paralyzed by negative thoughts (*I'm not ready; I don't have enough time; I'm not smart enough; I don't want to think about the GRE test*), you are going to have a hard time getting yourself to do the work you need to do.

On the other hand, if you can somehow get yourself to stop thinking those unproductive thoughts, you can start real preparation. The very act of *doing* something may make you feel better and lead to more positive *thoughts*, which makes it easier to continue working.

Therefore, it makes sense to just begin work. The place to start is with the study plan you based on the times you have available to study and on your assessment of your practice test results (see the study plan discussion earlier in this chapter). A study plan is easy. You have time to do it. It doesn't require genius-level performance. Once you have it in place, just follow it. You choose success. If you haven't already made your study plan, what are you waiting for?

Once your study plan is made, stick to it as though you have no choice. Of course, you do have a choice. You are choosing how you want your future to unfold. You are doing this for you.

STAY HEALTHY

If you were preparing to run a marathon, you would be thinking about how to take care of your body. You would want to eat well, get enough rest, and condition your body for its endurance test. Taking the GRE test is much like running a marathon. You will need to perform at your mental maximum for three hours on test day. Your body and your mind both need to be ready. Here are the basics of caring for your marathon machine:

1. *Get Enough Rest.* Some people need more sleep than others. You know how much sleep you need to feel rested. Is it eight hours? Or do you need more? Is six enough? Or does that make you feel like a zombie the next day? Whatever your individual need is, make sure that you leave yourself enough time every day to get enough sleep. It's also important to remember that too much sleep can leave you feeling equally groggy. Get the amount you need to feel rested and no more.

    If you find yourself having trouble sleeping, first establish a bedtime routine. Maybe a warm bath helps you relax, or a glass of warm milk. Whatever you do, don't get interested in a good book just before bed. Anxious thoughts can also keep you awake, so bedtime is a good time to practice a calming visualization, or a series of visualizations, using the techniques previously discussed. Finally, if nothing seems to be helping you fall asleep, simply get up and study. If you can't sleep, you might as well be productive.

2. *Eat Well.* You know that athletes have to pay attention to what they eat. A marathon runner, for example, maintains a healthy diet during training as well as just before the race. Your brain also needs good food to function at its peak. A well-balanced diet based on the food pyramid will keep your body and your brain in top form. You are better off avoiding fast food laden with grease, sugar, and empty calories. Rather than junk-food snacks, try substituting the following:

INSTEAD OF THIS	EAT THIS
donuts	low-sugar, multigrain cereal
chips	carrot sticks
cookies	natural granola bar
ice cream	low-fat yogurt
soda	fruit juice
coffee	herbal tea

Remember that caffeine interferes with sleep when consumed past midafternoon. It is also an additive substance that tricks you into feeling more alert. If you feel you need coffee, maybe what you need is more rest.

3. *Exercise.* Unless you have a daily workout routine, you may not be meeting your body's need for exercise. Our bodies appreciate a good aerobic workout every day. Exercise helps you sleep more soundly and feel more relaxed throughout the day. Vigorous exercise is a great way to combat anxiety because it releases endorphins—the body's natural feel-good chemical.

Light exercise, such as a walk, can also double as study time. You can study your flashcards during a walk around the neighborhood. You can record an audiotape for yourself to listen to as you run through the park. Get in the habit of identifying times you can double up on study and another activity to maximize your productive time.

If you take care of your body and your brain by getting enough sleep, eating healthily, and exercising adequately, your brain and body will take good care of you during the GRE test. You are in training now: Get with the program.

▶ Multiple-Choice Strategies

As mentioned previously, the nice thing about multiple-choice test is that the answer is provided for you—all you have to do is identify it.

Avoid Distracters

Most of the questions on the GRE test are multiple-choice questions. There are two Analytical Writing questions, and the remaining questions are all multiple-choice. The good news about multiple-choice questions is that they provide you with the answer. The bad news is that ETS always provides *distracters* in addition to the correct answer. Distracters are wrong answers designed to look like possible right answers. In the Quantitative and Verbal chapters of this book, you will find detailed strategies for separating the correct answers from the distracters. Here is an overview of the basic technique:

1. *Read the question carefully.* Be sure you know *exactly* what is being asked. Many questions on the GRE test are missed because the test taker tried to answer a question other than the one that was being asked. In particular, look for wording such as "All of the following are true about the author's purpose EXCEPT." Train yourself to notice any word in the question that is in all capital letters. Such a word will often completely change the meaning of the question. In the example above, if you do not notice the word "EXCEPT," you will be looking for answers that are true about the author's purpose. In that question, you want to look for the one answer that is not true about the author's purpose.

2. *Circle or underline key words and phrases in the question.* These are words and phrases that help you pick the one correct answer. Think of them as clues. You are the detective and you must examine each question closely for clues to the correct answer. For example, if you have a reading-comprehension passage about improvements in bicycle safety and then the question, "The modern bicycle has all the following safety features EXCEPT," the key words are "modern," "safety features," and "except." After you mark these words and phrases, look in the passage for the safety features of the modern bicycle. Then choose the answer that is not mentioned in the passage as a safety feature of the modern bicycle.

3. *Rule out incorrect answers.* In the previous example, as you identify safety features of the modern bicycle from the passage, you will mark off each one as a possible choice. Because this is such a helpful technique, you will want to seriously consider setting up your scratch paper with choices **a** through **d**, or **a** through **e**, depending on the number of choices in that question. The reason it's important to actually mark the answer as you eliminate it from your choices is so that you will know it's not the answer and won't waste time considering it again. You may be able to eliminate only one or two incorrect answers, but every wrong answer you eliminate increases your chances of picking the correct answer.

4. *Watch out for absolutes.* ETS, through years of practice, has gotten very skillful at encouraging test takers to choose the wrong answer when they are not sure of the right one. Fortunately for you, there are several categories of distracter answers that tend to recur on the GRE test. An example of a distracter is an absolute word such as *always, never, all,* or *none* included within an answer. While it is *possible* to find a correct answer that uses such an absolute, if you are unsure, it is wise to avoid an answer that uses one of these words. You will learn in Chapters 4 and 5 how to identify other types of distracters and eliminate them from your answer choices.

To Guess or Not to Guess

If you aren't sure about the answer to a question, should you guess? In a nutshell, the answer is yes. On the GRE test, you are penalized for an incorrect answer exactly the same as you would be if you left the question blank. If you guess, even wildly, you might get lucky and increase your score. So eliminate as many wrong answers as possible, then guess.

▶ The Endgame

If you are reading these words several weeks or more before you take the GRE test, you may want to bookmark this page and come back to it the week before the test (got your sticky notes handy?). Your routine during the last week should vary from your study routine of the preceding weeks.

The Final Week

Exactly one week before you take the GRE test is a good time for your final practice test. Then you can use your next few days to wrap up any loose ends. This week is also the time to read back over your notes on test-taking tips and techniques.

During the final week, however, it's a good idea to actually cut back on your study schedule. Cramming on vocabulary words and math concepts or frantically writing essays now will only make you feel less prepared and more anxious. Anxiety is your enemy when it comes to test taking. It's also your enemy when it comes to restful sleep, and it's extremely important that you be well rested and relaxed on test day.

What you want to substitute for study is more visualization and relaxation. Visualize yourself sitting at the computer in the testing center, working your way through the test in a calm and focused way. You are buoyed by the confidence that you have prepared for this test. You remain confident even though you don't know all the answers. When you don't know an answer, you apply the techniques you have practiced as you worked your way through this book. Picture yourself smiling and stretching as you finish the test, feeling good about the work you have done. Then imagine the reward you have waiting for yourself after the test. Don't forget to tell yourself out loud, especially if you are an auditory learner, how proud you are of your hard work and how confident you are of your success. If you sound unsure of yourself at first, repeat your words until you sound convincing—then you will believe yourself.

During that last week before the exam, make sure you know where you are taking the test. If it's an unfamiliar place, drive there so you will know how long it takes to get there, to park, and to walk from the parking lot to the testing center where you will take the GRE test. Do this in order to avoid a last minute rush to the test and its accompanying anxiety.

Be sure you get adequate exercise during this last week. It will help you sleep soundly, and exercise also helps rid your body and mind of the effects of anxiety. Don't tackle any new physical skills, though, or overdo any old ones. You don't want to be sore and uncomfortable on test day.

Check to see that your test appointment confirmation and your personal identification are in order and easily located. You will not need anything else because you are not allowed to bring anything in with you to the testing area.

T Minus One

It is the day before the GRE test. You have done your preparation and you are as ready as you are going to be. Here are some dos and don'ts:

DO:
1. Relax!
2. Find something amusing to do the night before-watch a good movie, have dinner with a friend, read a good book.
3. Get some light exercise. Walk, dance, swim.
4. Get all of your test materials together: confirmation of your appointment and proper identification.
5. Practice your visualization of GRE test success.
6. Go to bed early. Get a good night's sleep.

DON'T:
1. Study. You have already prepared. Now relax.
2. Party. Keep it low key.
3. Eat anything unusual or adventurous—save it!
4. Try any unusual or adventurous activity—save it!
5. Allow yourself to get into an emotional exchange with anyone—a sibling, a friend, a parent, a significant other. If someone starts something, remind him or her that you have a GRE test to take tomorrow and you need to postpone the discussion so you can focus on the test.

Test Day

On the day of the test, get up early enough to allow yourself extra time to get ready. If you have a morning appointment, set your alarm and ask a family member or friend to make sure you are up. Even if your appointment is later, make sure you don't sleep longer than you usually do. Too much sleep can actually make you feel tired all day.

Eat a light, healthy breakfast, even if you usually eat nothing in the morning. If you do usually eat breakfast, eat whatever you normally eat. Remember that sugary things are likely to let you down during the test. Protein-rich foods, such as eggs and cheese, are more apt to keep on giving your brain fuel throughout the test. If you don't normally drink coffee, don't do it today. If you do normally have coffee, have one cup. More than that may make you jittery today.

If you have scheduled an afternoon test, eat a light but satisfying lunch. Be sure not to stuff yourself before going in. Digestion drains blood from your brain, so it's best to eat at least an hour before test time. Again, it's best to eat protein because that will give you sustained energy. Stay away from sugar—you can always promise yourself a sweet treat after the test.

Give yourself plenty of time to get to the testing center and avoid a last-minute rush. Plan to get to there ten to fifteen minutes early.

Once you are settled at your computer, you will have as much time as you need to run through the testing procedures. They will be identical to the ones you have practiced in POWERPREP. Your timed exam will start only when you are ready to begin it. Just before you begin the actual test is a good time to visualize success one more time. Remember to breathe. Inhale fully into your abdomen and exhale at least as fully. If you feel your body tensing up, practice your relaxation exercises, tensing and releasing muscle groups to help them relax. Breathe.

Once the test begins, don't waste time reading the directions. You will know the directions from your preparations; the directions are always the same.

Remember not to spend too long on questions you don't understand. You want to answer every question presented to you. On the other hand, take your time on the first ten to fifteen questions. You want to answer them correctly so that the computer will place you in the highest possible range.

You can hide the onscreen clock if you want to, but do check in with it periodically in each section to see how you are doing on time. You don't want to suddenly realize you have only five minutes and a lot of unanswered questions.

If you find yourself getting anxious during the test, remember to breathe. If you need to, take a minute or two to slip into your relaxation visualization or your visualization of success. You have worked hard to prepare for this day. You are ready.

After the GRE Test
Celebrate! Reward yourself for a job well done.

► In a Nutshell

As you go through this review book, as you make your study plan, as you prepare to take the GRE test, always remember why you are doing these things. You are doing them for your future, for your dreams, whatever they may be. Whenever you hit a snag, when you feel weary and unmotivated and are tempted to give up, remember why you committed yourself to this path. Call up your vision of yourself, with your graduate degree in hand, living your dreams. Only you can make that vision a reality, but this book is here to help you take your first step. Read on.

CHAPTER

3 ▶ The GRE Analytical Writing Section

▶ Pretest

The following Analytical Writing Assessment pretest contains two tasks: the first is to present your perspective on an issue and the second is to analyze an argument. These two tasks provide you with practice for the same kinds of prompts you will see on the actual exam. This pretest is designed to give you a sense of what the Analytical Writing section will be like and to help you assess your strengths and weaknesses for this portion of the exam.

First, you will be given an opportunity to practice presenting your perspective on an issue. On the official exam, you will have 45 minutes to complete this task. Take your time on this pretest; it is intended to familiarize you with the task so you know what to expect. You will have plenty of time later in your studies to practice under more official conditions. You will be asked to choose one of the two given prompts and decide what position you will take on the given issue. Then you will be required to write an essay supporting your position.

Second, you will be given an opportunity to practice analyzing an argument. This task gives you brief directions and a short paragraph, which presents an argument. Your job is to analyze and evaluate that argument and present your critique of it in writing. On the official exam you will have 30 minutes to complete this task. Take your time on this pretest; it is intended to familiarize you with the argument task. You will have more time later to practice writing under conditions closer to those you will encounter on test day.

When you are finished, compare your essays to the scoring guide on pages 57–58 and the sample top-score essays below. The results of this pretest should help you plan your study time effectively and determine the areas in which you need the most careful review and practice. Now, you can get started!

Present Your Perspective on an Issue

Read the following prompts and choose *one* of them on which to take a position. Use relevant reasons and examples as evidence to clearly express and support your point of view throughout your essay.

Prompt: "Fiction should not be a required form of reading."

Prompt: "Grades should be abolished from the education system because the competition they feed reduces the amount of actual learning."

Analyze an Argument

Read the following argument. Analyze and comment on how logical and/or reliable you find this argument.

Prompt: The following appeared in a letter to the editor in the sports pages of a community newspaper.

A teacher can't earn more than $50,000 a year doing one of the toughest jobs in the world. These saints work a lot harder and deserve to get paid a lot more for the miracles they perform on a daily basis. The average salary for professional athletes is $650,000. That's more than ten times what the average public high school principal makes. Basketball players can earn millions in just one season, and football players can earn hundreds of thousands for just a 30-second commercial. Even *benchwarmers* make more in a month than teachers make. Who is more important—the woman who taught you how to read and write so that you can succeed in life or the jock who plays for a living?

Top-Score Sample Issue Essay

Prompt: "Fiction should not be a required form of reading."

Response:

Remember the last book that captured your imagination and transported you to another place and time? Remember a book that made you fall in love with its characters, made you feel their pain and joy? Remember a story that taught you an important lesson or that helped you better understand others and make sense of the human condition? Fiction, unlike a user manual, a magazine article, or newspaper editorial, doesn't present you with facts. It doesn't inform you of current events or give you advice on how to cultivate a better garden. It probably won't help you decide which candidate to vote for or which product to buy, but that certainly doesn't mean it shouldn't be a required form of reading. Indeed, fiction serves three crucial functions for human beings: It helps us understand the human condition—both ourselves and other people with whom we come into contact on a regular basis. In addition, it cultivates our imaginations. It can also teach us about history, psychology, even biology and other sciences.

Compassion for others is rooted in understanding and acceptance, and a good story brings us into the inner world of its characters so that we can understand them. In Toni Morrison's novel *The Bluest Eye*, for example, Morrison peels away the layers of her characters' histories piece by piece, like an onion, until we see into their cores and understand what drives them. They may still do awful things to each other, but she shows us *why* they do the things that they do, and we learn that we shouldn't judge others until we understand their pasts. Their stories are sad and painful, and we learn to love even the outcast Pecola. In fact, we learn that those outcasts are the ones who need our love the most.

Many stories and novels also help us understand ourselves better. Joseph Conrad's dark and powerful novel *Heart of Darkness* helps us understand the dark side that inhabits all humans. Conrad shows us that we need to acknowledge and explore this dark side in order to control it. It makes us question just how civilized we are and even what it means to be civilized in the first place. This piece of fiction helps us understand what it means to be human and to negotiate the real world by presenting a specific story that illustrates what it means to be a part of the world.

Furthermore, good fiction cultivates our imagination, which is more significant to us than some might think. Without imaginations, we would lead sad, empty lives. Imagination is central to human emotional health and is a key aspect of human intelligence. Facts are one thing; but facts can be of no real use unless coupled with imaginations. Fiction can help us by keeping our imagination fresh and active. In a story like Franz Kafka's "Metamorphosis," for example, we are asked to imagine that Gregor, the main character, wakes up one morning, having turned into a giant bug. On first glance this idea sounds crazy, but once we accept this premise and imagine Gregor as a five-foot-long cockroach, we can feel his family's horror and imagine his agony as he finds himself trapped in his room and abandoned by those he loves. This story helps us stretch our minds so that we can more fully understand the world around us.

Through fiction, people can also grow to understand scientific concepts or historical events that they might never have considered before. Fiction opens our minds to the world of possibility—it often explores "what could have been" or "what might be" through historical or science fiction. Fiction such as *Jurassic Park* can even help us understand scientific concepts like DNA. Although many scientists believe that it is not possible to recreate a dinosaur based on DNA from dinosaur blood preserved in fossilized mosquitoes, Michael Crichton introduced the concept to many people who might never have thought about it before. The book sparked my own interest in learning about a scientific concept in a more engaging context than a scientific journal or biology textbook. For example, after reading the book, I decided to do a little of my own research about DNA and how scientists use it.

Fiction should definitely be a required form of reading for all students. Not only does it provide an opportunity to escape our daily lives, it also presents a different perspective of the world, one we might never have thought of before, while still informing us about the human condition. Fiction also has the potential to awaken our interest in parts of the world we may never have explored and in learning more about science or history in a more engaging way.

Top-Score Sample Argument Essay

Prompt: The following appeared in a Letter to the Editor in the sports pages of a community newspaper.

A teacher can't earn more than $50,000 a year doing one of the toughest jobs in the world. These saints work a lot harder and deserve to get paid a lot more for the miracles they perform on a daily basis. The average salary for professional athletes is $650,000. That's more than ten times what the average public high school principal makes. Basketball players can earn millions in just one season, and football players can earn hundreds of thousands for just a 30-second commercial. Even *benchwarmers* make more in a month than teachers make. Who is more important—the woman who taught you how to read and write so that you can succeed in life, or the jock who plays for a living?

Response:

The author of this piece drives home the idea that professional athletes get paid too much, especially in comparison to teachers, who help you "succeed in life." As much as anyone may believe that teachers deserve to be paid more than they earn, or that some professional athletes are grossly overpaid, the argument this author makes is not very effective. Much of the evidence and reasoning used by the author of this piece is flimsy and illogically reasoned—there is a shaky conclusion, counterarguments are not addressed, and the premises the author uses to support the conclusion are not reasonably qualified.

The conclusion drawn in this argument is, "These saints work a lot harder and deserve to get paid a lot more for the miracles they perform on a daily basis." This sentence raises several red flags. First, the author draws a comparison between teachers and saints. It is true that teachers do noble work, and arguably this work improves individuals and sometimes even society; however, neither of these duties makes teachers "saints." Second, the author uses the word *miracles* to describe the results of teachers' work. This word is emotionally charged, implying that a teacher's work is amazing and fantastic. The connotation of the word *miracle* suggests bias in the author's opinion of the teaching profession. Juxtaposed to calling the work of professional athletes "play," this word draws on the reader's compassion, appealing to emotional rather than presenting impartial evidence. Finally, this claim is incomplete. Teachers work harder than whom? Deserve to get paid more than whom? Although the answer "professional athletes" is implied, the claim does not explicitly state this.

The argument as given is weakened by the fact that it does not address any counterarguments or note any other perspectives. It could have addressed the positive role models many athletes play to youth, the community outreach many professional athletes do for free, or the generous charities many athletes set up and donate money to. By stating some of these counterarguments and refuting them, the author could have gained more credibility, showing that insight and logic played into his or her argument. As it is, the argument appears biased and one-sided.

What's more, the premises on which the author bases his or her conclusions seem unreasonably qualified. For example, the average salary given for professional athletes doesn't seem like the appropriate measure to use in this situation. There are many professional sports, professional table tennis or volleyball, for example, where the salaries for even the top players don't approach $650,000. If you were to survey all professional athletes, you'd probably find that the *typical* player doesn't come close to a six-figure salary. However, because players like Shaquille O'Neal and Tiger Woods make millions of dollars, the *average* is higher than the *typical* salary. Therefore, this piece of evidence the author chooses seems loaded.

In addition, sources are not provided for this salary statistic. Furthermore, the author does not cite sources for the $50,000 teacher's salary or that benchwarmers make more than teachers. (Besides, it is unlikely that table tennis team benchwarmers make larger salaries than teachers!) Because this evidence lacks sources, the author's credibility is weakened, since the evidence cannot be verified as fact. If the figures can be verified, then the premises are reasonable; however, for all the reader knows, the author simply made everything up.

Overall, this argument is not well reasoned. The conclusion of this argument seems biased and the word choice seems suspect, appealing to emotion, rather than to logic. Additionally, the argument does not consider alternate viewpoints, further weakening its position. Finally, the evidence presented in the argument weakens its credibility because it doesn't cite a source to verify its validity. Although many people believe that teachers deserve to be paid a better salary, this particular argument isn't effective. The logical conclusion would be to suggest some type of change or solution to this problem, but the incomplete conclusion, appealing to emotion, makes it sound like the author is complaining rather than making a good case for a teacher salary increase.

▶ Introduction to the GRE Analytical Writing Section

Good writing skills go beyond the GRE General Test. They are essential for success both in graduate school and beyond. This chapter of the book will help you understand what to expect from the Analytical Writing section of the GRE General Test, how to do your best on this section of the exam, and how the test is scored. You will learn specific tips and strategies for answering the two different types of questions presented on the writing test and for doing your best possible writing in the time allotted to you. You will also practice and assess your own writing.

No matter how confident you are about your writing, it is essential to seriously prepare for the Analytical Writing section of the GRE test. The Analytical Writing section of the exam is always the first part of the General Test. It is 75 minutes long, and is given in two parts, which may appear in any order. The two parts are as follows:

- *Present Your Perspective on an Issue*—45 minutes. You must clearly and thoughtfully communicate how you feel about a given issue of general interest, taking any point of view you believe you can best support. You will choose only one of two writing prompts.
- *Analyze an Argument*—30 minutes. You must clearly and thoughtfully critique and analyze a given argument. Your job is only to offer your own analysis of the argument, *not* to offer your own opinions. For this portion of the test, you will not have a choice of prompts.

Both of these essays test your critical thinking abilities, while also examining how well you can organize, formulate, articulate, support, and/or analyze a given argument or issue in writing.

▶ About the Analytical Writing Section

What to Expect

The Analytical Writing section is different from the other parts of the exam because it assesses your ability to think critically and logically about a topic of general interest. Unlike the Verbal or Quantitative sections your knowledge of specific content is not being tested. Instead, more abstract skills—such as critical thinking and analytical writing skills, which are skills essential to successful graduate students—are being tested. Much of graduate-level work consists of formulating, supporting, and critiquing arguments central to a chosen field of study, so the creators of the GRE test devised a section of the General Test that measures this ability in graduate candidates.

The two tasks in the Analytical Writing section assess your abilities in complimentary ways. The first task—Presenting Your Perspective on an Issue—gives you a choice of two prompts of general interest. Your job is to choose *only one* topic, take a point of view, and give specific, appropriate reasons and examples that support this point of view; in other words, your challenge is to construct a persuasive argument, backing up your point of view with specific evidence. The second task—Analyzing an Argument—requires you to examine and evaluate the validity of *someone else's* argument and evidence. The given argument *intentionally* contains flaws that you must identify, think about, and understand. Then, you should analyze the reasoning of this argument and clearly express your critique of this argument in writing.

Neither task is testing your objective knowledge in a particular area or course of study. The prompts are meant to test how well you can both create and analyze persuasive arguments about topics of general interest. In fact, the topics are chosen specifically so that GRE test takers, no matter what field of study they plan to pursue or what special interests they have, can address the topic with no trouble. For the Issue task,

In addition to preparing for the test with the practice prompts on pages 70–73 of this book, you can help yourself prepare for the Analytical Writing section by familiarizing yourself with the collection of writing prompts from which your official prompt will be selected. The GRE program has published a complete list of writing prompts online.

But do not get too excited—there are over 300 prompts given for each task, and the wording might differ slightly when you see the prompt on the actual exam. So, while it is good to familiarize yourself with the prompts and even practice by answering or discussing some of them with friends, family, or teachers, you will not be able to have a stock answer ready for each prompt in the pool.

To see the collection of Issue topics, go to www.GRE.org/issuetop.html. To see the collection of Argument topics, go to www.GRE.org/argutop.html. You can also write to the GRE Program to receive a hard copy of these topics.

GRE Program
P.O. Box 6000
Princeton, NJ 08541-6000

you will not have to hold particular knowledge or have been through specific training to write an effective essay. Likewise, for the Argument task, you will simply evaluate and assess another person's argument. You should not take a perspective on this argument, but rather you should evaluate its logic and reliability.

How the Analytical Writing Section Is Administered

Because the entire GRE General Test is administered on the computer, you will see the writing prompts and enter your response on the computer. ETS has created a simple word-processing program so that no advantage or disadvantage is given to people who are used to any particular word-processing program. There is no spell-check or grammar-check on this program. In this program, you will be able to delete text, insert text, cut and paste text, and undo a previous action. You can practice using this word-processing program with POWERPREP software, available to download at www.GRE.org/pprepdwnld.html, or available from ETS—they will send it to you when you register for the test. You will also have time to familiarize yourself with the program interface at the test center before you begin the test.

Finally, there is always the Help button, which you can click on during the test to review the directions and/or give you a summary of the tutorial—however, keep in mind that this will take away from your precious test-taking time. It's best to be prepared; if at all possible, familiarize yourself with the program before you go into the test.

How to Budget Your Time

Because you have a limited amount of time to complete each task, it is important to plan your time carefully. Be sure to leave enough time to plan, write, and revise your essay. For the 45-minute Issue task, you will need to parcel your time carefully to include these steps:

- Read both prompts.
- Choose one of the two prompts.
- Decide which perspective you will take.
- Plan your response.
- Write your essay.
- Revise and edit your work.

For the Argument task, you will need to set aside time to first analyze the given argument, then plan and write your evaluation of that argument.

In addition, don't forget to allow time to review and proofread your writing for errors—on both tasks. Your score will not change because of a few minor errors, but many obvious errors will affect and lower your final score. Again, errors give the impression of sloppy reasoning or weak writing. A good general rule is to divide your time on the essay test in the following manner:

PERCENT OF YOUR TIME	ISSUE TASK	ARGUMENT TASK
1/4 of your time planning	10 minutes	8 minutes
1/2 of your time writing	25 minutes	15 minutes
1/4 of your time revising and editing	10 minutes	7 minutes

You don't need to follow this guideline to the letter, but it's probably smart to follow it generally.

How the Test Is Scored

Whether you choose to handwrite your essays or type them into the computer, your writing will be scored by trained college-level writing instructors. These scorers have been specifically trained to read and evaluate GRE-level writing using a six-point holistic rubric. Two readers will score each essay, and your final score will be the average of both readers' scores for both essays. For example, if, on the Issue essay, one reader gives you a 4 and one gives you a 5, your score will be 4.5.

The two readers do not know the score the other reader has given your essay, and if there is a discrepancy of more than one point (for example, if one reader scores your essay a 4 and the other a 6), then a third reader will be asked to score your essay.

While scoring an essay is far more subjective than correcting a multiple-choice exam, the GRE program has developed a detailed scoring rubric to guide readers through the essay-scoring process. This rubric lists specific criteria that essays should meet to attain each score. The complete GRE Analytical Writing scoring guide is available to download for your review at: www.GRE.org/pracmats.html#awprep, in the document entitled *An Introduction to the Analytical Writing Section of the GRE General Test.* Be sure to review the scoring guide carefully. The more you know about what is expected of you in the essay, the better you will be able to meet those expectations. You can review adapted GRE Analytical Writing rubrics on pages 57–58.

Unlike the Verbal and Quantitative sections of the General Test, on the Analytical Writing section of the exam you will not receive your scores immediately because the scorers need time to read and evaluate your writing. It usually takes 10–15 days after you take the test to receive your score for this section of the test.

► The Analytical Writing Process

The Analytical Writing section asks you to complete two separate but complimentary tasks. Each task is testing your analytical writing skills, including the assessment of your critical thinking skills; however, completing the two tasks requires two different abilities. The Issue task requires you to construct and support your own point of view on a prompted issue, while the Argument task requires you to analyze an argument that someone else has constructed. In order to be successful on this part of the GRE test, you will need to understand the nature of each task and thoroughly demonstrate that understanding to the readers of your essays. The next section of the chapter will help you understand how to complete each task effectively, starting with the Issue task.

► Present Your Perspective on an Issue—Attack Mode

This 45-minute task in the Analytical Writing section tests your ability to communicate and support your point of view on a particular topic. You will be given *two* persuasive writing prompts—general claims about topics, which are designed to provide an issue on which you will take a perspective—and you may choose *only one* of these prompts to address in your essay. Your job will be to clearly express and support your point of view throughout your essay.

It is likely that you have already done a lot of persuasive writing in your undergraduate career, so this section of the chapter will serve as a review of the essential things to keep in mind as you develop this particular persuasive essay. Remember, on this task, you must think about a topic critically, decide which perspective to take, and then plan and write a thoughtful essay in a limited amount of time.

Purpose of the Issue Task

The Issue task directions tell you to "present your perspective on the issue below, using relevant reasons and/or examples to support your views." The purpose of this task, then, is to see how well you can create and support a compelling argument on a given topic. So the first thing you need to do is choose between the two topics. The more quickly you can choose which claim to address, the more time you will have to focus on the planning, writing, and revising of your essay.

Choosing the Claim You Will Address

Choosing the topic you can best support is one of the most challenging parts of *Presenting Your Perspective on an Issue*. However, once you commit to a topic, you will find that it is much easier to calm your brain and begin to think logically about your writing. Often, one of the claims will speak more to your own personal experiences and you will immediately begin to think of support for that idea. These simple steps should help you choose your claim:

1. **Read each claim carefully.** Make sure you understand the claim thoroughly before you choose to write about it for your essay.
2. **Think about how your own personal experiences relate to each claim.** Think about things you have observed or experienced in daily life, read about in newspapers or magazines, or even heard about from your friends and family members.
3. **Decide which claim you have the most support for.** These experiences will serve as support for your theme, so it is best to choose the claim for which you can immediately think of more support.

As you read and think about each claim, remember that there is no "right" claim to choose or "right" position to take on the claim. The Analytical Writing section assesses how well you can communicate and support an interesting and convincing argument. The topics are specifically designed to make you think critically about an issue and present your case, so start thinking critically as you prepare for the test.

For example, if one of the claims states that "at the college and university level, students should work frequently in small groups because people learn best when they pool their resources and share knowledge among themselves in the spirit of collaboration," and you have had numerous positive experiences learning in small groups, it might be easy for you to come up with many specific pieces of support for this claim. Or, you may have had negative experiences working in small groups, in which case you can easily come up with many examples that *disagree* with this claim.

On the other hand, if you completed your undergraduate degree through distance learning, you may never have had to collaborate with other students to do your coursework. You might not have any experiences to support or refute that claim so it may be better for you to choose another topic. Moreover, you might not feel strongly one way or another about this issue, in which case, it would also probably be better for you to choose the other topic.

What If Neither Topic Speaks to You?

If neither topic grabs your attention, or you cannot immediately think of any personal experiences or examples, then look more closely. Ask yourself the following questions:

- How can I relate my own experiences, either academic or personal, to this topic?
- Which topic is more interesting to me?
- What might _____ think of saying? (Insert the name of the best debater you know!)
- What are any examples or reasons I can think of to support each topic?

It may be that you are simply choosing the lesser of two evils; however, once you encourage yourself to look more closely, you may find that you have more to say on the issue than you originally thought. An original example can spark you to think of several more, solid pieces of support for the issue.

As you examine each claim, engage your critical thinking skills by asking yourself the following questions:

- What is the main issue?
- Do I agree or disagree with the claim?
- Does the claim make any generalizations that are illogical or false?
- Are there conditions under which I disagree with the claim? If so, how might these conditions affect my argument?
- Can I think of experiences from my own life, or the lives of my friends and family, that support or refute the claim?
- Can I think of newspaper or magazine articles I have read that could help me support my case?
- Are these examples relevant and convincing?
- What are some other positions on this issue?
- How can I logically address opposing views in my writing?

If these questions seem overwhelming to think about now, do not worry too much. Learn these questions now, and when you are faced with the two issues (or claims), it will be easy to apply the questions. Go to the website and practice applying these questions to the sample essay prompts. However, it is best to begin to consider them now, so that you have some of these ideas in mind as you begin to formulate your defense.

Again, it is essential to remember that there is no "right" answer to this task. The scorers are not judging your position on the issue; rather, they are looking to see how well you have employed your critical thinking skills and how well you can establish and support a claim.

The choice is yours, so let your experiences guide you. Naturally, it will be much easier to write on a topic for which several pieces of support come to mind. Remember, the more you practice for this task, the easier it will be to decide quickly which issue you can support better. Use the sample Issue prompts at www.GRE.org or the practice Issue prompts at the end of this chapter to help you gain more confidence in choosing an Issue topic.

Deciding Your Position on the Issue

After you have considered your own experiences in relation to the claim, you should find it easier to decide what point of view to take. You have a lot of latitude with this task—you can agree or disagree *completely* with the claim or you can agree or disagree *conditionally* with the claim.

Deciding on the position you want to take is the best time to think about those last couple of questions you asked yourself when you were choosing the topic itself:

- What are some other positions on this issue?
- What might someone who opposes my position say, and how can I address those views in my writing?

You want to be sure that you can really support the position you take, so it is helpful to play your own devil's advocate and to think about your position in a more complex manner. Thinking about the issue from several different points of view will help you solidify your case and be certain that the evidence you choose is really supporting the position you take on the issue.

Planning Your Response

If you have carefully thought about and answered the questions provided to you in the *Choosing the Claim* and *Deciding Your Position* sections, you are really ready to get down to business. Planning your essay should be a snap now. You probably already know the following basic formula for a good essay:

1. Introduction—Your introduction should *always* include a clear, thoughtful, thesis statement and a brief overview of your position on the issue you plan to discuss.
2. Body—The body of your essay is where you will provide support for your thesis statement, or your argument. You will provide clear, relevant examples that support your case, and defend against an opposing point of view.
3. Conclusion—Your conclusion should sum up your main points, providing a satisfactory wrap-up of what you set out to prove in your essay.

The form of the essay you write for the Issue task of the Analytical Writing section might not be the traditional five-paragraph essay or another standard type of essay you learned how to write in your undergraduate studies. In fact, you have a lot of freedom in how you choose to *present* your writing. For example, you might do one or more of the following:

- Present several, short pieces of evidence to support your position.
- Choose one, extended example which backs up your argument.
- Describe a scenario.
- Pose and answer a series of questions relating to your topic.

The effectiveness of your presentation—your skill at clearly expressing your position and defending that position—are most important. Further, it is a pleasure for people to read a well-organized essay. No matter how you choose present your ideas, keep the basic framework in mind. Then you will continue to state your argument clearly and support it throughout your essay.

No matter how you choose to present your ideas, you should still keep the basic framework in mind. You will still need to clearly state your argument and support it throughout your essay.

STEP ONE: THE THESIS STATEMENT—YOUR POSITION

The good news is, you have already started to formulate your thesis—the main idea of your essay. You know what position you are going to take on the issue, and this idea will form the core of your essay. This idea, the argument you make, will control what you write and what kind of support you will provide for that idea throughout your essay. Your argument should not simply paraphrase the claim or prompt, and it should not just make a general statement about the topic. It should be a clear, personal position on the issue.

For example, take the following prompt: "The most important quality of a good teacher is his or her ability to interest you in the subject he or she is teaching." What are some good thesis statements for this claim? Consider what a thesis statement *is not*. The following statements are not thesis statements. They do not take a clear, personal position on the particular prompt.

- Teachers should know a lot about the subjects they teach.
- Teachers should never talk about their own perspectives on an issue.
- What makes a good teacher?

In contrast, the following thesis statements correspond directly to the issue. They clearly state the author's position on the topic.

- Good teachers must be able to interest their students in the subjects they teach; however, this ability alone does not ensure that someone will be a good teacher.
- Contrary to popular belief, the most important quality of a teacher is not his or her ability to interest students in the subject he or she is teaching; equally vital, are other abilities, such as the ability to listen to and provide encouragement and support for each individual in the classroom.
- In today's classrooms, it is hard to attract the attention of apathetic and distracted students, so the most important ability good teachers should possess is the ability to interest their students in the subjects they teach.

The issues you will address on this task on the Analytical Writing section are sometimes more complex than the example above, but no matter how complex the issue, when you formulate your thesis statement, you must still clearly and succinctly state your position, and mention any conditions of that position. Then, you will need to break the claim down analyzing it closely and thinking about any questions the claim raises.

For example, if you were to formulate an argument for the claim mentioned previously, you might think of the following questions to analyze the claim and formulate your thesis:

- What makes a good teacher?
- Is getting students' attention the *most* important quality of a teacher?
- What are some other significant qualities that a good teacher possesses?
- Which quality in a teacher is essential to you? Why?
- What have your past experiences with teachers shown you about what it takes to be a good teacher?
- Do you know any teachers personally? What would they say about this claim?
- Would someone who is a teacher have a different perspective than I have?
- Are there other people, such as parents, other students, members of the school board, or principals, who might have a different perspective than I have?
- What might people in different parts of the world say about the most important quality of teachers?

Once again, to formulate a good thesis, you must *think critically* about the issues the claim raises in order to formulate the position you can best support in your essay. These types of questions will not only help you shape your own position on the topic, but they might also help you think of examples that will support your claim.

STEP TWO: GATHERING YOUR SUPPORT

Just as you had a head start formulating your thesis statement when you chose your claim and decided on your position, you probably have a good idea of what pieces of evidence you want to present to your audience. You want to choose the examples and reasons you determine will *best* support your position. So think back to the questions you answered when you were choosing your claim and deciding which position to take:

- Can I think of experiences from my own life, the lives of my friends and family?
- Can I think of newspaper or magazine articles I have read that could help me support my case?
- Are these examples really relevant and convincing?
- What are some other positions on this issue?
- How can I logically address opposing views?
- What did you think about when you were choosing the prompt and deciding which position to take?

These questions will help you brainstorm and elaborate on ways to support your claim.

Think back to the sample prompt: "The most important quality of a good teacher is the ability to interest you in the subject he or she is teaching." You have definitely had experiences with teachers, so thinking

As you gather and jot down your evidence, you can organize your evidence into two areas: evidence that supports the topic and evidence that supports an opposing view point. If you find that the evidence for an alternate viewpoint is stronger than the claim you originally made, you might want to consider changing your position. You may change your position completely, or you may decide to apply a more complex or a more limited set of conditions than the claim originally outlined using evidence from *both* the supporting and opposing perspectives to support your new position. Remember, there is no "right" answer to the Issue task; it is vital that you take the position you feel that you can support the best.

about your own experiences in the classroom in relation to what makes a good teacher will guide your position. Brainstorm a list of experiences that will support your position. For now, simply jot down everything that comes to mind.

Next, you will need to narrow down all those experiences; your job is to come up with the most compelling experiences to support your position. Thinking about some opposing viewpoints will help you choose the best evidence—both to support your claim and to refute the opposing claim.

Step Three: Create a Detailed Outline

Now that you know what you are going to say, you have to decide how you are going to say it. It will make the actual writing part of this task go much more smoothly, as much of the thinking will already have been done. You will be able to put your ideas into a logical, effective order and then fill in any gaps in your support.

Even if you are not planning to write your essay in a traditional five-paragraph format, it is best to create your outline according to the basic structure of a traditional essay:

Introduction
Body
Conclusion

Your outline, however, will be much more detailed. For example, you will add your thesis statement, or position, to the introduction portion of the outline, and the body will be broken down into all the examples and reasons you have chosen to support your thesis.

These reasons and ideas will make up your supporting paragraphs, so when you have placed everything into outline form you will be able to see if you are missing any evidence or support. To help develop these vital supporting paragraphs, you should expand your outline. For each main supporting idea—or topic sentence—list at least one specific detail or example to support that idea.

For example, your detailed outline for the topic above might look something like the following:

1. Introduction:

Thesis: Contrary to popular belief, the most important quality of a teacher is not his or her ability to interest students in the subject he or she is teaching; equally essential, are other abilities, such as the ability to listen to and provide encouragement and support for each individual in the classroom.

2. Evidence: Ms. S., my first grade teacher—she paid attention to each child's individual needs, while also keeping us engaged in academic matters.

    a. Lots of kids learned to read in their own time, on their own level.

    b. Everyone was accepted for who they were no matter at what level they were reading.

    c. We had lots of meetings where she got to hear from each of us what we were thinking about. She probed us with questions that would expand our thinking.

3. Evidence: Mr. L., my high school history teacher—he helped each of us individually connect to our history in our exploration of the Vietnam War.

    a. While all his assignments really interested us and his enthusiasm for exploration of the topic was catching, it was more his understanding of what would make this subject come alive for a group of high school students, understanding what *we needed*, that made him such a unique and wonderful teacher.

    b. Assignment to interview people we knew personally who had firsthand experience with war, even if it was being a conscientious objector. Made this war that happened before we were born seem more present and real.

    c. Shared his personal experience during that time so that we understood him better and as a result we all shared our ideas freely with him.

4. Conclusion: These were teachers who were widely recognized in my school community as good teachers. While I loved to go to school every day to see what I was learning next because they made learning interesting, it was also their abilities to understand what their students needed and to support and encourage our learning that made them good teachers.

Your outline might look different depending on the number of examples (the amount of evidence) you choose to include as support for your position. The critical thing is that you get your ideas out, so that you can see where you might be missing support, or even if you have too much or irrelevant support. The more detailed your outline, the easier it will be for you to fill in the blanks as you write your essay.

That said, you do have a limited amount of time to complete your entire essay, and you should probably spend no more than one fourth of your time planning the essay. Remember that you will have already done a lot of brainstorming on the topic as you were choosing your topic and deciding on your position. The brainstorming you have already done will make your outline flow more smoothly and quickly. If it helps, you can create a basic outline while you choose the topic, decide on a position, and gather your evidence. Then, simply add more detail and fill in any gaps before you actually get down to writing.

The tone you take in persuasive writing is essential. Establish your credibility by writing in a rational, thoughtful, and logical manner. You must clearly present your point of view to those who both agree and disagree with you. In addition, you must defend your position against those who disagree with you. You should have already brainstormed reasons why people might not agree with your perspective, so be sure to acknowledge and refute those reasons in your essay. This is when it is critical to write in an even-handed tone. You want to sound logical and rational, as if you have carefully and thoughtfully considered other points of view, but with the reasons and examples you have uncovered, the support for your claim is the strongest so you have decided to take this position.

Keep in mind that, with 45 minutes to complete this task, the scope of your essay will be limited. So while it is vital to include as many details and as much support as possible, remember that you have a limited time to write. Your outline should help you gauge the scope of your essay before you start writing. If it seems like you have too much in your outline, try to pick the best examples to support your position. You can always add more if you find that you have time.

Like choosing your topic and taking a position, creating a good outline takes practice. As you complete the practice prompts at the end of this chapter, be sure to practice making an outline. The more practice your have under your belt, the more automatic these steps will seem when it is time to take the official GRE General Test.

Writing Your Essay

You already have lots of practice writing essays, so this is where you get into the details about how to actually construct your essay. What is most essential to remember when you are working on the Issue task is that you are writing a persuasive piece. Ask yourself these questions:

- Who is my audience?
- Of what do I want to convince them?
- How do I want to say that?
- Am I maintaining my position consistently throughout my writing?

When you write a persuasive piece, your audience is *not* someone who necessarily agrees with your position. Your job is to convince people, sometimes people who do not necessarily see the position from the same point of view, that your position is logical, well reasoned, and thoroughly developed. You will want to clearly state your position at the outset of your essay, and then follow through by logically providing examples and reasons that support your point of view.

Keep this checklist in mind as you write your essay. It should help you focus your writing and keep you on track.

- Use an interesting lead-in sentence to open your essay—if you can think of one fast. You only have a limited amount of time, so don't waste precious moments coming up with something clever. It's better to get writing. You can always add a catchy opening later.
- Make sure you have clear topic sentences that refer explicitly to your position, or thesis.
- Support your topic with facts and examples from a combination of sources: personal experiences, experiences of friends, family, or other people you know, and facts, data, or expert opinion (from readings or lectures).
- Acknowledge other points of view in a reasonable, logical manner, clearly explaining why your position is more persuasive.
- Conclude the essay in an effective way—summarize your main points, demonstrating that you have proven your position and drawing all that you have written about together. Think about why this issue is significant and address its significance in your conclusion. Think about the questions this issue raises, and address the implications of the issue in your conclusion.

Remember, the purpose of the Issue task is to thoroughly examine the issue and come up with a position on that issue. The scorers will be looking at how well you use examples to develop and support your argument. In addition, they are looking at the organization, language, flow, and word choice in your essay—in other words, how well you can sustain and organize the focus of your writing, connecting your ideas logically and fluently.

Revising and Editing

In the 45 minutes you have to put your essay together, you should leave some time to go over your writing, briefly revising and editing your work. You won't have time to polish and perfect your work the way you would in an untimed writing assignment; however, it is essential not to skip this crucial step.

When you have finished your draft, quickly and carefully read over your essay and make changes to improve it, focusing on improving the content and style of your writing. When you revise, you concentrate on the big picture: your ideas and how you have organized and presented them in your essay. Of course you will want to check for obvious grammatical, mechanical, and usage errors, but you can still get a top score and have a couple of minor errors in your writing. The scorers understand that you have a short amount of time to plan, write, and revise your piece, so make sure that you have thought critically about the topic and that your position was clearly stated—that you have provided adequate support, addressed alternate points of view, and connected your ideas logically while maintaining good focus.

You don't have time to rewrite paragraphs or add new ones, but you should have a couple of minutes to change word order, adjust word choice, and correct obvious grammatical and mechanical mistakes. This final polishing step can help make your ideas come across much more clearly for your readers, strengthen your writing, and ensure that you have done your best work.

Assessing Your Writing

Compare your essay to the following rubric, adapted from the official Present Your Perspective on an Issue rubric, to assess your writing. The rubric lists the criteria by which each official GRE reader assesses your work.

SCORE 6

An essay with a score of 6 expertly develops and supports a compelling argument on a given topic. The position is skillfully analyzed and written.

The essay at this level includes the following attributes:

- a perceptive position on the issue
- compelling and persuasive examples and reasons
- a well-developed, well-focused, and well-organized analysis and point of view
- ideas that logically connect to each other
- effective vocabulary, word choice, and sentence variety, communicating ideas fluently and precisely
- adept skill at using the conventions (i.e., grammar, usage, and mechanics) of standard written English, perhaps with minor errors

SCORE 5

An essay with a score of 5 is thoughtful and well developed. It analyzes the issue and presents a position clearly and effectively using good examples.

The essay at this level includes the following attributes:

- a thoughtful position on the issue
- a well-developed position using logically sound reasons and/or compelling examples
- generally good organization and focus
- clearly connected and communicated ideas
- appropriate vocabulary and sentence variety
- skillful use of the conventions of standard written English, perhaps with minor errors

SCORE 4

An essay with a score of 4 reveals a proficient analysis of the issue. The writing sufficiently articulates meaning.

The essay at this level includes the following attributes:

- a clear, developed position on the issue
- relevant reasons and/or examples
- sufficient focus and organization
- ideas that are usually presented acceptably clearly
- general control of the conventions of standard written English, with some errors

SCORE 3

An essay with a score of 3 reveals some competent analysis of the issue and communicates some meaning, but contains apparent flaws.

The essay at this level contains **at least one** of the following flaws:

- vague or limited analysis of the issue
- weak development of a position on the issue
- weak or irrelevant reasons or examples selected
- shaky focus and organization
- lack of clarity due to poor language use and sentence structure
- occasional major errors or recurrent minor errors in grammar, usage, or mechanics that may confuse the reader and obstruct meaning

SCORE 2

An essay with a score of 2 reveals significantly weak analytical writing skills.

The essay at this level contains **one or more** of the following flaws:

- unclear, limited, weak development of a position on the issue
- poor presentation of analysis of issue
- few, if any, reasons or examples selected—if evidence is presented, it is weak and irrelevant
- lack of focus and/or organization
- significant problems in the use of language and sentence structure that regularly obscure meaning
- major errors or repeated minor errors in grammar, usage, or mechanics that repeatedly confuse the reader and obstruct meaning

SCORE 1

An essay with a score of 1 shows essential absence of analytical writing skills.

The essay at this level contains **one or more** of the following flaws:

- little or no indication of understanding and analysis of the issue
- little or no indication of the ability to develop an organized piece of analytical writing
- critical problems in language and sentence structure—errors persistently interfere with meaning
- ubiquitous errors in grammar, usage, or mechanics resulting in unintelligible writing

SCORE 0

An essay with a score of 0 does not relate to the topic, is written in a foreign language, is a restatement of the prompt, or is illegible, blank, or otherwise totally incomprehensible.

Practicing

By now, you should be ready to practice for *Presenting Your Perspective on an Issue*. There are 20 sample prompts at the end of this chapter to use as practice. Keep in mind what you have read in this section as you begin practicing. For the first couple of prompts, take your time choosing an issue, deciding on a position, planning, and writing your essay. After you feel more comfortable, try to stick to the 45-minute time limit by which you will be forced to abide on the official Test. Remember, this writing task is a test of your critical thinking skills and how well you express yourself in writing. If you practice sensibly, using the steps outlined in this section, you should be prepared to ace this test come test day.

► Analyze an Argument—Attack Mode

This 30-minute task in the Analytical Writing section requires you to analyze an argument that someone else has constructed. Unlike the Issue task, you will not be taking a position on and writing about an issue in this task. For this task—the Argument task—you will be required to critically examine the reasoning and evidence used in someone else's argument.

You will be given a short passage, about a paragraph in length, that makes a case. The author will present evidence and reasons to support his or her position. Your job is to carefully examine the case, looking critically at the support provided, the specific claim that was made, and any assumptions the author made without providing support or evidence. Look at the structure of the argument, examining the author's line of reasoning for logical connections and logical fallacy.

Purpose of the Argument Task

The purpose of this task is to see how well you can understand, analyze, and evaluate an argument in writing. As a graduate student, you will be required to analyze readings insightfully and explain your analysis effectively to your professors and academic peers. Therefore, this task assesses your ability to evaluate the logic and reliability of an argument, while employing your critical thinking, perceptive reading, and analytical writing skills.

It is easy to forget what you are *not* being asked to do on this task. Unlike the Issue task, you will *not* be required to formulate a position on the issue. In fact, in your Argument essay, you should not talk about whether you agree or disagree with the argument, or even whether the report the author gives is accurate. You *should* do the following:

- Talk about the *argument* the author makes.
- Examine whether the conclusions drawn and line of reasoning employed by the author are valid.
- Analyze the thinking that went into the argument.
- Scrutinize the logical accuracy of someone else's argument.

Parts of an Argument

As you break down the argument into different parts, it may be helpful to know the following terms:

- **claim:** an assertion about the truth, existence, or value of something
- **argument:** a discussion of a position, claim, or case that is supported by reasons and evidence
- **conclusion:** the main or overall claim in an argument
- **premise:** claim that supports the conclusion

While you will not be required to know these particular terms for the test, it is helpful to understand the different parts of an argument. Your analysis will flow more easily if you think of breaking the argument down and discussing each of these pieces.

In this task, you will be revealing your abilities to identify assumptions, weaknesses, and fallacies as you analyze an argument.

The task directions tell you to "discuss how well reasoned you find this argument." So your first order of business is to examine the given passage.

Examining the Argument

For the Argument task, you will not be required to know any technical analytical terms or systems of analysis. You may have learned some terminology for fallacies or analysis in your undergraduate classes, but you are not required to have any specific kind of knowledge of any particular subject matter. Instead, you will be assessed on how well you understand, analyze, and evaluate an argument, as well as on how well you convey your analysis in writing.

According to *Merriam-Webster's Collegiate Dictionary*, an argument is "discourse intended to persuade." It is a discussion of a position, claim, or case that is supported by reasons and evidence. You have already practiced this type of persuasive discussion in the Issue task. In fact, you have learned how to formulate and support an argument or claim. Now, for this task, you will need to start by breaking down the argument into its various parts in order to understand what the claim is really saying. You want to understand how all these individual parts work together to produce the argument.

To examine the argument you are given, you will need to read the claim carefully, most likely more than once. Start by identifying the issue (or issues) presented, and the position the author takes on that issue. Then, you can begin to break down the argument into its individual components.

First, name as many claims, assumptions, and conclusions as possible. Identify each individual piece of evidence and support that the author presents in the argument. Make special note of any assumptions—something that is taken for granted to be true; it may or may not be explicitly stated—the author makes in the passage.

Once you have identified the individual parts of the argument, see whether or not these pieces of support actually support the point the author is trying to make. Think of what kinds of evidence you might select if you had been the author of the passage:

- Would they have been the same kinds of examples?
- Would you have chosen different ones? Why?
- Does the author's evidence or data really support the conclusion?
- What other evidence can you think of that the author did not include?
- Would this evidence have supported or weakened the author's claim?
- Are there other explanations, besides the ones given, that they author did not address?
- Is there a particular kind of evidence that you know of that contradicts the author's evidence?
- What changes might make the author's reasoning more logical or sound?
- Does the conclusion seem logical given the evidence or data the author provided?

By making note of the answers to these questions as you read through the argument, you will have an easier time deciding what to address in your critique. Remember, the argument you will be given in this task *purposely* includes flaws in reasoning and logic, so if you break down the argument into its parts, you should be able to see where these flaws lie.

Identifying Flaws in Logic and Reasoning

Now that you have broken the argument down, it should be easier to identify the parts of the argument you want to critique. When you present your critique, you want to critique the *major flaws* of the argument, so you are looking for serious errors in the argument. Do not worry whether or not the claim seems correct or true, and do not mention whether you agree or disagree with the claim. This is not the point of the task. Your assignment is to evaluate how the pieces of the argument are put together, whether they are logically sound, and how well each piece of evidence supports the claim.

There are several different kinds of flaws you are likely to see in the arguments given in this task. The following list will explain the most common logical flaws found in this task.

COMMON FLAWS

Using circular reasoning, or assuming to be true what you are supposed to be proving
Example: That restaurant is the best one in town because I like it.

Claiming that one event caused another when there may be no logical connection
Example: When I got home from my vacation my fish was dead, so I know that my roommate did not feed it.

Claiming that most people do something, so it must be OK
Example: It is OK to take office supplies from your office because everyone does it, so it is not stealing.

- Evaluate any statistics or data in relation to the sample size and population. The numbers might not actually represent what the author claims they do.

- Keep in mind that an argument must have a premise and a conclusion, but the premise or conclusion may be unstated.

- If the premise is missing, ask yourself if there are any assumptions that must be true in order for the argument to be valid. Find the missing link between the premise and conclusion.

- Remember that a premise for one conclusion can be the conclusion of a subargument.

- Conclusions must be based on the evidence in the passage. If there is no relevant evidence for an option, it cannot be the correct answer.

- Stick to the statements and claims in the argument that has been presented. Do not let your opinion on the matter influence your critique of the argument.

- You do not need to name a fallacy or flaw in logic—you just need to be able to recognize that something is wrong with the argument.

Using a biased or inadequate sample of data as evidence

   Example: I know five people from Los Angeles and they are all superficial, so everyone from
                L.A. must be superficial.

Suggesting only one or two alternatives when the issue is more complex and might have more alternatives than those described

   Example: I did well in school because my brother did too.

Presenting a non sequitur, where the second part of the claim does not logically follow the first

   Example: Dayjon has an IQ of 180, so he will get an A on the test.

Attacking a person instead of that person's ideas

   Example: You are a woman; therefore, you do not know what you are talking about.

Using someone's popularity to prove a point about which they might have little or no authority

   Example: That NBA superstar says that standardized tests will improve schools' accountability, and that is why we should implement standardized tests in every school in
                the country.

Comparing two similar things that might not share all the same traits

   Example: Because the books are both 500 pages and are on the same topic, they are equally
                good.

When you read through the argument you are given in the Argument task, be sure to look for these common fallacies.

Narrowing Your Scope

Now that you have identified the major flaws in the argument, you are ready to narrow your scope and develop your essay. You may want to discuss the argument line by line, or you may want to develop a critique of one critical flaw in the argument. On the other hand, you might want to briefly summarize the argument and then identify several main flaws in the critique in order of importance. Furthermore, throughout your essay, you should be analyzing the reasoning of, the premise of, and/or the assumptions made in the argument you are critiquing. However you decide to present your critique, what is crucial is how well you reasoned your analysis and how well you can articulate your analysis.

Planning Your Essay

Like planning for the Issue task, your Argument essay should also include the main parts of an essay: an introduction, body, and conclusion. You already know how to construct a thesis statement, gather support, and create an outline for an essay. However, the way you actually present your critique is a bit different from the way you present a persuasive writing piece. You can look at the sample top-score Argument essays at the end of this chapter for the various forms this task might actually take.

THE INTRODUCTION

Use the introduction to set up your critique. Start out by summarizing the argument, and then outline the argument's line of reasoning. Discuss how logically convincing the argument is and identify the major flaws you plan to address in your critique. If you can, write a thesis statement that summarizes the main issues you will address in the rest of your critique.

THE BODY

The body of your essay is where you will analyze the argument. You have already broken down the argument, identified its major flaws, and narrowed the scope of your critique. In the body, you will make an in-depth analysis of the flaws, providing examples from the passage that support your critique. Be sure to consider the premise of the argument in addition to the assumptions and the types of reasoning made in the argument.

THE CONCLUSION

The conclusion is where you will sum up your critique by restating the main issues you addressed in the body. This is not the time to bring up any new points. You may want to address what parts of the argument made sense to you, and then summarize your critique by briefly discussing how the author could have improved his or her reasoning and support.

THE OUTLINE

As in the Issue task, you should plan by sketching out a brief outline from your notes and thoughts listing the following elements:

1. introduction: summary of argument, thesis statement
2. first point (assumption, flaw in reasoning, or premise) and evidence
3. second point and evidence
4. third point and evidence
5. conclusion

Writing Your Essay

Just as you did when you were writing your Issue essay, you should clearly and explicitly use the evidence you uncovered in your analysis to support the points you make in your critique. However you choose to present your critique, be as clear as possible, presenting your analysis in a logical order. Summarize the argument and identify its major flaws. Then present each point of analysis with evidence from the Argument prompt.

When you write your essay analyzing an argument, you will want to do all of the following:

- Identify the main points you will cover in your critique.
- Be sure you have clear topic sentences that refer explicitly to your position, or thesis.
- Support your points with facts and examples.
- Comment explicitly on the underlying reasoning, premises, and assumptions of the argument.
- Discuss what makes the reasoning weak, flawed, or illogical.

Remember, the scorers are looking at how insightfully you analyze the argument you are given. In addition, they are looking at the organization, language, flow, and word choice in your essay—in other words, how well you can sustain and organize the focus of your writing when analyzing and criticizing someone else's argument logically and fluently.

Revising and Editing

Again, you are working under time constraints, so you won't have a lot of time for revising and editing. Leave a few minutes at the end of your allotted time to catch any obvious errors. Take a couple of minutes to change word order, adjust word choice, and correct obvious grammatical and mechanical mistakes. It can help convey your ideas more clearly for your readers, showing how strong your critical thinking skills are, and showcasing your analytical writing abilities.

Assessing Your Writing

Compare your essay to the following rubric, adapted from the Analyze an Argument rubric used by the official scorers of the Analytical Writing section of the GRE test, to assess your work. The rubric lists the criteria for each score that trained readers use to assess your work.

SCORE 6

An essay with a score of 6 reveals a rational and coherent analysis and critique of the argument. The writing is clear and expertly communicates meaning.

The essay at this level includes the following attributes:

- identification and insightful analysis of the essential aspects of the argument
- ideas that are clearly and logically developed, organized, and connected with clear transitions
- skillful support of the main points of the critique
- effective vocabulary, word choice, and sentence variety, communicating ideas fluently and precisely
- expert control of the conventions (i.e., grammar, usage, and mechanics) of standard written English, perhaps with minor errors

SCORE 5

An essay with a score of 5 analyzes the argument insightfully and presents a logical, well-developed, and effective written critique.

The essay at this level includes the following attributes:

- clear and perceptive identification and analysis of significant aspects of the argument
- clear and logical organization, connecting ideas fluently with appropriate transitions
- rational and logical support for the main points of the critique
- good control of language—suitable word choice and sentence variety
- skill at using the conventions of standard written English, perhaps with minor errors

SCORE 4

The essay with a score of 4 critiques and analyzes the argument proficiently, while adequately communicating meaning.

The essay at this level includes the following attributes:

- identification and analysis of essential aspects of the argument
- satisfactory development and organization of ideas; however, ideas may not be well connected with transitions
- understanding of the main points of the critique
- adequate control of language—reasonably clear expression of ideas
- general control of the conventions of standard written English, perhaps with some errors

Score 3

An essay with a score of 3 reveals some skill at critiquing and analyzing the argument. It communicates some meaning, but contains noticeable flaws.

The essay at this level contains **at least one** of the following flaws:

- most of the critical aspects or features of the argument are not identified or analyzed, but contain some analysis of the argument
- unrelated or nonessential analysis of an issue or weak reasoning
- weak or limited logical development and organization of ideas, offering support of little relevance and value for points of the critique
- ideas that are not clearly expressed
- occasional major errors or recurrent minor errors in grammar, usage, or mechanics that may confuse the reader and obstruct meaning

Score 2

An essay with a score of 2 reveals significantly weak analytical writing skills.

The essay at this level contains **one or more** of the following flaws:

- logical analysis of critique is not present, or writer presents his/her own position on the argument
- weak development of ideas, or poor organization and/or logic employed
- little, if any, relevant or reasonable support
- serious difficulty in use of language and in sentence structure, problems frequently obstruct meaning
- major errors or repeated minor errors in grammar, usage, or mechanics repeatedly confuse the reader and obstruct meaning

Score 1

An essay with a score of 1 reveals essential absence of analytical and writing skills.

The essay at this level contains **more than one** of the following flaws:

- little or no indication of understanding and analysis of the issue
- little or no indication of the ability to develop an organized piece of analytical writing
- critical problems in language and sentence structure-errors persistently interfere with meaning
- pervasive errors in grammar, usage, or mechanics resulting in unintelligible writing

Score 0

An essay with a score of 0 does not relate to the topic, is written in a foreign language, is a restatement of the prompt, or is illegible, blank, or otherwise totally incomprehensible.

▶ Tips and Strategies for the Official Test

Now you are ready to practice this task. Take a few minutes to go over the tips and strategies on the next few pages, and then go for it. In the practice section of this chapter, there are 10 practice prompts for you to analyze and critique. Feel free to flip back to this lesson at any time. Remember, on the official exam, you will have just 30 minutes to complete this task. When you are practicing, take as long as you need on the first couple of practice essays you write. Once you feel comfortable, try to complete the task in the time you will be allotted on the official exam. If you practice sensibly, using the formula presented here, you will be well prepared to succeed on the official exam.

The following list will serve as an easy reference as you complete the practice prompts on the subsequent pages and as you continue to prepare for the Analytical Writing section of the GRE General Test. The bulleted points that follow indicate what to remember as you complete both the Issue and the Argument tasks.

The Issue task is 45 minutes and the Argument task is 30 minutes. Be sure to budget your time on the official exam. A good general rule is to divide your time on the essay test accordingly:

PERCENT OF YOUR TIME	ISSUE ESSAY	ARGUMENT ESSAY
$\frac{1}{4}$ of your time planning	10 minutes	8 minutes
$\frac{1}{2}$ of your time writing	25 minutes	15 minutes
$\frac{1}{4}$ of your time revising and editing	10 minutes	7 minutes

The Issue Essay

Remember, there is no "right" answer to the Issue essay. You are required to present and support a position. Your abilities to think critically and support a position effectively in writing are being examined—you are not being judged on the point of view you present.

Don't forget that your job is to defend your position against those who disagree with you. Establish your credibility by writing in a rational, thoughtful, and logical manner.

Choose quickly which claim you will address. The more time you have to formulate your position, choose your evidence, and write and revise your essay, the better it will be. For guiding questions to help you present and support a well-developed position, see the bulleted list on page 49.

Be sure to think of and address two to four counter claims or opposing arguments. Doing so will prove to the scorers that you thought deeply about the issue and came up with some conflicting ideas, but that the evidence for your position refutes opposing arguments. Try to think about the questions this issue raises, and address the implications of the issue in your conclusion.

When you are planning your essay, don't forget the outline, and be sure to include the following pieces:

- an introduction with a strong thesis statement that presents your position
- a body that consists of strong, well-developed paragraphs using specific evidence (reasons and examples) to support your position
- a conclusion that sums up your position, drawing all your evidence together

Leave about a quarter of the time allotted to go over your writing, briefly revising and editing your work. Even though you do not have a lot of time, use the following checklist to strengthen your writing, verify that your ideas are clear to your readers, and ensure that you have done your best work.

CHECKLIST FOR ISSUE ESSAY

Remember that while you should look for obvious spelling, grammar, or mechanical mistakes, it is essential that you present the big picture clearly. Check all of the following:

- The introduction holds the reader's attention.
- The position is expressed clearly and early on in the piece.
- Each paragraph discusses only one main idea.
- Each paragraph relates to and supports the position.
- The piece follows a logical order.
- Transitions are used effectively within sentences and between paragraphs, so your writing flows.
- The conclusion successfully brings the piece of writing to a close.

Use the adapted or official rubrics to assess your writing. Enlist the help of friends, family, or teachers to help you assess your writing according to the same standards GRE test scorers will use on the official exam.

The Argument Essay

On the Argument essay, be sure that you are critiquing and analyzing the written argument by commenting on the logic and reasoning that went into the position. You are *not* being asked to reveal your own views on the argument.

Read the claim carefully, more than once. Start by identifying the issue (or issues) and the position the author takes on that issue. You will need to identify as many claims, assumptions, premises, and conclusions as possible.

Determine whether or not these are valid pieces of support for the author's position. Use the questions on page 61 to guide your analysis of the evidence.

Identify and critique the *major* flaws in the argument. Don't waste valuable time on minor, insignificant points. Remember, you have only 30 minutes to complete this task, so you really need to focus your critique on the major flaws in logic and reasoning. (For help identifying these flaws, see the list of Common Flaws on pages 61–62.)

Plan for your writing using an outline that includes the three main pieces of an essay:

- an introduction that summarizes the argument and includes a thesis statement summarizing the main issues and flaws you will address in the rest of your critique
- a body that presents an in-depth analysis of the flaws in logic and reasoning, providing examples from the passage that support your critique
- a conclusion that sums up your critique by restating the main issues you addressed

You should also be sure to take seven minutes at the end of your allotted time to confirm that your essay does all of the following:

- identifies the main points you will cover in your critique
- contains clear topic sentences that refer explicitly to the main points of your critique
- supports your points with facts and examples
- comments explicitly on the underlying reasoning, premises, and assumptions of the argument
- discusses what makes the reasoning weak, flawed, or illogical

Once again, you will want to leave a few minutes at the end of your allotted time to catch any obvious errors in your writing. Make sure your essay demonstrates your strong critical thinking skills and showcases your analytical writing abilities.

Use the rubrics provided to assess your practice attempts. Recruit friends, family, teachers, or other good writers you know to help you evaluate and improve your writing.

Now that you know what to expect, you should be on your way to earning a top score on the Analytical Writing section of the GRE test. Take a deep breath, and jump right into the exercise. The practice prompts following these tips and strategies give you a chance to practice what you have learned in this chapter of the book. Remember, good writing skills go beyond the GRE test; they are essential to your future success—in school and beyond.

▶ Practice

In this practice, you will put together all the strategies and skills you have acquired in this chapter. Feel free to flip back to the lessons on how to complete the two kinds of tasks and to the tips and strategies for excelling in analytical writing.

Challenge yourself here with 20 Issue prompts and 10 Argument prompts. Then, review the five sample level-6 Issue essays and five sample level-6 Argument essays. These prompts have been adapted from the list of official GRE test prompts and provide topics similar to those you might see on the official exam. Use the sample essays and the adapted rubrics to help you assess your own writing. If you do not feel comfortable assessing your writing on your own, show it to a friend, family member, or a writing teacher. This outside feedback might be helpful—allowing you understand how well your writing meets the criteria GRE test scorers use on the official exam.

For the first couple of practice essays, take your time and thoroughly complete each step of the task. As you grow more confident, try to complete the tasks in the time that will be allotted to you on the official exam—45 minutes for the Issue task and 30 minutes for the Argument task.

Good luck!

Present Your Perspective on an Issue—20 Sample Prompts

The following prompts require you to take a position on a given issue that you feel you can support well. Use relevant reasons and examples as evidence to clearly express and support your point of view throughout your essay.

1. "The U.S. government should pay for the college and university tuition of anyone who wishes to complete higher education."

2. "Receiving a good education is a privilege, not a right."

3. "Reward systems—systems where good behavior is positively reinforced with rewards—are the best way to maintain order in a classroom, home, or workplace."

4. "To make democracy work, we must be a nation of participants, not simply observers. One who does not vote has no right to complain."—*Louis L'Amour*

5. "It's not what you do once in a while; it's what you do day in and day out that makes the difference."—*Jenny Craig*

6. "Scientific, not artistic, creations should be the indicator of the value of civilization."

7. "Studying the whole of a subject or skill leads to a greater understanding of it than an in-depth investiation or discovery of a particular slice of the subject or skill."

8. "Someone who is feared makes a better leader than someone who is loved."

9. "An individual's greatness should be judged by whether or not that individual is the first to accomplish something great."

10. "A work of art is worthy of merit only if it holds common appeal. In order for a work to be considered great, it should be able to be universally understood."

11. "The increased access to knowledge on the Internet leads people to think and reflect less, since a simple search can provide countless pages of information on any one topic. People feel less need to contribute to the intellectual community since there is already so much information out there that is easily accessible."

12. "Our classrooms should provide a balanced program in which kindness and compassion for others, in addition to concern for the community at large, is a central emphasis—as important to success in the world as basic reading, writing, science, and math skills."

13. "The more universal access to knowledge provided by the Internet and other information technologies, the more positive the effect on worldwide pursuit of lifelong learning and intellectual growth."

14. "Being alone is the best way to get to know yourself. People need little help from others to uncover their true selves."

15. "Public resources should not be spent on pursuit of the arts while there are starving and unemployed people, struggling systems of education, and crime in the streets."

16. "The worth of something should be judged by its practical application in the world. We shouldn't waste time and money on anything that does not serve a practical purpose."

17. "As Charles F. Kettering said, 'The price of progress is trouble.'"

18. "A judgment on the worth of something should not be accepted unless it comes from an expert in that field."

19. "Over the past 20 years, technology has only made our lives easier."

20. "Good things come to those who wait, but better things come to those who go out and get them."

Analyze an Argument—10 Sample Prompts

Analyze and comment on how logical and/or reliable you find the following arguments.

1. The following was found on an Internet chat room about the rising costs of healthcare.

> Doctors in large cities make more money than doctors in small towns or rural areas. Just because a doctor's office is in a fancy building or at a fancy address, he or she can charge patients more. Of course, some medical schools cost more than others, but basically all doctors spend a lot of money and a long time in school. There's no proof that graduates of more expensive schools practice in big cities and graduates of less expensive schools practice in small towns. All doctors should charge the same. Whether a patient goes to a doctor in a big city or small town, the cost should be the same.

2. The following is taken from an editorial in the *Colton Times*.

> Giving children computers in grade school is a waste of money and teachers' time. Even if computers are getting cheaper, these children are too young to learn how to use computers effectively and need to learn the basics, like arithmetic and reading, before they learn how to play on the computer. After all, a baby has to crawl before he or she can walk. Students' grades in the schools in my neighborhood have gone down because students now have computers in the classroom.

3. The following is an excerpt from an article in the Friends of the Oakville Library's quarterly newsletter.

> Every few decades for more than 140 years, the public library has endured a cycle of change. We are in the middle of one of these cycles today as librarians try to be responsive to the trends of the times. The Internet and CD-ROM technology are changing public libraries in significant ways.

4. The following appeared in an article in *Managing Today* magazine.

> Today's work force has a new set of social values. Ten years ago, a manager who was offered a promotion in a distant city would not have questioned the move. Today, a manager in that same situation might choose family happiness instead of career advancement.

5. The following is a memo from the manager of Cook's Books, a local bookstore.

> New evidence suggests that many more people are becoming vegetarians. At Johnson's Supermarket, sales of red meat and poultry have gone down 40% over the past three months.

Furthermore, last month's survey of Johnson's customers revealed that they were unhappy with the quality of meat they bought from the store. In addition, over the past two months, *Gourmet* magazine, in which there was a special section on healthy vegetarian recipes, sold out here and at several other locations across town. All of this evidence suggests that our buyers will purchase more vegetarian cookbooks in this month's order, and we should expand our vegetarian cookbook collection.

6. The following is part of a business plan developed by Yoga for Life, a new yoga studio that wants to open a location in downtown Smallville.

Studies show that, in the past five years, more and more Americans are trying to get fit and beat stress. A recent poll at SmallvilleOnline.com showed that 60% of those polled would be interested in taking up yoga. Furthermore, as a result of the recent economic downturn, many people in Smallville are being forced to work longer and harder hours because companies are scaling back and cutting costs. Now, more than ever, there is a demand for a relaxing form of exercise at the end of the day. A yoga center with certified instructors in downtown Smallville will provide this relaxing exercise for city residents.

7. The following appeared in an article in *Science Times* magazine.

Close-up images of Mars by the Mariner 9 probe indicated networks of valleys that looked like the streambeds on Earth. These images also suggested that Mars once had an atmosphere that was thick enough to trap the sun's heat. If this is true, something happened to Mars billions of years ago that stripped away the planet's atmosphere. Thus, a large meteor must have crashed into Mars's atmosphere billions of years ago and thinned its atmosphere so that those streams evaporated.

8. The following appeared in an article on school cafeteria menus in a parenting magazine.

In this day and age, an individual's eating habits often reflect his or her identity—55% of all high school students are vegetarians. Students have the right to be served foods that fit their life choices. Unfortunately, school cafeterias mimic all-too-popular fast-food menus in an effort to provide appetizing food to young people, serving items such as burgers and fries, pizza, hot dogs, and fried chicken. Many of the lunch selections currently offered by most school cafeterias could be made healthier with a few substitutions. Veggie burgers, for example, offered alongside beef burgers, would give both vegetarians and the health conscious more options. A salad bar would also serve the dual purpose of providing both vegetarians and low-fat food eaters the opportunity for a satisfying meal.

9. The following appeared in a newsletter on physical fitness.

Pilates is the best way to help clients improve their core strength—specifically strengthening muscles in the legs, back, and abdominal region. It improves flexibility and strength for the entire body. Not surprising, when it is integrated with rehabilitation exercises and physical therapy, Pilates speeds up the healing process of soft-tissue injuries, improving alignment, tone, and breathing. A combination of mind and body exercises, the workout is also refreshing and energizing for its participants.

10. The following appeared in a letter to the editor of the Noxville newspaper.

> In the next mayoral election, residents of Noxville should vote for Joanne Burgess, a former teacher and principal, instead of Lijuan Jackson, a member of the Noxville city council, because the current members of the city council are not improving our education system. In fact, for the past four years, test scores have dropped significantly, violence in schools has increased 25%, and more children than ever before are being held back. If we elect Joanne Burgess as our next mayor, the education problems in Noxville will certainly be solved.

Sample Issue Essays

4. "To make democracy work, we must be a nation of participants, not simply observers. One who does not vote has no right to complain."—*Louis L'Amour*

Voting is the privilege for which wars have been fought, protests have been organized, and editorials have been written. "No taxation without representation" was a battle cry of the American Revolution. Women struggled for suffrage, as have all minorities. Eighteen year olds clamored for the right to vote, saying that if they were old enough to go to war, they should be allowed to vote. Yet Americans have a deplorable voting record.

Interviewing people about their voting habits is revealing. There are individuals who state, almost boastfully, that they have never voted. They somehow set themselves apart from the requirements of citizenship in a democracy. Many who avoid voting do so consciously. It is not as if they were ill or unavoidably detained on Election Day. Often they claim that their votes don't matter. "What's one vote?" they ask. Perhaps one vote may not count as much in some elections, but there have been results determined by one or very few votes. However, the total number of single votes that are *not* cast can add up to a significant difference in a particular race. Some people say they do not vote because they don't know enough about the issues. Others say that they avoid learning about the issues because it is too depressing. But then I always hear them complaining about the situation of our country. In a democracy, we can express our opinions to our elected leaders, but more than half of us avoid choosing these people who make policies that affect our lives.

One of the effects of this statistic is that politicians will cater to the groups that do vote in large numbers, giving more weight to their needs than to those of other groups or of the general population. Since so many do *not* vote, elected officials can, with impunity, promote policies that benefit the special interests that financially contribute to the election campaigns. Another effect of not voting is the free rein given to those in office to disregard the expressed opinions of constituents. For if you do not vote, why should the candidate worry about you?

It seems ironic that in this most democratic of societies, we abrogate the privilege for which so many have struggled. How many countries do not have a choice of candidates, yet their citizens are forced to participate in sham elections? In the United States, we do have choices. We can vote to fire an officeholder who does not live up to our expectations by voting for his or her opponent at the next election, and we are free to choose someone whose ideas appeal to us.

Perhaps a major reason for not voting is the failure to convey that the right to vote is precious and unique and that each and every vote is important. The major effect is that we are voluntarily giving up our right as citizens to elect officials that truly represent us. If we have not done our part in choosing them, we are, in effect, telling these officials that we don't care enough to bother to vote.

5. "It's not what you do once in a while; it's what you do day in and day out that makes the difference."
—*Jenny Craig*

As a teenager, I wanted to get a job so that I could purchase a car when I turned sixteen. My father sat me down at the kitchen table and said, "I think that's a great goal. I have only one condition for you: 10% of every paycheck must go into a savings account; you cannot touch that money except in an emergency." I argued with my dad, "If I have to put 10% away, how will I ever save enough money to buy a car?"

"You will have enough," he replied. "And you will soon see how important it is to set money aside for savings. It's a habit that's worth every penny."

Jenny Craig says, "It's not what you do once in a while; it's what you do day in and day out that makes the difference," and my father's savings condition demonstrated the importance of Craig's statement. Although I often resented having to put that 10% in a separate account, I upheld my end of the bargain. I always put 10% of each paycheck into a savings account, and I never touched it. Two years later, when the transmission on my car blew, I didn't have to fret about coming up with the money for repairs. With the money I had saved over the years and placed into that 10%-of-each-paycheck savings account, I was able to cover the cost of the car repairs without hassle, and I began to see the wisdom of my father's rule, which I adopted as my own. This habit has helped to provide me with a secure financial future, which I might not have had without my father's prudent advice as a regular influence in my life.

As tight as my budget was at times, I learned that it's important to get started right away. When I moved out on my own, and I was barely scraping by—every last penny went to bills and my expenses. I began by saving just 5%, and as soon as I got a raise, I moved up to 10%. For example, when I was earning $500 a week, I put $25–$50 of that paycheck in my special for-emergencies-only savings account. At first, I had to make do by clipping coupons, renting a movie instead of going to the theater, or ironing my own shirts instead of taking them to the cleaner. I thought carefully about ways I could save just a few dollars—I knew that just a few dollars from each pay-check is all it takes to build up a solid savings account. This good habit prevented me from being caught unprepared when I had to fly home unexpectedly when my dad went into the hospital.

I know that some people get by without saving regularly. They might put in $25 here or there, but some of my friends who didn't make saving a regular part of their routine got caught unawares when a financial emergency came up, such as an unexpected car repair, a family emergency, or their apartment getting robbed. I have heard from my friends, time and time again, "I wish I had money put away like you do." My saving habit has provided me with more security than many of my friends. I feel prepared for almost anything.

Although at times, 10% of each paycheck seemed (and still seems!) like a lot, when I automatically took it right out of each paycheck, I found I didn't miss it. When my salary was $40,000 a year, I thought of it as $36,000 per year. I learned from my experience as a car owner that I can't afford *not* to save 10% of each paycheck. You never know when you are going to need an extra $100 or $1,000; life is full of surprises, and lots of them are expensive. If, like some of my friends, I had simply put in $25 here and there, I might never have saved enough money to feel secure or prepared for an emergency. This habitual practice has assured me of a stable future, something I might not have had if I hadn't regularly put money away, ready for anything that might come my way.

9. "An individual's greatness should be judged by whether or not that individual is the first to accomplish something great."

Just as there are many definitions of success, there are also many definitions of greatness. The Scottish poet Alexander Smith said that a great person is someone who does a thing for the first time. He's right, and the list of those great people is long and includes the likes of Neil Armstrong, Jackie Robinson, and Thomas Edison. But this definition of greatness isn't broad enough to include many other people who are also great. Greatness can also be attained by working to improve the lives of others.

Mother Teresa is the first person who meets this broadened definition of greatness. Mother Teresa, who received the Nobel Peace Prize in 1979, dedicated her life to helping the poor, the sick, and the hungry. She left her homeland of Yugoslavia to work with the impoverished people of India, whom she selflessly served for almost 70 years. She became a nun and founded the Missionaries of Charity sisterhood and the House for the Dying. She embraced those that many in society chose to disdain and ignore: the crippled and diseased, the homeless and helpless. She gave them food, shelter, medical care, and the compassion that so many others denied them. She was not the first to dedicate her life to the care of others, but she was certainly a great woman.

Another great person who also won a Nobel Peace Prize was Dr. Albert Schweitzer, a German doctor who, like Mother Teresa, also selflessly served the poor and sick. Schweitzer dedicated himself to the people of Africa. In Africa, he built a hospital and a leper colony, a refuge for those who had been rejected by society. Again, he was not the first to offer care and comfort for the sick and suffering. But he certainly was great.

Harriet Tubman was also a great woman. She risked her life over and over again while leading hundreds of American slaves to freedom along the Underground Railroad. She gave them the greatest gift one can offer: freedom to live a better way of life. She wasn't the first to escape, and she wasn't the first to go back for others. But she was the one who continued to go back. She knew that each time she returned for another person, she was risking her life. But like Mother Teresa and Dr. Schweitzer, Harriet Tubman was utterly dedicated to improving the lives of others.

Greatness comes in many forms, and we are lucky to have numerous examples of greatness upon which to model our lives. Some great people are those who were able to be the first to accomplish something marvelous, while others, like Mother Teresa, Albert Schweitzer, and Harriet Tubman, are great because they worked tirelessly to ease the suffering of their fellow human beings.

19. "Over the past 20 years, technology has only made our lives easier."

In today's world, the first place people turn to when there is a question to be answered, information to be located, or people to be contacted, is often the Internet. This technology has become rapidly accessible over the past 20 years. People can access the Internet from home, school, the office, the public library, and even Internet cafes. It has expanded human communications capabilities. Who could have predicted 20 years ago that communication would change as radically as it has? Gone are the days when people had to stay near a telephone waiting for an important call or even search for a public phone while traveling. Technology has not only increased our speed of communication, making it faster and easier to communicate with each other, it has also provided a virtually boundless source of information that is easily accessible from almost anywhere, making life easier.

In the last twenty years we have benefited from tremendous changes in telecommunication. The relatively simple change to portable phones enabled us to roam around the house while chatting, unlimited by the length of the cord that attaches the receiver to the base of the telephone, while the beeper and the cellular telephone allow us to talk to anyone around the world at any time. New cellular technologies also allow people to send text messages and check e-mail from a handheld cell phone.

Improved telecommunication technology is not the only technology that has made our lives easier. Written communication is also instantaneous. We can send an e-mail or message instantly to someone not only from a computer, but also from a cellular telephone. Or perhaps you have a piece of writing or a form that must be sent but cannot be conveniently sent via the computer. Facsimile (fax) technology has also made sending the written word faster and easier. The document is transmitted to the receiver at once—it's almost like *handing* the copy to the recipient.

Furthermore, the Internet has supplanted the traditional encyclopedia as well as a number of other sources of service and information. We can make reservations, plan vacations, play interactive games, learn a language, listen to music or radio programs, read the newspaper, and find out about a medical condition, with just the touch of a button. There is no limit to the subject matter you can research on the Internet. Finding an answer or uncovering knowledge is as simple as going to a search engine such as Yahoo or Google and typing in a few keywords or a Web address. You will probably summon links to more sources than you could have imagined, in only seconds. You can also join Internet chat rooms or discussion groups to ask questions or join in on a fun or intellectual discussion.

Furthermore, the Internet saves people time shopping and running errands, no matter what they need to purchase or accomplish. You can place prescriptions online and purchase clothes and food on websites. You can even buy stocks and purchase a house online. If you are looking for a bargain or an unusual item, you can go to a popular auction site and either sell or buy. This ease in shopping makes life more flexible and easy.

It is possible to communicate instantly with anyone, anywhere, as long as there is an Internet connection. In a world where people frequently travel, and where families do not necessarily live in the same neighborhoods, e-mail is a means of making simple, inexpensive, and immediate contact. Not only do we send verbal messages, but now digital cameras take pictures that can be stored and then instantly transmitted on the Internet.

One caveat is the individuals who subvert the opportunities offered by this technology. They are less than honest, disguise their identities, bilk people in financial scams, and entice unsuspecting people, including children, into giving them personal information. Warnings about these problems are currently being publicized so those Internet users will not be victimized.

Of course, the Internet providers, such as AOL, hope to make a profit, and there is usually a monthly fee for the connection. To increase the profits, the providers sell advertising, which may pop up on the subscriber's screen and require the user to stop and respond, either positively or negatively, to the ads.

When you consider that, among other things, you can hear a concert, read a book, visit a museum and view its contents, visit the websites of numerous individuals and organizations, play a game with one or more people, and pay your bills, you will realize that the uses of the Internet are too vast for a short list. Most people would agree that much ease has been added to people's lives by the advances of technology over the past 20 years. With so much happening in such a short amount of time, we can only begin to imagine what new possibilities will be explored in the future that can make our lives easier.

20. "Good things come to those who wait, but better things come to those who go out and get them."

Growing up, I was always told, "Good things come to those who wait." For a long time, I believed it, but now that I am older, I believe that sometimes it's better to go after what you want instead of just waiting for it.

I think the saying "Good things come to those who wait" teaches us an important lesson in patience. For example, when I was 12 years old, I desperately wanted to go to the beach. Coming from Indiana, I had never seen the ocean before, and it was a long and expensive trip for us. I was really into the *Anne of Green Gables* series, and Anne lived on Prince Edward Island. I wanted to be Anne, but even more, I wanted to understand what it was like to live near the dunes and walk along the seashore. My family lived more than 300 miles from the coast, and we didn't even have a car. All spring and early summer, I begged my parents, but they told me that they couldn't afford it. "We'll go someday, but not now," they said. All summer long, I waited and waited. By the time August came around, I had given up hope; I had resigned myself to waiting. Two weeks before we had to go back to school, my parents surprised me with a family trip to Cape Cod. I had a great time, and I still remember the trip fondly.

However, that trip didn't just "happen" for our family because I waited. The money didn't just fall from the sky, and the trip didn't magically plan itself. That summer, I thought that because I had waited, a good thing happened. Now that I know more about the world, I realize that my parents had to work hard to make that trip happen. First of all, they had to scrimp and save money. They also had to postpone other plans they had, such as buying a new washing machine or a new school wardrobe for me and my sister. Instead of several new outfits, we only got a few new things. My parents worked overtime for most of the summer, and they also had to find inexpensive accommodations and entertainment so that we could afford the trip.

Over time, I have also discovered that it is better to be proactive, to make things happen for yourself. For example, when I graduated from college and I needed a job, I knew that it wasn't likely that a great job would just fall into my lap if I waited long enough. I worked hard—I spent hours in the career services office of my college, and I researched companies, built a network of contacts in publishing, and spent long hours writing cover letters and revising my resume. I also spent hours pouring over the employment classifieds, and pounding the pavement looking for work. I practiced for my interviews, and made sure my references were impeccable. Finding a job became a job unto itself. Eventually, I found a great job as an editorial assistant at a large publishing company, but not because I just waited. I hunted that job down. I found people I knew who knew someone who worked at the company, and my resume was perfect because I worked long and hard on it. I didn't want to take any chances waiting for something to happen.

The expression "Good things come to those who wait" implies that good things just happen to us if we wait, without any outside force or direction. The expression implies we are not agents of our own destinies. Sometimes, good things do just happen to come along if we are patient. On occasion, we do happen to meet the right person or be in the right place at the right time, but I also believe that we have the power to make good things come our way. We make choices and set up our circumstances to make it more likely for certain things to happen to us. Good things may come to those who wait, but I believe better things come to those who go out and get them.

Sample Argument Essays

1. The following was found on an Internet chat room about the rising costs of healthcare.

Today, doctors in large cities make more money than doctors in small towns or rural areas. Just because a doctor's office is in a fancy building or at a fancy address, he or she can charge patients more. Of course, some medical schools cost more than others, but basically all doctors spend a lot of money and a long time in school. There's no proof that graduates of more expensive schools practice in big cities and graduates of less expensive schools practice in small towns. Whether a patient goes to a doctor in a big city or small town, healthcare should cost the same.

The claim in this argument, that healthcare should cost the same no matter where doctors live, or how much money they owe in student loans, is obvious to the reader. As much as any reader believes that healthcare is too expensive, the argument itself is not very effective. The author's reasoning is flawed because it is based on assumptions, not hard evidence.

First of all, the argument's claim is based on the idea that doctors determine the cost of healthcare. Certainly doctors are involved in deciding how much money they charge for their time and services; however, the term healthcare means more than doctor's visits. It includes getting tests done, getting X-rays, purchasing medicine, staying in the hospital, and many other services. In today's healthcare web, full of HMOs, expensive insurance, and malpractice lawsuits, much more is involved in the cost of healthcare than where a doctor lives or how much that doctor owes in student loans.

Furthermore, the author never provides evidence to support the general statement upon which the argument is based: " . . . doctors in large cities make more money than doctors in small towns or rural areas." The author just makes that statement without presenting any hard evidence or qualifying it. It's hard to believe such a generalized argument without proof.

The passage is also based on the assumption that no matter where doctors live, the care they give should cost the same amount. Even if we disregarded the author's assumption about doctors being the sole determiner of the cost of healthcare, the argument doesn't make sense. The author doesn't take into account the different costs of living in cities and small towns and rural areas. In general, rent is higher in cities, and a doctor's staff expects a higher salary because there is a higher cost of living—in general, it costs more to run a healthcare practice in the city. Additionally, it makes sense that because there are more people who live in cities, doctors see more patients. Therefore, even if doctors in both cities and small towns charged the same, doctors in the city would see more patients and would probably make more money.

Finally, the argument is also partly based on the assumption that healthcare is so expensive because all doctors have large student loans to pay off. To begin with, not all doctors *have* large student loans to pay off. Besides, there is no evidence to suggest that large debt due to student loans is a major factor in determining the cost of healthcare.

In short, the reasoning in this argument leaves much to be desired. It is based mostly on assumptions, not evidence or fact. Finally, the evidence provided does not seem relevant to the author's claim—doctors aren't the only people making cost decisions concerning healthcare, and it costs more to run a practice in the city, so it makes sense to charge more in the city. It doesn't mean that it's fair, but it is logical.

2. The following is taken from an editorial in the *Colton Times*.

Giving children computers in grade school is a waste of money and teachers' time. Even if computers are getting cheaper, these children are too young to learn how to use computers effectively and need to learn the basics, like arithmetic and reading, before they learn how to play on the computer. After all, a baby has to crawl before he or she can walk. Students' grades in the schools in my neighborhood have gone down because students now have computers in the classroom.

The author of this argument concludes that it is a waste of money and teachers' time to give children computers in grade school because they need to learn basic skills before they can learn how to effectively use a computer. The author doesn't provide any real evidence, but rather makes a thin analogy between a baby learning to crawl before it walks, and students learning basic skills before they learn how to use a more complicated machine.

First of all, the author's analogy is weak. Learning to crawl before you walk is a proven, developmental progression, while learning how to use a computer effectively is not. Perhaps if the author had presented a study about developmental reasons why grade-school students cannot effectively learn how to use the computer, the argument would be more convincing.

Secondly, the author concludes that children should not have computers in grade school. It is difficult to tell from the author's language whether she or he means that computers have no place in grade school classrooms or curriculum, or whether she or he means that grade-school-aged children should not have access to them. This point is unclear, and therefore weakens the argument. Further weakening the argument is the reference to how computers are getting cheaper. This fact has no relation to the main issue of whether computers belong in the grade school classroom—it is irrelevant to the topic at hand.

Finally, the last statement of the argument states, "The grades of schools in my neighborhood have gone down because students now have computers in the classroom." The author provides no logical connection between the fact that the grades of students in schools in his or her neighborhood have decreased and the fact that there are computers in the classroom. The author fails to consider other causes of the drop in grades. There are numerous other reasons why grades may have dropped, totally independent of the fact that there are computers in the classroom.

All in all, the argument is not well reasoned. The author provides a weak analogy and also presents flawed evidence to support the argument. However, the argument could be strengthened by evidence that using computers makes learning to read or do math more difficult—this evidence would back up the author's contention that using computers interferes with learning basic skills. In sum, the author doesn't present compelling evidence that supports the claim that children shouldn't use computers before they know how to read and do math. After all, there are many math and reading computer games that help grade school students improve their basic skills.

5. The following is a memo from the manager of Cook's Books, a local bookstore.

New evidence suggests that many more people are becoming vegetarians. At Johnson's Supermarket, sales of red meat and poultry have gone down 40% over the past three months. Furthermore, last month's survey of Johnson's customers revealed that they were unhappy with the quality of meat they bought from the store. In addition, over the past two months, *Gourmet* magazine, in which there was a special feature on healthy vegetarian recipes, sold out here and at several other locations across town. All of this evidence suggests that our buyers will purchase more vegetarian cookbooks in this month's order, and we should expand our vegetarian cookbook collection.

The author of this piece concludes that the bookstore should expand its vegetarian cookbook collection because meat and poultry sales at a local supermarket have recently decreased, customers are unhappy with the quality of meat from the supermarket, and a magazine with a feature on vegetarian cooking has sold out for the past two months. However, the evidence presented contradicts itself, the support isn't compelling, and the author fails to consider alternate points of view.

First of all, although the report from Johnson's Supermarket does say that sales of meat and poultry have decreased a significant amount, it also says that customers were unhappy with the quality of the meat they found at Johnson's. This evidence suggests that the sales in meat decreased so significantly because customers were unhappy with the *quality* of the meat, not just the meat itself. Thus, this piece of evidence does not support the claim that many people in the town are becoming vegetarians. Perhaps they are not buying meat from Johnson's because it was of poor quality.

Furthermore, we don't know the circumstances of this statistic. Perhaps Johnson's Supermarket is a small neighborhood shop. This record would be more significant if it were a large supermarket at which many people shopped. Also, 40% is a large drop in meat sales, so the number seems fishy.

Secondly, the manager suggests that selling out of *Gourmet* magazine two months in a row, when there were features on vegetarian cooking, was also significant indication that many more people are becoming vegetarian. The magazine's selling out is not adequate indication that many people are deciding to become vegetarians. Perhaps many people became interested in vegetarian cooking from the past two issues; however, perhaps there were other compelling features or articles in the issues. Or, the order size could have been small—if there were only 20 copies ordered and it's a popular magazine, they all could have been sold—or there could have been special bulk sales of this issue. There are many other possibilities that the author doesn't entertain.

This lack of reflection on alternate points of view is also a problem with the argument. The author fails to mention other possibilities in his or her argument, such as a change in season— people tend to eat lighter in the summer, so perhaps more people were cooking without meat. The author even includes evidence about the quality of Johnson's meat that refutes the very evidence provided to back up the claim.

All in all, this piece presents an unsupported argument. The evidence presented isn't very compelling as support for expanding the vegetarian cookbook collection at Cook's Books. In addition, the author leaps to conclusions based on weak evidence. Finally, there is no evidence that the author has considered alternative possibilities or looked at the issue from multiple perspectives. Cook's Books is, after all, a business, so this argument should be more critically examined.

6. The following is part of a business plan developed by Yoga for Life, a new yoga studio that wants to open a location in downtown Smallville.

> Studies show that in the past 5 years, more and more Americans are trying to get fit and beat stress. A recent poll on SmallvilleOnline.com showed that 60% of those polled would be interested in taking up yoga. Furthermore, as a result of the recent economic downturn, many people in Smallville are being forced to work longer and harder hours because companies are scaling back and cutting costs. Now, more than ever, there is a demand for a relaxing form of exercise at the end of the day. A yoga center with certified instructors in downtown Smallville will provide this relaxing exercise for city residents.

The argument above claims that there is demand in downtown Smallville for a yoga center because, not only are more people trying to "get fit and beat stress," but the economic downturn has also introduced a need for a relaxing, energizing form of exercise. Although all of these pieces taken together may be true, the connections between pieces of evidence are shaky.

To begin, the author cites evidence that Americans are trying to "get fit and beat stress." First of all, America is a large country, so it is illogical to make the leap that because unnamed studies show that *Americans* want to get fit, Smallville citizens are also looking to improve their health and fitness. Because the studies cited are unnamed, the reader cannot assume their validity—the reader doesn't know the sample size, the institutions that conducted the surveys, or what kind of fitness and stress—busting these polled Americans want.

In addition, although the statistic provided by an online poll of Smallville residents says that 60% of residents would be interested in taking yoga, the reader does not know the sample size or the population of the people polled. What if some respondents voted more than once? What if only ten people participated in the poll, and six of those people are interested in taking yoga? What if only 5% of Smallville can go online, and only 10% of those who can, did? Because the author doesn't account for these discrepancies, the reader cannot assume that this poll is an accurate indication of the wishes of the entire Smallville population.

The argument is further weakened by the leaping conclusion made in the third and fourth sentences. The author says that people are working hard and are stressed out, and so they want a relaxing form of exercise. The leap is made based on the assumptions that *if* Smallville citizens are being forced to work longer and harder hours, and *if* they want to get fit, then they will want to do yoga. It doesn't follow that they will necessarily want to do yoga. Finally, although 60% of those polled were *interested* in yoga, even assuming there was a reasonable sample size, it doesn't mean that they *are* going to do yoga. Also, the author doesn't consider the fact that yoga sessions may be an unwanted expense for people who are working "longer and harder hours" just to make ends meet.

Thus, before a decision is made on whether or not to open the yoga center, a more complete understanding of the actual customer base is needed—what the downtown area is like, and what the exercise and fitness goals of the community really are. Overall, an argument that addresses these issues would be stronger than the one given.

10. The following appeared in a letter to the editor of the Noxville newspaper.

> In the next mayoral election, residents of Noxville should vote for Joanne Burgess, a former teacher and principal, instead of Lijuan Jackson, a member of the Noxville city council, because the current members of the city council are not improving our education system. In fact, for the past four years, test scores have dropped significantly, violence in schools has increased 25%, and more children than ever before are being held back. If we elect Joanne Burgess as our next mayor, the education problems in Noxville will certainly be solved.

On first glance, the idea that a teacher/principal would make a more effective member of the city council, solving the problems of the education system in Noxville, than a current member of the city council, seems to be an obvious assumption. However, upon deeper analysis of the argument, several pieces of it do not successfully support the claim.

To begin with, the premise that a teacher/principal will be able to solve the problems with the education system in Noxville provides a fragile base from which to found the argument because this supposition is founded on the idea that a current member of the city council is not a good candidate only because the current town council hasn't improved education. The assumption that a teacher/principal is suited to being mayor based solely on her expertise in the area of education presents too many problems. There is much more to being mayor of a city than improving the education system—being mayor is a political, not educational, office— besides, Burgess's expertise alone will not help her solve the education problems of Noxville.

In addition, the premise that Jackson alone represents the achievements of the entire city council does not make sense. The premise is based on the entire council's track record, which may or may not indicate Jackson's personal ideas or set of values. The author lumps Jackson together with the city council—it is important to remember that decisions the council makes are not his decisions alone. In fact, he may have supported measures to improve education that the entire council didn't pass. The connection between the relationship of a single city council member and problems with the education system is unsupported and weakens the author's argument. Jackson alone is not responsible for the outcome of city council decisions— other members have say in the decisions and intentions of other members of the town council.

Furthermore, the information the author provides about the city council's failings is unqualified. The author lists three problems with education as it stands: test score decline, school violence, and more children who are held over, repeating grades. First of all, the author does not say whether these problems were being addressed by the city council. Additionally, the source of these figures is not provided to the reader, so the reader has no way of judging their validity. For example, what exactly does *significantly* mean? It is a broad, subjective term, and without knowing the actual figure the reader cannot take for granted the definition of significantly.

Therefore, the argument's reasoning is loosely connected, founded on assumptions and unqualified premises. Alone, the evidence provided to support the position is not tentatively related to the author's main argument, that an expert in education will solve Noxville's education problems, and that the city council's record alone reflects Jackson's neglect of the education system.

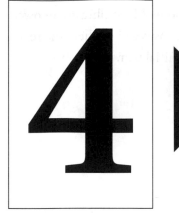

The GRE Verbal Section

▶ Pretest

One way to increase your chances for GRE test success is to become familiar with the test itself. This section focuses on the Verbal test questions. The following is a pretest that will help you assess what your strengths and weaknesses are, when it comes to the verbal skills assessed on the GRE test. Take this test before moving ahead in the book. Don't worry if you don't do as well as you would like; there's no better way to focus your studies than by seeing your strong points and your not-so-strong points.

ANSWER SHEET

1.	ⓐ ⓑ ⓒ ⓓ ⓔ	8.	ⓐ ⓑ ⓒ ⓓ ⓔ	15.	ⓐ ⓑ ⓒ ⓓ ⓔ
2.	ⓐ ⓑ ⓒ ⓓ ⓔ	9.	ⓐ ⓑ ⓒ ⓓ ⓔ	16.	ⓐ ⓑ ⓒ ⓓ ⓔ
3.	ⓐ ⓑ ⓒ ⓓ ⓔ	10.	ⓐ ⓑ ⓒ ⓓ ⓔ	17.	ⓐ ⓑ ⓒ ⓓ ⓔ
4.	ⓐ ⓑ ⓒ ⓓ ⓔ	11.	ⓐ ⓑ ⓒ ⓓ ⓔ	18.	ⓐ ⓑ ⓒ ⓓ ⓔ
5.	ⓐ ⓑ ⓒ ⓓ ⓔ	12.	ⓐ ⓑ ⓒ ⓓ ⓔ	19.	ⓐ ⓑ ⓒ ⓓ ⓔ
6.	ⓐ ⓑ ⓒ ⓓ ⓔ	13.	ⓐ ⓑ ⓒ ⓓ ⓔ	20.	ⓐ ⓑ ⓒ ⓓ ⓔ
7.	ⓐ ⓑ ⓒ ⓓ ⓔ	14.	ⓐ ⓑ ⓒ ⓓ ⓔ		

Instructions: There are 20 questions in this section. Set a timer for 20 minutes. Stop working at the end of 20 minutes and check your answers in the explanations section that follows.

Analogies

Instructions: In the questions that follow, there will be an initial pair of related words or phrases followed by four answer pairs of words or phrases, identified by letters **a–e**. Choose the answer pair where the relationship of the words or phrases most nearly matches the relationship of the initial pair.

1. BREACH : WHALE
   a. whistle : dog
   b. dunk : doughnut
   c. shoot : target
   d. ride : horse
   e. fly : bird

2. QUIXOTIC : PRAGMATIC
   a. murky : clear
   b. callous : insane
   c. limp : frightened
   d. tender : poignant
   e. unflappable : sensitive

3. LIBEL : SMEAR
   a. represent : discount
   b. doubt : verify
   c. heed : consider
   d. countermand : titillate
   e. persevere : abandon

4. PILOT : FERRY
   a. plumber : pipe
   b. carpetbagger : carpet
   c. teacher : chalk
   d. physician : heal
   e. author : book

5. LIMP : INJURY
   a. stiff : cast
   b. incarceration : conviction
   c. integrity : honesty
   d. normality : congruence
   e. paralysis : wheelchair

Antonyms

Instructions: In each of the following questions you will be presented with a capitalized word followed by four answer choices lettered **a–e**. Select the answer word or phrase that has a meaning most nearly *opposite* to the initial word.

Some of these questions will require you to discriminate among closely related word choices. Be sure you choose the answer that is most nearly opposed to the capitalized word.

6. AMPLE:
  a. complete
  b. insufficient
  c. quiet
  d. supple
  e. wistful

7. AERATE:
  a. ground
  b. placate
  c. destroy
  d. calibrate
  e. suffocate

8. PAUCITY: -
  a. excess
  b. height
  c. certainty
  d. pulchritude
  e. modesty

9. RESPLENDENT:
  a. illuminated
  b. dowdy
  c. hideous
  d. delightful
  e. magnanimous

10. SAGACITY:
  a. incredulity
  b. belligerence
  c. stupidity
  d. tolerance
  e. independence

Sentence Completions

Instructions: Each of the following sentences contains either one or two blanks. Below each question are answer choices lettered **a–e**. Select the lettered choice that best completes the sentence, bearing in mind its intended meaning.

11. Ball lightning is a _____ phenomenon; it typically limits its dazzling electrical displays to about ten seconds.
   a. incomprehensible
   b. incomparable
   c. stereoscopic
   d. polymorphous
   e. transitory

12. The renowned daredevil was, in fact, temperamentally quite _____, as evidenced by the fact that he declined to _____ until nearly two years of age.
   a. circumspect..perambulate
   b. incredulous..incarcerate
   c. gullible..villify
   d. pernicious..inculcate
   e. elusive..concentrate

13. It is difficult to be an iconoclast; for _____ the world whips you with its _____.
   a. flamboyance..imprisonment
   b. nonconformity..displeasure
   c. disrespect..intervention
   d. ostentation..opprobrium
   e. procrastination..misfortune

14. Our land is young; but our day of _____, our long _____ to the learning of other lands, draws to a close.
   a. dependence..apprenticeship
   b. presumption..deference
   c. possibility..capitulation
   d. flagellation..perfidy
   e. competence..hardship

15. That which is apprehended by intelligence and reason is always in the same state; but that which is conceived by _____, with the help of _____ and without reason, is always in a process of becoming and perishing and never really is.

   a. tribunal..analogy

   b. opinion..sensation

   c. catastrophe..dissidence

   d. precedent..insouciance

   e. perfidy..catastrophe

Reading Comprehension

Instructions: Read the passage that follows. After the passage, answer the content-based questions about it. Each question must be answered using only the information that is either *implied* or *stated* in the passage.

(1)   It is generally allowed that Guiana and Brazil, to the north and south of the Para district, form two distinct provinces, as regards their animal and vegetable inhabitants. By this it means that the two regions have a very large number of forms peculiar to themselves, and which are supposed not to have been derived from other quarters during modern geological times. Each may be considered as a centre of

(5)   distribution in the latest process of dissemination of species over the surface of tropical America. Para lies midway between the two centres, each of which has a nucleus of elevated tableland, whilst the intermediate river valley forms a wide extent of low-lying country. It is, therefore, interesting to ascertain from which the latter received its population, or whether it contains so large a number of endemic species as would warrant the conclusion that it is itself an independent province. To assist in deciding

(10)   such questions as these, we must compare closely the species found in the district with those of the other contiguous regions, and endeavour to ascertain whether they are identical, or only slightly modified, or whether they are highly peculiar.

16. The author's main point is that

   a. the fauna and flora of Para are distinct from both the flora and fauna of Guiana and the fauna and flora of Brazil.

   b. Para supports a very large number of ecological distinct habitats.

   c. ecological considerations override all others with respect to Para.

   d. it has not yet been determined whether or not Para is an ecologically distinct district.

   e. the government of Para has historically not been supportive of biological expeditions.

17. The scientific methodology the author of this passage recommends following is

   a. tracking migration patterns from both Guiana and Brazil to Para.

   b. disseminating information about indigenous species to the scientific community.

   c. comparing and contrasting Para's indigenous species to those of Guiana and Brazil.

   d. hunting for peculiar species of flora and fauna, wherever they may be located.

   e. initiating a longitudinal study of species evolution.

18. The author of this passage would agree with which of the following statements?

    I. Both Guiana and Brazil are ecologically distinct provinces in South America.

   II. Both Guiana and Brazil are centers of distribution for the dissemination of species into Para.

  III. Para consists of a nucleus of elevated tableland and a low-lying river valley.

    a. I, II, and III

    b. I and II only

    c. III only

    d. II and III only

    e. I only

19. It can be inferred from this passage that the main criterion for declaring any given area a distinct province in terms of its flora and fauna is

    a. the particulars of the district's geographical features, including its isolation or lack thereof.

    b. the number of peculiar species endemic to the district.

    c. the district's proximity to natural populations of endemic species.

    d. the number of identical species inhabiting contiguous regions.

    e. the diversity of species within geographical boundaries.

20. This passage supports all of the following statements EXCEPT:

    a. Guiana is a center of distribution for the dissemination of species.

    b. Careful attention to detail will be essential in resolving the questions raised about the Para district's flora and fauna.

    c. Brazil's natural geographic features include a nucleus of elevated table land.

    d. Guiana is a distinct province with regard to fauna and flora.

    e. Para is situated between two distinct river valleys.

▶ Pretest Answers

The following are the answers for each of the previous sections.

Analogies

1. e. The pair of answer choices with the same relationship is *fly : bird*. *Breach* is the action of a *whale*. *Fly* is the action of a *bird*.

2. a. The relationship of *quixotic* to *pragmatic* is one of opposites. *Murky* is the opposite of *clear*.

3. c. To *libel* is to *smear*. To *heed* is to *consider*. The word pairs are synonyms.

4. d. A *pilot's* job is to *ferry* passengers. A *physician's* job is to *heal* patients.

5. b. An *incarceration* is caused by a *conviction*. A *limp* is caused by an *injury*.

Antonyms

6. b. *Ample* means plenty. *Insufficient* means not enough.

7. e. *Aerate* means to give air to. *Suffocate* means to deny air to.

8. a. *Paucity* means not enough. *Excess* means too much.

9. b. *Resplendent* means splendid (note the common root). *Dowdy* means shabby.

10. c. *Sagacity* means wisdom. *Stupidity* is the opposite of wisdom.

Sentence Completion

Note: In the explanations, any reference to sentence *units* is a reference to sections of the sentence as denoted by punctuation, such as commas and semicolons.

11. e. The second part of the sentence is a restatement of the first part. *It* refers to *ball lightning*. The fact given, that *it . . . limits its . . . displays*, tells us that *ball lightning is a transitory* (passing) *phenomenon*.

12. a. *In fact* signals a contrasting relationship. In this case the first blank contrasts with our expectations of a daredevil's temperament. The second blank illustrates *(as evidenced by)* the concept of carefulness expressed by the word *circumspect*. To *perambulate* is to walk.

13. b. The second unit of the sentence expands on the idea in the first unit, so think of it as a restatement. A key word in the second unit is *whips*. The first blank tells what the world whips for: a synonym for *iconoclast*. The second blank tells what the world whips with: *displeasure*, a figurative whipping, not a literal one.

14. a. The word *but* in the second unit of the sentence signals a contradiction to the idea in the first unit. The contrasting idea, however, is in the final unit: *draws to a close*. The blanks in the second and third units tell us what is drawing to a close: our *dependence* and *apprenticeship*.

15. b. The first unit of the sentence speaks of *intelligence* and *reason* as means of understanding. The second unit begins with *but*, signalling a contrast. Both blanks must be filled with words that contrast with *intelligence* and *reason*.

Reading Comprehension

16. d. The author's main point in this passage is to set forth the need to investigate the ecological status of Para and the means by which the investigation should proceed.

17. c. The author states *we must compare closely the species found in the district with those of the other contiguous regions*.

18. b. Statements I and II are both contained in the first half of the paragraph. Statement III is not correct for Para, though it is correct for both Guiana and Brazil.

19. b. The author suggests evaluating Para to see if it *contains so large a number of endemic species as would warrant the conclusion that it is itself an independent province*.

20. e. It is suggested that Guiana and Brazil each have elevated tablelands, which descend to a single river valley and that Para is located within this valley.

▶ Introduction to the Verbal Section

The Verbal section of the GRE test presents you with questions very much like those on the preceding sample test. As you can see from the pretest, a good vocabulary will help you immensely. In addition, there are numerous strategies that can help you maximize your chances of correctly answering the questions; this chapter will discuss how to utilize those strategies.

The Verbal section of the GRE test is timed for 30 minutes. In that time you will be presented with 30 questions, each with answer choices **a–e**. Because the exam is a computer-adaptive test (CAT), every test taker will receive a different set of questions. If you answer a given question correctly, you will then be presented with a more difficult question. If you answer incorrectly, you will receive a less difficult question. The harder the questions you successfully answer, the more points you receive. That means your answers to the first 10 or 15 questions are particularly important, because the CAT program is finding the general range within which you correctly answer questions. Once the program has determined your general score range (e.g., are you in the 500s, the 600s, the 700s?), it uses the remaining questions to fine-tune your score (e.g., 620? 640? 660?). That means you want to be especially careful with your answers on the first half of the Verbal section.

Remember that you may also have an additional section (which could be presented as a Verbal or a Quantitative section). If so, one of the two Verbal (or Quantitative) sections will be a research section that will not count toward your score. However, you will not be able to tell which of the two similar sections is the scored section and which is the research section. It is important to treat each one as though it were the scored section.

▶ What to Expect on the GRE Verbal Section

As you saw in the pretest, there are four kinds of Verbal section questions: **analogies**, **antonyms**, **sentence completions**, and **reading comprehension questions**. These questions are designed to test your comprehension of the logical relationships between words, as well as your ability to understand and think critically about complex written material.

Analogies test your vocabulary and your ability to identify relationships between pairs of words (and the concepts they represent). In each analogy question, you will be presented with a pair of words in all capital letters, in a format that looks like this:

PAGE : BOOK

Then you will be given five answer choices, **a–e**, in the same format but in lowercase letters. You must choose the answer choice that contains words with the same relationship to each other as the initial pair has. There are straightforward techniques that can help you divine the relationships, and they are easily mastered with practice. You will have the opportunity to get familiar with these techniques later in this book.

The relationship of all *antonyms* is one of *opposition*. You want to pick the answer choice (i.e., the word or concept) that is most nearly the opposite of the question word. The question word will be presented in all

Don't Get Personal

Remember that on the GRE test, you must assess arguments and answer questions based only on the information presented on the test. For the moment, forget what you might know or how you might feel about the topic or issue. Base your answer only on the argument and evidence in front of you.

capital letters, for example, FLOOD. The answer choices will consist of either single words or phrases, lettered **a–e**, and you must select the word or phrase that is most nearly opposite in meaning to the initial word. Obviously, this is also a test of vocabulary. In order to understand the relationships of the words, you must know their meanings and their nuances.

Sentence-completion questions test your ability to follow the logic of complicated, though incomplete, sentences. Often the sentences are long and difficult to follow, and each contains either one or two blanks. Though the vocabulary used is sometimes challenging, these questions primarily test your ability to use words and phrases as *clues* from which to construct meaning. The following pages of this chapter contain information about these clues, including how to identify and use them to make logical predictions and successfully complete the sentences.

Reading comprehension questions present you with a passage taken from the humanities or the social or natural sciences. You are then asked a series of questions that test your understanding of what is stated or implied in the passage. You will be asked to draw inferences from the author's words, but you will not need to call upon any outside information you may possess or resources other than the passage itself.

If you have ever taken the SAT exam, you will be somewhat familiar with three of these four question types. (There are no antonym questions on the SAT exam.) Each type of question comes in varying levels of difficulty, starting with a question considered to be about average in difficulty. Once you answer the initial question, the computer will administer either a harder or an easier follow-up question and then continue to repeat that process with subsequent questions.

▶ The Four Types of Verbal Section Questions

Analogies

There are roughly six to eight analogies on the Verbal section. You will see instructions on your screen, which read something like the following:

> In the questions that follow, there will be an initial pair of related words or phrases followed by five answer pairs of words or phrases, identified by letters **a–e**. Choose the answer pair where the relationship of the words or phrases most nearly matches the relationship of the initial pair.

Analogy questions test your ability to establish the relationship between the pairs of words or phrases. In the example from the previous section, PAGE : BOOK, the first thing you should do is read those words to yourself in this format: PAGE is to BOOK as what is to what? Then you should think: what is the relationship of *page* to *book*? You might say, a page *is part of* a book; or you might say, a book *is made up of* pages. Then you look for the answer choice that reveals the same relationship. In this case, it would be something that is one of the identical component parts of a larger whole, for example, as *drop* is to *water*.

There are certain types of relationships that recur with some regularity on the GRE test:

- part to whole
- contrasting/antonyms/opposites
- cause and effect
- type of
- degree of
- use or purpose of
- tool to worker

These relationships will be discussed in the extended lesson on analogies later in this chapter.

Antonyms

You probably know that a **synonym** is a word or phrase that means the same as another word or phrase. An **antonym** is a word or phrase that means the opposite of another word or phrase. Think of the prefix *anti*, meaning *against* or *not*.

There are seven to ten antonym questions on the GRE test. The directions for those questions will read something like the following:

> In each of the following questions you will be presented with a capitalized word followed by five answer choices lettered **a–e**. Select the answer word or phrase that has a meaning most nearly *opposite* of the initial word. Some of these questions will require you to discriminate among closely related word choices. Be sure you choose the answer that is most nearly opposed to the capitalized word.

Your strategy for antonym questions is to first determine the meaning of the capitalized word and to then think to yourself what the opposite of that word would be. The opposite of the word FLOOD, for example, would be a word such as *drought*. *Drought* has a connotation of extreme dryness, the opposite of *flood's* connotation of extreme wetness. It is vitally important to remember that many words have more than one meaning and to consider all possible meanings when looking at your answer choices. You will learn other strategies for correctly answering antonym questions in the lesson on antonyms later in this section.

Sentence Completions

Sentence completion questions test your ability to follow the logic of complicated sentences. Each of these questions has either one or two blanks within a single sentence. Often the sentences are long and difficult to follow, but with practice you can learn to master them. There are between five and seven of these questions on the GRE test.

At the beginning of the sentence completion portion of the Verbal section, you will find instructions along the lines of the following:

> Each of the following sentences contains either one or two blanks. Below each question are answer choices lettered **a–e**. Select the lettered choice that best completes the sentence, bearing in mind its intended meaning.

These instructions, which are paraphrased from the exam's actual instructions, tell you that the test makers believe that each incomplete sentence contains enough clues to its meaning for you to understand it, even with one or two blanks. That means you have to use the overall context of the sentence to determine the meaning(s) of the missing word or words. You will see in the lesson on sentence completion questions that there are easily mastered techniques for deciphering the clues within each sentence, using the syntax of the sentence to guide you.

Reading Comprehension

Reading comprehension questions test your understanding of complex passages, such as those you might encounter in graduate school. The exam will present you with two to four passages, drawn from writings in the humanities, social sciences, and natural sciences. Each passage, typically 300 to 1,000 words in length, is followed by from four to eight questions, with answer choices **a–e**; you can expect somewhere in the neighborhood of 15 reading comprehension questions.

There are a variety of writing styles, including narrative, expository, and persuasive. The writing will typically be dense and contain difficult vocabulary. You will have to analyze each passage using advanced techniques:

- making inferences from the author's statements
- interpreting the author's purpose in writing
- drawing logical conclusions with which the author would agree

The directions for reading comprehension questions will read something like the following:

> Read each of the passages that follow. After each passage, answer the content-based questions about it. Each question must be answered using only the information that is either *implied* or *stated* in the passage.

In the lesson on reading comprehension questions, you will gain insight into the types of passages used and the kinds of questions posed. You can practice answering these types of questions using the sample test in this book; it would also be a good idea to practice using these reading comprehension strategies anytime you read.

The Verbal Section at a Glance

The Verbal section of the GRE test has 30 questions. There are four kinds of questions:

Antonyms test your understanding of vocabulary by using pairs of words with opposite meanings.

Analogies test your understanding of the relationships between pairs of words.

Sentence completion questions test your ability to use the information found in complex, but incomplete, sentences to determine meaning and correctly complete the sentences.

Reading comprehension questions test your ability to understand the meaning of material in a passage and to draw inferences from what is stated.

▶ A Lesson a Day Makes the Test Go Your Way

There's not enough time to memorize the dictionary to prepare for the Verbal Section, but you can easily boost your vocabulary, practice critical thinking skills, and learn to be a good guesser. This section explains how.

The Power of Words

As you have seen, all four kinds of verbal questions test your knowledge of and ability to use words. It is no surprise, then, that success on the Verbal section of the GRE test depends largely on both the size of your vocabulary and your facility with using it.

What if you don't consider yourself a word person? Don't despair. The fact is, we are all word people. Words guide our everyday lives. Words shape our perceptions of the world. Even math can be thought of as another language—a language that is explained through the use of words.

No matter what kind of word power you already possess, your GRE test verbal score will improve as you increase your vocabulary. Other than using this book as a study guide, the single most productive way to prepare for the Verbal section is to learn additional vocabulary. The best way to go about this is to work with a

Tip

Want to build your vocabulary? Try setting your Internet browser homepage to one of these word-a-day websites:

- www.mywordaday.com
- dictionary.reference.com/wordoftheday
- oed.com/cgi/display/wotd
- www.nytimes.com/learning/students/wordofday
- www.wordsmith.org/awad

test-prep book or computer program. There are a variety of software programs, websites, cassettes, and CDs that teach vocabulary building. A good starting place is a vocabulary book like LearningExpress's *Vocabulary and Spelling Success in 20 Minutes a Day,* which makes it easy to boost your vocabulary and your Verbal section score.

Try these strategies to help build your vocabulary for the GRE test:

1. Practice determining the meaning of unfamiliar words in context.
2. Maintain your own vocabulary list and review it regularly.
3. Study prefixes, suffixes, and word roots. Many GRE-level words have Latin or Greek word roots. Knowing these word bases and common beginnings and endings can give you an edge in determining the meaning of unfamiliar words.

Think It Through

At least as important as the size of your vocabulary, however, is your ability to use words as logical tools. In other words, the GRE test assesses your ability to think clearly and logically.

As you have progressed through school, you have moved from *memorizing* facts, to *researching* and *organizing* them, to *interpreting* and *expanding* them. In graduate school you will be required both to evaluate others' ideas and arguments and to generate your own. Authors often present ideas in artful fashion—perhaps to disguise their arguments' weaknesses. You will need to lift the curtains of artifice and peer through to the essence of the arguments.

The GRE test's Verbal section, therefore, is designed to assess your skill with words. Whether you are comparing concepts (analogies), contrasting concepts (antonyms), deducing meaning from available clues (sentence completion questions), or interpreting and extending meanings (reading comprehension questions), you are being asked to use words as logical tools.

Fortunately, there are guidelines for these skill sets. This chapter lays out those guidelines for you. You will learn attack strategies for each of the four types of questions, as well as techniques for questions that seem to resist analysis. With practice these techniques and strategies will become second nature and will remain in your repertoire of logical tools as you enter graduate school.

▶ How to Approach Analogies

An analogy question asks you to find the relationship between a pair of words. Words, of course, represent concrete or abstract things; so you are being asked to discover relationships between things. Once you understand

If you don't see the answer pair that parallels the relationship you are trying, see if there is another way to state the relationship between the words in the stem pair.

the relationship between the initial pair of words, you must find the answer pair with an analogous (the same kind of) relationship.

An analogy is presented in a standard format that can be confusing to the uninitiated, but is simple once you get the hang of it. GRE test analogies will appear in the following format:

DENIM : COTTON

a. sheep : wool
b. uniform : boots
c. linen : flax
d. silk : rug
e. fur : coat

The way to read an analogy to yourself is: *Denim* is to *cotton* as *blank* is to *blank.* You are looking for a parallel relationship between denim and cotton, and the correct answer pair. First you determine the relationship between denim and cotton (or between cotton and denim, if that's easier for you). *Denim* is a material made from the *cotton* plant, so the correct answer is **c.** *Linen* is a material made from *flax.*

Relationships

Word relationships are like their human counterparts: They can be difficult yet rewarding. You have to be patient and flexible, but once you understand what you need to do, everything gets a lot easier!

There are certain types of relationships you will find over and over on the GRE test. Here are some of the more common ones:

1. **Part to Whole**. An example of this would be *leaf : tree.* A *leaf* is a part of a *tree.* A *chapter* is part of a *book.* A *finger* is part of a *hand.* A *circuit* is part of a *computer.*
2. **Contrasting/Antonyms/Opposites.** *Light : dark* is an example of a contrasting relationship. *Fast* is an antonym of *slow. Previous* is the opposite of *subsequent.*
3. **Cause and Effect.** *Crime : punishment* is an example of cause and effect: He committed a *crime*; the result was his *punishment. Rain : wet* is another example (when it *rains,* things get *wet*), as is *study : success* (when you *study,* the result is *success*).
4. **Type of.** An example of type is *trumpet : horn.* A *trumpet* is a type of *horn.* A *recliner* is a type of *chair.* A *Siamese* is a type of *cat.*

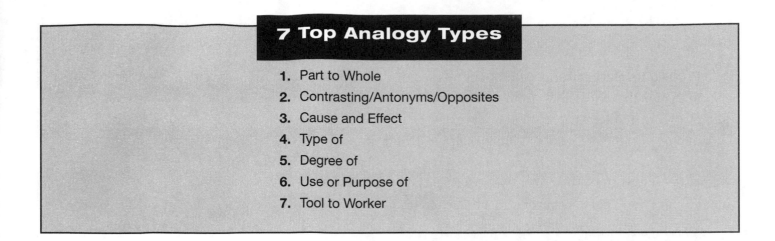

7 Top Analogy Types

1. Part to Whole
2. Contrasting/Antonyms/Opposites
3. Cause and Effect
4. Type of
5. Degree of
6. Use or Purpose of
7. Tool to Worker

5. Degree of. *Hot : blistering* is an example of a degree analogy. *Difficult* is a (lesser) degree of *impossible*. *Mountain* is a (greater) degree of *hill*.

6. Use or Purpose of. An example of use or purpose is *microwave : heating*. A *microwave* is used for *heating*. A *pen* is used for *writing*. The purpose of a *train* is *transportation*.

7. Tool to Worker. *Hammer : carpenter* is an example of tool to worker. A *spatula* is a tool used by a *cook*. A *photographer* uses a *camera*.

There are many other types of relationships, but these are among the ones most commonly found on the GRE test.

Analogy Strategies

THE SENTENCE

Your single most useful strategy in tackling analogies is to make a sentence using the *stem* (or initial) words. Use one stem word at (or near) the beginning of the sentence and the other stem word at (or near) the end. The sentence must reveal their relationship with some degree of specificity. The more difficult the analogy is, the more specific the sentence must be in revealing the words' relationship. Here is an example:

TOOTH : MOUTH

    a. eyebrow : face
    b. bark : bite
    c. orthodontist : dentist
    d. toothbrush : holder
    e. stalactite : cave

You might start out by saying: *A tooth is part of a mouth*. That reveals a part-to-whole relationship. Then, check the answer pairs for a parallel relationship by substituting each pair in your sentence. *An eyebrow is part of a face*. That's true, so it's a possibility. *A bark is part of a bite*. No; rule it out. *An orthodontist is part of a dentist*. A dentist could also be an orthodontist, but it's more likely that this answer was put in as a distracter because of its connection to teeth and mouths. Rule it out. *A toothbrush is part of a holder*. Again, it seems likely to be a distracter because of its relationship to teeth. Rule it out. *A stalactite is part of a cave.* A stalactite is a formation that hangs down from the ceiling of a cave, so the sentence is true and therefore a possibility.

Now you have two possible answer choices, **a** and **e**, either of which works with your sentence. That means your sentence is not specific enough and needs to be reworked. One technique that will help you come up with specific sentences is to use active verbs. Notice that the verb in *A tooth is part of a mouth* is a state-of-being verb, the verb *is.* An active verb would be more helpful.

It's worth pointing out here that you have already dramatically improved your chances of a right answer. Through the process of elimination you have boosted your potential for guessing correctly on this question from 1 in 5 to 1 in 2. Of course, you do not want to have to guess; you want to answer correctly. So you get more specific.

First, think about *tooth* and *mouth.* A tooth enables a mouth to perform one of its functions, chewing. Try that angle. Does an eyebrow enable a face to perform a function? That doesn't sound quite right, though eyebrows and faces certainly both have several functions. Does a stalactite enable a cave to perform a function? Not right either. Try again.

Sometimes it helps to form a visual image. A tooth grows from the bottom or the top of the mouth, which resembles a . . . cave! Your sentence could be *A tooth grows in a mouth and a stalactite grows in a cave.* Answer choice **e** is, in fact, correct.

PART OF SPEECH

Another conceptual tool for analogies is to think about what parts of speech your stem words are. Remember, though, that many words have two or more meanings; and that, often, a different meaning of the same word classifies the word as a different part of speech. For example, in the analogy BOARD : TRAIN, *board* could be a noun meaning (1) the kind of board from which floors are made, or (2) a group of people in charge, such as a board of directors. *Board* could also be a verb meaning (1) to cover up with boards or (2) to get on or enter. *Train* could be a noun meaning (1) a long, trailing part of a dress or (2) a mode of transportation, or it could be a verb meaning (1) to teach or (2) to trail, or drag. Each of these words also has additional meanings, both as nouns and as verbs.

Get in the habit of thinking about the various ways common words can be used. On analogy questions, it is very important to be flexible about the meanings of words. If one meaning or set of meanings is not working, try to find alternate meanings for the words. If they are common—that is, not difficult—words, their meanings are very likely to be their less common usages.

It is important to remember, however, even as you search for alternate meanings, that you are focusing on the *relationship* between the stem words, not on their *meanings.* The reason to think about meanings is simply to help you find the correct relationship. On the GRE test, there are often distracter answers that have words very close in meaning to the stem words. Just because a word in an answer choice has the same meaning as one of the stem words *does not* mean it is the correct choice. That word and its partner must have the same *relationship* as the stem words for it to be the right answer.

1. Focus on relationships, not on meanings.
2. To reveal the relationship, make a sentence using both stem words.
3. Try reversing stem words if necessary to find their relationship.
4. Remember, many words have more than one meaning.
5. See if forming an image using the two words will help.
6. Stay flexible. If one strategy is not working, try another.
7. Eliminate wrong answers as a way to find the right answer.

Even if you don't have any idea about the meanings of the words, knowing their parts of speech is one way of eliminating wrong answers. Take, for example, this analogy:

EXACERBATE : PROBLEM

    a. aggravate : symptom
    b. joyous : glum
    c. examining : patients
    d. exercise : confiscate
    e. automobile : drive

Even if you did not know the meaning of *exacerbate,* you would probably be able to designate *problem* as a noun. You can then eliminate any answer choices that do not have a noun as the second word of the pair. *Glum* is not a noun; it is an adjective. *Confiscate* is not a noun; it is a verb. *Drive* is also a verb. Therefore, you can safely eliminate answer choices **b, d,** and **e.** Now you look again at *exacerbate.* Both *aggravate* and *examining* are verbs, but only *aggravate* mimics the verb form of *exacerbate.* Therefore, **c** is not the answer; the correct answer is **a.** You were able to arrive at the correct answer in this instance through the process of elimination.

► How to Approach Antonyms

The logical relationship embedded in each antonym question is one of *opposition*. In each case, you are looking for the answer choice that is most nearly opposite the initial word. If you remember this simple principle and apply your vocabulary skills to decipher words you may not be familiar with, you will still do well on the antonym questions.

Always Opposed

An antihero is the opposite of a hero. An antibiotic is designed to inhibit or destroy life (*bio* = life). Antifreeze works against the tendency of liquids to freeze. The most important thing to keep in mind as you answer

As you learn new words,

1. See what kinds of outrageous contexts you can find in which to use your new words. Amaze your friends and confound your coworkers.
2. Find a buddy with whom you can play word games. Try to stump each other.
3. Learn vocabulary through associations. Use a thesaurus to look up synonyms for your new word. If your thesaurus has antonyms, you can then look up the antonyms, then the synonyms for each antonym, and so on. See how long you can keep expanding the web of synonyms and antonyms by picking words with slightly different shades of meaning. Draw the synonym/antonym web and post it where you can look at it.

---

antonym questions is that you are looking for a word or phrase that stands most directly in opposition to the stem word.

It is easy to become distracted by a synonym to the stem word and think that is the answer. However, a synonym will mean the *same as* the stem word, not the *opposite of* the stem. Train yourself so that alarms go off in your head when you see a synonym as one of your answer choices in an antonym question, and then toss out that choice. It will never be the correct answer to an antonym question.

It is also important to remember that many words do not have a diametrically opposed antonym. You must then choose the word or phrase that is *most nearly* opposite the stem word. The words in the antonym questions will most often represent *concepts*. You are looking, then, for the *concept* among the answer choices that most nearly opposes the *concept* of the stem word.

Eliminate and Create Context

Don't forget your trustworthy testing friend, elimination. To begin, you can eliminate any answers that do not have opposites. If an answer doesn't have an opposite, it doesn't have an antonym, and so cannot be the correct choice. In many cases you will be able to eliminate two incorrect answer choices, leaving you with two seemingly correct answers. When that happens, you must try to more precisely define the stem word. It will help if you remember the contexts in which you have seen this word. How is it used in a sentence? Try writing a sentence using the word. Now substitute the answer choices in place of the stem word. Which answer word or phrase does the best job of changing the meaning of the sentence into its direct opposite? That will be the correct answer.

Separate and Conquer

If you are unsure of a word's meaning, try breaking it into its component parts. Look at root words, prefixes, and suffixes (see Appendix B). Knowing the meanings of those elements will be of immense utility in tackling antonym questions. LearningExpress's *Vocabulary and Spelling Success in 20 Minutes a Day* contains

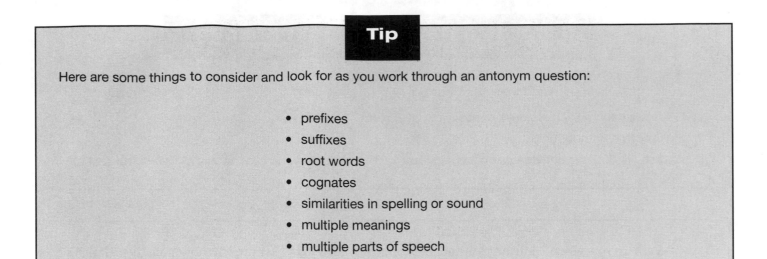

Tip

Here are some things to consider and look for as you work through an antonym question:

- prefixes
- suffixes
- root words
- cognates
- similarities in spelling or sound
- multiple meanings
- multiple parts of speech

extensive sections on prefixes, suffixes, and root words, which will be well worth your time to study. Also, if you are familiar with another language related to English, such as German, or any of the languages derived from Latin (e.g., Spanish, French, and Italian), you can often get a sense of a word's meaning by connecting it with a word you know in one of those languages. Look for similarities in spelling or even in sound. These words are called *cognates*: They are related in that they descend from a common root word.

Remember that many words have more than one meaning. (Did you misread the word *separate* in this section's heading?) You should be especially alert to multiple meanings: If you know what a stem word means and you know what the answer choices mean and you still can't determine which answer opposes the stem word, ask yourself whether any of those words has multiple meanings. You may not have considered the meaning the test makers had in mind when writing the question. This is especially true in the case of common words. Think, for example, how many different meanings a simple word such as *field* has. Now look it up in a dictionary. You probably forgot a few meanings. *Field* has multiple meanings as a noun, and it can also be an adjective and a verb. Most of the antonym questions, actually, will stick to those three parts of speech, but any individual word may switch parts of speech, depending on how it is used. Without the context clues provided by a sentence, you must be flexible in order to ensure correct identification of a word's meaning. Remembering that a word may be a noun, a verb, or an adjective can remind you to stay flexible.

Voracious Vocabulary Virtuosity

It bears repeating that success on the GRE test's antonym questions is largely dependent on your ability to accurately define the vocabulary in the questions. There are strategies and techniques to help you choose antonyms, but it's difficult to select the correct answer unless you have at least some idea about the meanings of the words in a question and in its answer choices. The more precisely you can define a word, the more certain you can be of its opposite.

If you have difficulty remembering new words, it is probably because you are not completely engaged in the activity of acquiring them. As you learn a new word, try to connect it to something in your life or your reading. Remember that words open doors to ideas and images. They enrich the way you experience the world.

Perhaps you have no difficulty learning words initially, but a week later you have forgotten them. If that's the case, make it a point to use each new word you learn as soon and as often as possible, either in writing or in conversation. As they say, use a word three times and it's yours.

One of the best ways to learn vocabulary is also the easiest: Make long lists of words you don't know and then break them down into short lists. Learn a short list every day. Also, remember to make use of nonstudy times to learn vocabulary. You can learn two words while you enjoy a (healthy!) snack. You can learn a word while you brush your teeth or sit on the bus. You can design and use flash cards, which is one of the best ways to study vocabulary.

▶ How to Approach Sentence Completion Questions

The sentence completion questions on the GRE test are, for the most part, long and complex. Each of these questions takes the form of a sentence that is missing either one or two words, represented by blanks. Over half of them are missing two words. Occasionally you may have a sentence with one blank, which will be completed by a phrase rather than a single word. You will have five answer choices, **a–e,** and must determine which answer best completes the sentence.

Sentence completions test two separate aspects of your verbal skills: your vocabulary and your ability to follow the internal logic of sentences. At first glance, these sentences can seem quite daunting. Fortunately, there are strategies that can greatly increase your score on these questions.

Sentence Detective

Although the sentence completions on the GRE test may seem difficult when you first encounter them, successfully answering them—like everything else worth doing—gets easier as you practice. Think of yourself as a detective trying to decode a secret message. Once you have the key to the code, it can be easy to decipher the message. The following sections will give you the keys you need to unlock the meanings of even the most complex sentences. The great thing is that these are master keys that can unlock any and all sentences, including the many complex sentences you will encounter in your graduate-level reading.

Sentence Structure

The single most important key to the meaning of a sentence is its structure. The best and easiest way to determine sentence structure is to look at punctuation. Sentence completion questions always have one or more commas or semicolons. The basic strategy is to separate the sentence into units divided by punctuation. Often, one of the units will express a complete thought, and at least one unit will have one or two blanks. The unit that expresses a complete thought will tell you what the unit(s) with blank(s) need to say.

For example, consider this sentence from the pretest:

> That which is apprehended by intelligence and reason is always in the same state; but that which is conceived by _____ with the help of _____ and without reason, is always in a process of becoming and perishing and never really is.

When you divide this sentence into punctuation-defined units you have:

> *That which is apprehended by intelligence and reason is always in the same state;*

and

> *but that which is conceived by _____ with the help of _____ and without reason,*

and

> *is always in a process of becoming and perishing and never really is.*

The first unit, which has no blanks, tells you that whatever is understood *(apprehended)* using *intelligence and reason* remains static *(in the same state)*. The second unit, the one with two blanks, tells you that there is another way of understanding *(conceiving)*, which does not involve reason. The word *but* at the beginning of the second unit tells you that you need words that contrast with *intelligence* and *reason*. The third unit confirms that the concepts in these contrasting words lead to understanding that is not static, but is impermanent *(becoming and perishing)*.

Now you are ready to use the first and third units to illuminate choices for the second. You are looking for words that will speak of another method of understanding, one that does not involve intelligence and reason. *What could that be?* you ask yourself. Feelings, intuition, and preconceptions are possible choices. You may think of others.

Your final step is to look at the answer choices to find the one that matches the idea you have formed about what needs to be in the blanks. When you have two blanks, it is important to remember that your answer choice, which will have two words or phrases, must fit both blanks. Distracter answers will often fit one blank but not the other. The correct choice may contain the words *opinion..sensation.* Those are very close to the words *preconceptions* and *feelings.*

Here is an example of a question from the pretest that does not divide neatly into a complete unit and an incomplete unit. This one has blanks in two of its four units:

> *The renowned daredevil was, in fact, temperamentally quite _____, as evidenced by the fact that he declined to _____ until nearly two years of age.*

In the first unit, *The renowned daredevil was, in fact,* the phrase *in fact* tells us that there is something unexpected going on. If *in fact* were to be removed from the sentence, there would be no way you could know what kind of words go in the blanks. *In fact* is a **clue phrase**, one that points you toward the meaning of the sentence. *In fact* is the phrase that tells you there is something unexpected going on in the next unit of the sentence, *temperamentally quite _____.* Thus we know that the *renowned daredevil* had an unexpected kind of temperament. What kind of temperament would you expect a famous daredevil to have? *Adventurous, bold,* or *daring?* Right. So the word that goes in the first blank will be one that has a contrasting relationship to the expected temperament. What kinds of words contrast with *adventurous, bold,* and *daring? Careful, cautious,* and *conservative* are the kinds of words you are looking for in the first spot of the answer choices.

The second unit of the sentence, *as evidenced by the fact that he declined to _____ until nearly two years of age,* uses a phrase of comparison, *as evidenced by,* to let us know that the word that goes in the second blank should illustrate the daredevil's nonbold temperament.

Now, think of the synonym you came up with for *not bold,* such as *cautious.* Put it in the first blank. Then read the sentence, using your word in the first blank. Think of something that, if not done before age two, would indicate that kind of temperament. The next thing you do is look at the answer choices for words that are similar to the ones you chose. The answer to this question is *circumspect .. perambulate.* Even if you didn't know that to perambulate is to walk or move about on one's own, you could be fairly confident that you had the right answer because *circumspect* (careful, cautious, and thoughtful) is such a good choice.

Sleuthing 101

The second vitally important skill you must master for sentence completion questions is the ability to **identify key words and phrases**. These are the words that most help you decode the sentence. Think of them as clues to a mystery. Among the most useful of these are the words that enable you to identify the logical relationship between the complete unit(s) of the sentence and the incomplete unit(s). As in the preceding example, sometimes you have to complete one portion of a two-blank sentence before you can work on the logical relationship of another unit. There are three types of logical relationships commonly expressed in sentence completion questions: **contrast, comparison,** and **cause-and-effect** relationships. These three relationships will help you decipher the sentence completion questions.

CONTRAST

Words that logically signal a relationship of contrast are words such as *though, although, however, despite, but,* and *yet.* Can you think of others? There are also **phrases that signal a contrast** between the units of the sentence, phrases such as *on the other hand, but, however, despite,* or *on the contrary.* Try making a sentence using these words and phrases. See how the two parts of your sentence oppose each other. This is the logical relationship of contrast, or opposition. No matter how complex a sentence completion sentence seems at first glance, when you see one of these words or phrases, you will know you are looking at a sentence that expresses one thought in its complete unit and a contrasting thought in its incomplete unit. First, decipher the thought in the complete unit, then fill in the blank in the incomplete unit with a word that expresses a contrasting thought. For example:

Although the tiger is primarily a solitary beast, its cousin the lion is a _____ animal.

Next, divide the sentence into two units, using the punctuation to guide you. Now you have as the first unit, *Although the tiger is primarily a solitary beast,* and the second unit, *its cousin the lion is a _____ animal.* The first unit tells you by the use of the word *although* that the second unit will express a relationship of opposition or contrast. You can see that tigers and lions are being contrasted. The word that goes in the blank has to be an adjective that describes *animal* in the way that *solitary* describes *beast.* Therefore the word that will contrast with the idea in the first unit is in opposition to *solitary.* What is an antonym of *solitary?* Solitary means *alone.* You might choose the antonym *social. Friendly, gregarious,* or *sociable* are other options, all meaning not solitary. Then, look for the word in the answer choices that is a synonym of the word you chose.

COMPARISON

There are two kinds of comparison relationships: comparison by similarity and comparison by restatement. Words that signal comparison are words such as *likewise, similarly,* and *and* itself. Phrases that introduce comparisons include *just as, as _____ as, for example, as shown,* and *as illustrated by.* An example of a comparison by similarity sentence would be: *Always be sure to treat other people _____; for example, hold the door open for the person behind you.* You know that holding the door is a kind or polite thing to do, so you will be looking for a word like *politely, kindly,* or *respectfully* to complete the first part of the sentence.

Words and phrases that precede restatement are *namely, in other words, in fact,* and *that is.* One example of a comparison by restatement sentence would be: *Julie was ____ over the outcome of the election; in fact, it was all she could do to keep from screaming.* The complete part of the sentence tells you that Julie was very upset, so you know that you will be looking for an answer choice like *angry, livid,* or *frustrated* to complete the idea in the first half of the sentence.

Relationships of logical comparison are straightforward. The idea expressed in the complete unit of the sentence is similar to or the same as the idea that needs to be expressed in the incomplete unit. When you know what the complete unit says, you know what the incomplete unit needs to say—the same thing, or very nearly so. Here is an example of a comparison sentence:

Until he went to military school, Foster never stood up straight, as illustrated by his _____ in this photograph.

This sentence has three units, two complete and one incomplete. The first two units tell you that before military school, Foster slouched. The blank in the third unit, therefore, needs to be filled by a word that will illustrate his slouching. The correct answer will be *posture, slouch,* or a synonym.

CAUSE AND EFFECT

A third kind of logical relationship often expressed in sentence completion questions is the cause-and-effect relationship. In other words, the sentence states that one thing is a result of something else. Again, you can rely on key words to point you in the right direction. Words such as *thus, therefore, consequently,* and *because* and phrases such as *due to, as a result,* and *leads to* signal a cause-and-effect relationship. Try making some cause-and-effect sentences to see how they work.

Here's an example of a cause-and-effect sentence:

Scientific knowledge is usually _____, resulting often from years of hard work by numerous investigators.

The complete unit of the sentence, *resulting often from years of hard work by numerous investigators,* tells you that the other unit results from *numerous investigators* working *hard* for *years.* The incomplete unit, the one with the blank, tells you that you are looking for a word to describe *scientific knowledge* that resulted from those years of hard work. You know that whatever word the test makers are looking for must have something to do with *the accumulation of* lots of stuff, because years of hard work by numerous investigators would produce a lot of something. The answer choice that was correct for this question, you may remember, was *cumulative,* which, of course, applies to *the accumulation of* lots of stuff.

Transitions

Transitions are an essential element of effective writing, and they are important clues to organizational patterns and meaning. Transitions signal the relationships between ideas, that is, they connect ideas within sentences and between sentences or within paragraphs and between paragraphs. They tell us the order in which things happened, whether one idea is more important than another, or how one item is similar to or different from something else.

For example, notice how transitions guide us through the following paragraph:

(1) Why do we punish those who commit crimes? (2) There are two main theories of punishment: retribution and deterrence. (3) *The first,* retribution, argues that people who commit crimes deserve to be punished and that the punishment should fit the crime. (4) *In other*

words, it is an "eye for an eye" philosophy. (5) Deterrence theory, *on the other hand*, posits that punishing offenders will help prevent future crimes.

The transitions here show us that sentence 4 offers an explanation for sentence 3 and that sentence 5 offers an idea that contrasts with the idea in sentence 3.

Certain transitions work best for specific functions. For example, *for example* is a great transition to use when introducing a specific example. Here is a brief list of some of the most common transitional words and phrases to watch for—and to use in your own writing.

IF YOU WANT TO:	USE THESE TRANSITIONAL WORDS AND PHRASES:		
introduce an example	for example	for instance	that is
	in other words	in particular	specifically
	in fact	first, second, third	
show addition	and	in addition	also
	again	moreover	furthermore
show emphasis	indeed	in fact	certainly
acknowledge another point of view	although	though	granted
	despite	even though	
show rank	more importantly	above all	first and foremost
	most importantly	first, second, third	
show cause	because	since	created (by)
show effect	therefore	hence	so
	consequently	as a result	
show comparison	likewise	similarly	like
	in the same way	in a like manner	just as

(continued)

Signal Words

Contrast: although, but, despite, however, yet, though

Comparison: likewise, just as, similarly, for example, as illustrated by, and, as . . . as

Restatement: in other words, namely, that is

Cause and Effect: as a result, due to, therefore, thus, leads to, because, consequently

IF YOU WANT TO:	USE THESE TRANSITIONAL WORDS AND PHRASES:		
show contrast	unlike	however	on the other hand
	whereas	instead	rather
	but	on the contrary	conversely
	in contrast	yet	
show the passage of time	then	next	later
	after	before	during
	meanwhile	while	soon
	eventually	finally	afterward
	in the meantime	immediately	suddenly

Putting It All Together

Once you learn how to identify the complete and incomplete units of a sentence, using punctuation to guide you, you have made a good start. Next, by determining the logical relationship of the units, using key words and phrases, you then understand what the sentence is saying, even if there's some vocabulary you don't understand. But if you keep working on building your vocabulary, chances are you will understand the crucial words.

▶ The Top Seven Steps for Answering Sentence Completion Questions

When you break up sentences using punctuation as a guide, you end up with more-or-less manageable chunks of words. Nevertheless, when you have a 25-word sentence, which is not that uncommon on the GRE test, and you break it into two units, you can still easily have a 12-to-15-word unit. On the real GRE test, there have even been 20-to-30-word sentences with no punctuation except for the period at the end.

These long sentences are further complicated by the fact that they often include difficult vocabulary. Seeing words you don't know may send your anxiety level soaring, and nobody does their best work when he or she is anxious. With practice, though, you can learn to take those long sentences and unknown words in stride. Try following these seven steps:

1. Start small. Don't tackle the whole sentence at once. There are several techniques to help you **break sentences into smaller units**. Using punctuation to guide you, as demonstrated in the previous section, is the most obvious method. If the guiding commas and semicolons aren't there, however, you will need to look for other places to break a sentence. One technique is to find a verb and gradually incorporate the words around it into an increasingly longer phrase as you decipher its meaning. The verb provides an anchor for the meaning because it tells you what is being done.

You can also use trial and error to find islands of meaning in a sentence. Find a word or a phrase you understand and start adding a word or two on either side. As you discover several such islands and gradually enlarge each one, you will eventually see how they fit together, and then you will understand the dynamics of the whole sentence.

2. If the vocabulary in a sentence is a problem, **look at the words around it**. Usually you can figure out what function a word is serving in the sentence. Ask yourself if it's an action word. If so, it's a verb. Is it describing something? Then it's an adjective or adverb. Is it the subject—the person, place, or thing performing the action in the sentence? It's a noun or pronoun. Use the surrounding context to help you guess the meaning or at least the part of speech of an unfamiliar word.

3. As you are reading a sentence with blanks or with words you don't know (which might as well be blanks!), it can ease your anxiety to **substitute words or sounds of your choosing in place of the unknown words**. The words *something* and *whatever* work well in many situations. You may find you prefer nonsense words instead, such as *yada yada* or *blah blah*. As the meaning of the sentence gradually becomes clear, you can start substituting words that might work in the sentence. Eliminate all answers that do not have the correct part of speech for the blank.

4. Now that you have a good idea about the gist of the sentence, it's time to think about filling in the blanks. It is crucial at this point that you **do not look at the answers!** Because the GRE test has so many distracter answers that will look right if you have not deciphered the meaning of the sentence, it would be a mistake to look at the answers to see what word(s) might go in the blank(s). You have to decide first what the answer needs to express. Then you can look at the answer choices to find one that matches your idea. It is not important that you come up with the perfect single word to express your idea. A phrase is fine, as long as you are clearly expressing the *meaning* you think the correct answer choice will express.

5. As you are deciding on the correct idea for the blank or blanks to express, **be sure you are sticking to what is expressed in the sentence**. Don't let the idea(s) in the sentence lead you off into another area. Perhaps the sentence reminds you of something you have read or heard that would perfectly complement the idea(s) in the sentence. Your information may be true, but it's a mistake to use your outside knowledge in completing a sentence. Remember that there will often be key words or phrases signaling the relationship of the various parts of the sentence. And there will *always* be enough information within the sentence so that you can answer without having any outside knowledge. Stick to the information within the sentence itself.

6. When you think you know what idea the answer word needs to express, **it's time to look at the answers**. If you see an answer choice that seems to match your idea, try plugging the answer into the sentence to see if it is internally consistent. That means, check to see if it fits into the sentence without introducing any new idea. If it seems to fit, but brings in an idea you can't find anywhere else in the sentence, it's the wrong answer.

7. If you can't settle on an absolutely correct answer, **use the process of elimination to help you**. Once you have deciphered the meaning of the sentence, break it apart and fit it back together. Chances are you will immediately see one or two answers that make no sense within the existing framework of the sentence. Eliminate all answers that don't fit the meaning of the sentence.

When you eliminate an answer, make a note of it. As you are working on a challenging question, use your scratch paper to write **a, b, c, d**, and **e** and then cross out incorrect choices, mark them off the list, eliminate them from your consciousness. You no longer need to consider them, so don't let those incorrect answers slow down your thought process by continuing to exist as possibilities. Promise yourself, however, that you will never eliminate an answer choice just because you don't know the vocabulary. Sometimes, in fact, you will be able to eliminate all the other answers, leaving you with the one answer you don't understand but which must be the correct choice!

A final warning about eliminating answers is that it must always be a conscious choice to eliminate an answer. Many times, distracter answers are positioned at **a** or **b** so that you see them, think hurriedly, "Oh, that's the one!" and move on without even looking at the other answers, including the correct one. Even if you think you see the correct answer, look at all the answer choices before making your final selection.

When a question has two blanks, you may be able to figure out the answer to one blank but not the other. If so, that's good—you can now eliminate all answers that do not fit in that blank. Then you can continue your efforts by focusing exclusively on the other blank.

▶ How to Approach Reading Comprehension Questions

The Verbal section of the GRE test contains at least two reading comprehension passages, each one followed by questions about the passage. Passages are excerpted from writings in the fields of the humanities and the social and natural sciences. Each prose passage is 300 to 1,000 words in length, and there will be several questions (most likely four to seven questions) regarding each one.

The reading comprehension questions test your ability to understand what you read. You will often be required to identify the author's main point or purpose in writing the passage. You will also have to accurately interpret secondary points and even the assumptions that underlie what is explicit in the passage. The questions will ask you to analyze each passage from several perspectives, including the kinds of research that might confirm or negate the author's conclusions.

GRE test passages are usually complex and densely packed with ideas and many are somewhat overwhelming at first glance. You must be able to extract information, both expressed and implied. You will be asked about the logical flow of the texts and about their consistency or lack thereof. You may also have to answer questions about the tone of the passages as well as their overall theme or meaning. You will see phrases such as *the passage implies that* . . . and *the author suggests that* . . . , which require you to extrapolate from the information given to form your own conclusions.

Finding the Main Idea

Standardized reading comprehension tests always have questions about the main idea of the passage, and for good reason: The main idea is the key concept or thought that the writer wants to convey in the text.

People often confuse the *main idea* of a passage with its *topic*, but they are two very different things. The topic or subject of a passage is *what the passage is about*. The main idea, on the other hand, is *what the writer wants to say about that subject*. For example, take a look at this paragraph:

> Although many social policies and much legislation is founded on this "greatest good" philosophy, there are several problems with utilitarianism as a basis for morality. First, happiness is not so easy to quantify, and any measurement is bound to be subjective. Second, in a theory that treats everything except happiness as *instrumentally* rather than *intrinsically* valuable, anything—or, more importantly, *anyone*—can (and should) be treated as a means to an end, if it means greater happiness. This rejects the notion that human beings have their own intrinsic value. Further, utilitarianism puts the burden of the happiness of the masses on the suffering of the few. Is the happiness of many worth the suffering of a few? Why do those few deserve to suffer? Isn't this burden of suffering morally irresponsible? This is the dilemma so brilliantly illustrated in LeGuin's story.

This paragraph is *about* "problems with utilitarianism," but that does not adequately convey the main idea. The main idea must say something more, make a specific assertion about that subject. And there are many things we could say about this topic: "There are not any problems with utilitarianism," for example, or "The problems with utilitarianism are an acceptable tradeoff for happiness," or "The problem with utilitarianism is its mathematical approach to happiness." In this paragraph, the writer makes his assertion (the main point) in the first sentence:

> Although many social policies and much legislation is founded on this "greatest good" philosophy, *there are several problems with utilitarianism as a basis for morality.*

A sentence like this—one that clearly expresses the main idea of a paragraph—is the **topic sentence**. A sentence that expresses the main idea of a longer text (an essay) is the **thesis statement**. Of course, main ideas are not always stated in topic sentences or thesis statements, and in much of what you read, main ideas will be inferred. We will deal with that scenario in a moment.

Whether explicit or implied, a main idea must be sufficiently **general** to hold together all of the ideas in the passage. Indeed, everything in the passage should work to explain, illustrate, or otherwise support the main

Topic/Subject: What the passage is about.

Main Idea: The overall fact, feeling, or thought a writer wants to convey about his or her subject.

idea. Thus, you can think of the main ideas as an umbrella that covers (encompasses) all of the other ideas in the passage. For example, look at the following choices for the main idea of the utilitarianism paragraph:

a. Utilitarianism is problematic because it treats people as a means to an end.
b. Utilitarianism requires that a few suffer so that many can be happy.
c. Utilitarianism is flawed as a foundation for moral action.
d. Utilitarianism is often used to determine social policy.
e. Utilitarianism does not adequately respect minority rights.

The only answer that can be correct is choice **c**, because it is the only idea that is general enough to hold together all of the information in the paragraph. Choices **a**, **b**, and **e** are all too specific to be the main idea; they are not broad enough to cover all of the ideas in the passage, which discusses three different problems with utilitarianism, including the problems cited in choices **a**, **b**, and **e**. Choice **d** is a contrasting idea used to introduce the main idea of the sentence, and how utilitarianism is used to determine social policy is not even discussed in this paragraph, so the idea expressed in **d** certainly does not hold together the entire paragraph. Only choice **c** is general enough to cover every sentence in the paragraph. It makes an umbrella statement that all of the sentences in the paragraph work to support.

Fortunately, the skills you are learning for the sentence completion questions will serve you well on the critical reading questions, also. Additionally, these critical reading and analysis skills will make your postgraduate career even more successful.

Ready, Set, Read!

If you are already skilled at quickly reading and understanding dense prose, good for you! If not, try this approach. Feel free to adapt it and change it to suit your needs and temperament. There's no one right way to read. The right way to do all of these things is the way that works for you; so as you practice, try variations on the method to see what suits you. But *do* practice; it's the only way to get better! In fact, you may want to seek out your own difficult reading passages and practice writing questions about them.

The first thing you may want to try is to skim the passage for its subject matter. With practice, you will find that topic sentences and key adjectives will practically leap out and grab your attention. Be sure to keep your pencil poised to write as you read. You will want to use your scratch paper to jot down key words and phrases as you see them. You may think you will save time by not making notes, but that is not the case! Think of yourself as a spelunker, exploring a dark cave. Your notes are your lifeline; they enable you to find your way back through the passage as you answer the questions. You don't want to have to wander around in the cave;

Using Context

If you encounter a word you don't know, try to figure out what the word means from its context.

- Find the clues the author provides in the sentence and surrounding sentences.
- Try to determine whether each clue word is positive or negative.
- Mark the page or write down the word somewhere so you can look it up later. See how closely you were able to guess its meaning.

The more you practice determining meaning from context, the more accurately you will be able to guess at those meanings and understand material at test time.

---

you need to know what territory you have already covered, so you can stride purposefully back through it. Your notes save you the wandering. They save you time.

Next, read the passage all the way through. As you finish each paragraph, ask yourself, "What was the main idea?" Then jot down a word, phrase, or diagram that expresses that idea. This is a note for yourself, one that will enable you to quickly tie the separate paragraphs into a coherent whole that will express the theme or point of the passage.

Writers often provide clues that can help distinguish between main ideas and their support. The following transitions are some of the most common words and phrases used to introduce specific supporting examples:

for example	for instance	in particular
in addition	furthermore	some
others	specifically	

Look for these transitions to help distinguish between main and supporting ideas.

As you read the passage, write down any words or phrases that seem particularly important or expressive. Also note the line numbers in which they are found. Often adjectives that set a mood or tone will help you understand the author's meaning, so be sure to jot them down as well. It's equally important to make note of details or pieces of evidence that support the author's main point(s). These notes are for you, so make them only as complete as you need them to be.

Don't write more than you need to, but be sure you can make sense of what you write. It's good to practice this technique before you actually need it. You can start with whatever you are reading, including this book.

If you were paying attention in English class when the teacher discussed topic sentences, you know that most well-written paragraphs have at least one sentence that sums up the main thrust of the paragraph. It is most often either the first or the last sentence, so if you are having trouble determining the author's point, reread the first and last sentences of each paragraph. You can't depend on that technique, though; use your judgment to determine if either of these sentences is truly the topic sentence.

Once you have carefully but quickly read the entire passage, it's time to tackle the questions. This is when the notes you have jotted will come in handy. Whenever you see words and phrases from your notes in the questions, you will know right where to look for them in the passage. You will want to cross-reference the passage, the questions, and your notes in order to determine the one best answer to each question.

Whenever you see a word or phrase such as *best, primarily, most closely,* or *most nearly,* it alerts you to the likely presence of particularly clever distracter answers. That is to say, there may be two or more answers that are close contenders—that both reflect language from the passage or are true about the passage. Rest assured, however, that with careful attention to the wording of both question and answer choices, you can determine which choice is truly best.

Making Inferences

Inferences are conclusions drawn based on evidence. For example, if you look up at the sky and see heavy black clouds, you might logically infer that it is going to rain. Reading comprehension questions like those you will see on the GRE test will often ask you to draw conclusions based on what you read in the passage. The key to drawing the right conclusions (making the right inferences) is the same as the key to finding the meaning of unfamiliar vocabulary words. You have to look for clues in the context. These clues include details, actions, and ideas described in the text (what has been stated, proposed, asked, asserted), sentence structure, and word choice.

Making logical inferences is largely a matter of looking objectively at the evidence in the passage. Remember, you are not being asked what *you* think about the writer or the passage but what is implied *by* the passage. What do the ideas and words add up to? What does the evidence suggest? For example, take a look at the following description:

> Dennis was scared. His knees were weak. He looked down . . . the water was twenty feet below. He looked up again, quickly. He tried to think of something else. He tried to reassure himself. "It's only twenty feet!" he said aloud. But that only made it sound worse. Twenty feet!

The writer could have said, "Dennis was scared. He was afraid of heights." Instead, the writer *suggests* how Dennis feels through details (*his knees were weak*), repetition (*twenty feet*), and the short, choppy sentence structure that reflects the panic Dennis is feeling.

Word Choice

Often, the best clues to meaning come from the specific words a writer chooses to describe people, places, and things. The writer's word choice (also called **diction**) can reveal a great deal about how he or she feels about the subject.

By looking closely at word choice, you will find clues that can help you better understand the text. Word choice clues can come in the following forms:

- particular words and phrases that the author uses
- the way those words and phrases are arranged in sentences
- word or sentence patterns that are repeated
- important details about people, places, and things

To see how word choice reveals the writer's attitude, read the two sentences below:

a. Higgins proposed a revolutionary idea.
b. Higgins proposed a radical idea.

It is not hard to see the difference between these sentences. In sentence **a**, the writer calls Higgins' idea *revolutionary*, while the writer of sentence **b** calls the idea *radical*. Though the sentences are similar, their word choice conveys two very different attitudes about Higgins' idea. Both writers agree that Higgins' idea is something unusual, different from the norm. But the way in which it is unusual differs significantly between sentences. A *revolutionary* idea is unusual in that it is new and unlike ideas that came before; it changes things dramatically. A *radical* idea, however, is unusual because it is extreme. From the word choice, we can infer that the writer of sentence **a** feels very positive about Higgins' proposal, while the writer of sentence **b** may feel concerned about the extreme nature of Higgins' plan. The writers don't need to spell out their feelings for you because their *word choices* make their positions clear.

DENOTATION AND CONNOTATION

Even words that seem to mean the same thing have subtly different meanings and sometimes not-so-subtle effects. For example, look at the words *dangerous* and *perilous*. If you say, "The situation is *dangerous*," that means one thing. If you say, "The situation is *perilous*," that means something a little bit different. That's because *dangerous* has a different **connotation** than *perilous*. Connotation is a word's *suggested* or implied meaning; it's what the word makes you think or feel. *Dangerous* and *perilous* have nearly the same **denotation** or dictionary definition—in fact, each word is used in the definition of the other. But *perilous* suggests more threat of harm than *dangerous* suggests. *Peril* has a more ominous ring to it than *danger* has and suggests a more life-threatening situation. *Perilous* and *dangerous*, then, have different connotations, and the word you choose to describe the situation can tell others a lot.

EUPHEMISMS AND DYSPHEMISMS

Another way writers use word choice to reveal their feelings is through the use of **euphemisms** and **dysphemisms**. A euphemism is a neutral or positive word used in place of something negative. A common example is to substitute the phrase *passed on* or *departed* for *died*. A dysphemism, on the other hand, uses a negative word or phrase (instead of something neutral or positive), such as saying *croaked* or *kicked the bucket* for *died*. To cite a business example, "I've been let go" is a euphemism and "I've been axed" is a dysphemism for "I've been fired."

Seven Strategies for Reading Comprehension Questions

1. **Read actively!** As you read, ask yourself at the end of each paragraph what it was about. Make notes about the passage; react to it on your scratch paper. Be an engaged reader. Try to become interested for a few minutes in the passage's subject.

2. If you have an especially good short-term memory, you may want to **look at the questions before you read the passage**. Jot down the words and phrases the questions ask about, then look for those words and phrases in the passage. When you find them, you can either go ahead and answer the question right then or note the area to come back to later.

3. If you don't understand what a question is asking, **rephrase the question, using your own words**. GRE test questions are written in a very precise, formal style in order to eliminate any ambiguity. Unfortunately, nobody talks that way, so the questions can be confusing at first glance. Once you have noted the key words and phrases, rewrite the question in a way that makes sense to you. Don't be afraid to add new words to the question; just be sure the words are expressing the same ideas that are already in the question and not changing the meaning of the question in any way.

4. Once you understand a question, **try to answer it in your own words before looking at your answer choices**. Distracter answers often take one of several forms:
   - they are close to the correct answer, but are wrong in some detail
   - they are true, but do not answer the question
   - they use language found in the text, but are not the correct answer

5. As with all the multiple-choice questions on the GRE test, **elimination is an important strategy for the reading comprehension questions**. Even if you don't know the answer to a particular question right away, you often will be able to eliminate one to three answer choices without even referring back to the passage. Then you know that one of the remaining answers is the correct one and you can more productively spend your time looking in the passage for information to back up your choice.

6. Expect to **refer back to the passage on virtually every question**. If you know the answer to a question without referring back, that's fine, although it might be a good idea to check the passage anyway, just to make sure you haven't fallen for a distracter answer.

7. **Remember to read between the lines!** With the sentence completion questions, you may remember that you must be extremely literal and never read anything into them or bring in any ideas that are not clearly expressed within the sentence itself. This is *not* true with reading comprehension questions. In fact, you will be called upon to interpret almost every passage, to draw conclusions from the text, and to extend the author's point of view in order to evaluate a statement that is not even in the passage.

▶ Tips and Strategies for the Official Test

Now you have tried your hand at some practice questions. You had read strategies for each of the four kinds of Verbal questions and started to absorb them. You have already learned some new vocabulary.

Here are the strategies you have learned for each type of question. As you read through the list, make sure you understand each one. If you encounter a strategy you don't understand, go back to the lesson for that type of question and read about the strategy one more time.

Analogy Strategies

- Find the relationship between the stem (initial) pair of words.
- Remember, words represent concrete or abstract things, which have relationships.
- Find the answer pair with the same kind of (an analogous) relationship.
- Be flexible about the meanings of words.
- Check for a *part-to-whole* relationship.
- Check for a relationship of *contrast/antonyms/opposites*.
- Check for a *type of* relationship.
- Check for a *degree of* relationship.
- Check for a *use or purpose* relationship.
- Check for a *tool to worker* relationship.
- To reveal relationship, make a sentence using both stem words.
- Try reversing stem words if necessary to find their relationship.
- If more than one answer is still a possibility, make your sentence more specific.
- The more difficult the analogy is, the more specific the sentence must be.
- One way to make more specific sentences is to use active verbs (not state-of-being verbs, such as *is*).
- Check the answer pairs for a relationship parallel to the stem words' relationship.
- Remember that many words have two or more meanings.
- Often, different meanings of the same word are different parts of speech.
- If a stem word is not a difficult word, its appropriate meaning is likely to be a less-common usage of the word.
- Check to make sure you are focusing on relationships, not on meanings.
- Don't choose distracter words with similar meanings to the stem words' meanings.
- Eliminate wrong answers as a way to find the right answer.
- Think about the functions of the stem words and the answer choices.
- Form visual images of the stem words and/or answer choices.
- Stay flexible. If one strategy is not working, try another.

Antonym Strategies

- The logical relationship embedded in each antonym question is one of opposition.
- Train yourself so that alarms will go off in your head when you see a synonym as one of your answer choices.

- If the stem word has no diametrically opposed antonym, choose the word or phrase that is *most nearly* opposite the stem word.
- Look for the *concept* among the answer choices that most nearly opposes the *concept* of the stem word.
- Eliminate any answer choices that don't have opposites.
- If you can't decide between two seemingly correct answers, try to more precisely define the stem word.
- Try to remember the contexts in which you have seen a stem word.
- Try writing a sentence using the word.
- Substitute into your sentence the possible answers. The answer word or phrase that does the best job of changing the meaning of the sentence into its direct opposite is correct.
- Use root words, prefixes, and suffixes to help determine a word's meaning.
- Remember that an unfamiliar word may be related to a word you know in another language.
- Be flexible. Remember that many words have more than one meaning.
- Use parts of speech to help you remember a word's various meanings.
- Improve your vocabulary! Make it fun by playing vocabulary games.
- Use new vocabulary in conversation or writing to help you remember it.

Sentence Completion Question Strategies

- Sentence completion questions test your understanding of logical relationships.
- The most important key to the meaning of a sentence is its structure.
- The easiest way to determine sentence structure is to use punctuation to guide you.
- First decipher the thought in the sentence unit without blanks, then fill in the blank(s) with a word or phrase that expresses a logically related thought.
- Sometimes you have to complete one portion of a two-blank sentence before you can work on the logical relationship of another unit.
- Signal words and phrases help you identify the logical relationship between the complete unit(s) of the sentence and the incomplete unit(s).
- There are three types of logical relationships common to sentence completion questions: *contrast, comparison,* and *cause and effect.*
- Words that signal a logical relationship of contrast are words such as: *though, although, however, despite, but,* and *yet.*
- Phrases that signal contrast are phrases such as *on the other hand* or *on the contrary.*
- There are two kinds of comparison relationships: *comparison by similarity* and *comparison by restatement.*
- Words that signal comparison are words such as *likewise, similarly,* and *and* itself. Phrases that signal comparisons are *just as, as _____ as, for example, as shown,* and *as illustrated by.*
- Words and phrases that signal restatement are *namely, in other words, in fact,* and *that is.*

- In restatement sentences, the idea expressed in the complete unit of the sentence is similar to or the same as the idea that needs to be expressed in the incomplete unit.
- A third kind of logical relationship often expressed in sentence completion questions is the cause-and-effect relationship, in which one thing is a result of something else.
- Words such as *thus, therefore, consequently,* and *because* and phrases such as *due to, as a result,* and *leads to* signal a cause-and-effect relationship
- *Start small.* Don't tackle the whole sentence at once.
- If the guiding commas and semicolons are not there, find a verb and gradually incorporate the words around it as you decipher its meaning.
- Find islands of meaning in a sentence and gradually enlarge each one.
- Use the surrounding context to help you guess the meaning or at least the part of speech of an unfamiliar word.
- Substitute words or sounds of your choosing in place of unknown words as you read.
- Don't look at the answers to see what word(s) might go in the blank(s); decide first what the answer needs to express.
- It's fine to use a phrase instead of a word, as long as you are clearly expressing the *meaning* you think the correct answer choice will express.
- Stick to what is expressed in the sentence. Don't incorporate other ideas.
- If you see an answer choice that seems to match your idea, check to see if it fits into the sentence without introducing any new idea.
- Look at all the answer choices before making your final selection.
- Use the process of elimination.
- Never eliminate an answer choice just because you don't recognize the word.

Reading Comprehension Strategies

- The reading comprehension questions test your ability to understand what you read.
- From each passage, you must be able to extract information, both expressed and implied.
- Phrases such as *the passage implies that . . .* and *the author suggests that . . .* require you to use the information given in order to form your own conclusions.
- First, skim the passage for its subject matter.
- Jot down important or expressive words and phrases as you see them, and note line numbers in which they are found.
- Adjectives that set a mood will help establish the author's tone.
- As you finish each paragraph, ask yourself what was its main idea. Jot it down.
- The main ideas of each paragraph can be quickly tied into a coherent whole that will express the theme or point of the passage.
- Make note of details that support the author's main point(s).
- Don't write more than you need, but be sure you can make sense of what you write.
- Include line numbers along with your notes, so you will know where to look in the passage.

- Try to become interested for a few minutes in the subject of each passage.
- Try looking at the questions before you read the passage or before you reread it.
- Jot down the words and phrases the questions ask about, then look for those words and phrases in the passage.
- If you don't understand what a question is asking, rephrase the question using your own words.
- Once you understand a question, try to answer in your own words before looking at the answer choices.
- Distracter answer choices may be close to the correct answer, but wrong in some detail.
- Distracter answer choices may be true statements, but not the correct answer to the question.
- Distracter answers may use language found in the text, but may still be the wrong answer.
- Elimination is an important strategy for reading comprehension questions.
- Expect to refer back to the passage on virtually every question, even if just to check to make sure you haven't fallen for a distracter answer.
- Read between the lines!
- Seek out your own difficult passages and practice writing questions about them.
- Practice these techniques before the exam.
- As you practice, try variations on the method to see what works for you.

▶ Practice

In our view, there's no such thing as too much practice. When you have practiced the techniques for each of the question types until you feel confident using them and you are answering the questions correctly, then you have practiced enough. Until then, keep working!

You are ready now to try your hand at some more practice GRE test questions. You might want to keep the list of strategies handy as you take the sample test, so you can practice them on difficult questions.

There are 20 questions of each type. Set your timer, estimating a minute per question. Keep in mind, however, that reading comprehension and sentence completion questions typically take longer to answer than antonym or analogy questions. Analyzing your average time per question on the four types of questions will give you valuable information that will help you pace yourself on the actual GRE test.

ANSWER SHEET

ANALOGIES

1. ⓐ ⓑ ⓒ ⓓ ⓔ
2. ⓐ ⓑ ⓒ ⓓ ⓔ
3. ⓐ ⓑ ⓒ ⓓ ⓔ
4. ⓐ ⓑ ⓒ ⓓ ⓔ
5. ⓐ ⓑ ⓒ ⓓ ⓔ
6. ⓐ ⓑ ⓒ ⓓ ⓔ
7. ⓐ ⓑ ⓒ ⓓ ⓔ
8. ⓐ ⓑ ⓒ ⓓ ⓔ
9. ⓐ ⓑ ⓒ ⓓ ⓔ
10. ⓐ ⓑ ⓒ ⓓ ⓔ
11. ⓐ ⓑ ⓒ ⓓ ⓔ
12. ⓐ ⓑ ⓒ ⓓ ⓔ
13. ⓐ ⓑ ⓒ ⓓ ⓔ
14. ⓐ ⓑ ⓒ ⓓ ⓔ
15. ⓐ ⓑ ⓒ ⓓ ⓔ
16. ⓐ ⓑ ⓒ ⓓ ⓔ
17. ⓐ ⓑ ⓒ ⓓ ⓔ
18. ⓐ ⓑ ⓒ ⓓ ⓔ
19. ⓐ ⓑ ⓒ ⓓ ⓔ
20. ⓐ ⓑ ⓒ ⓓ ⓔ

ANTONYMS

1. ⓐ ⓑ ⓒ ⓓ ⓔ
2. ⓐ ⓑ ⓒ ⓓ ⓔ
3. ⓐ ⓑ ⓒ ⓓ ⓔ
4. ⓐ ⓑ ⓒ ⓓ ⓔ
5. ⓐ ⓑ ⓒ ⓓ ⓔ
6. ⓐ ⓑ ⓒ ⓓ ⓔ
7. ⓐ ⓑ ⓒ ⓓ ⓔ
8. ⓐ ⓑ ⓒ ⓓ ⓔ
9. ⓐ ⓑ ⓒ ⓓ ⓔ
10. ⓐ ⓑ ⓒ ⓓ ⓔ
11. ⓐ ⓑ ⓒ ⓓ ⓔ
12. ⓐ ⓑ ⓒ ⓓ ⓔ
13. ⓐ ⓑ ⓒ ⓓ ⓔ
14. ⓐ ⓑ ⓒ ⓓ ⓔ
15. ⓐ ⓑ ⓒ ⓓ ⓔ
16. ⓐ ⓑ ⓒ ⓓ ⓔ
17. ⓐ ⓑ ⓒ ⓓ ⓔ
18. ⓐ ⓑ ⓒ ⓓ ⓔ
19. ⓐ ⓑ ⓒ ⓓ ⓔ
20. ⓐ ⓑ ⓒ ⓓ ⓔ

SENTENCE COMPLETION

1. ⓐ ⓑ ⓒ ⓓ ⓔ
2. ⓐ ⓑ ⓒ ⓓ ⓔ
3. ⓐ ⓑ ⓒ ⓓ ⓔ
4. ⓐ ⓑ ⓒ ⓓ ⓔ
5. ⓐ ⓑ ⓒ ⓓ ⓔ
6. ⓐ ⓑ ⓒ ⓓ ⓔ
7. ⓐ ⓑ ⓒ ⓓ ⓔ
8. ⓐ ⓑ ⓒ ⓓ ⓔ
9. ⓐ ⓑ ⓒ ⓓ ⓔ
10. ⓐ ⓑ ⓒ ⓓ ⓔ
11. ⓐ ⓑ ⓒ ⓓ ⓔ
12. ⓐ ⓑ ⓒ ⓓ ⓔ
13. ⓐ ⓑ ⓒ ⓓ ⓔ
14. ⓐ ⓑ ⓒ ⓓ ⓔ
15. ⓐ ⓑ ⓒ ⓓ ⓔ
16. ⓐ ⓑ ⓒ ⓓ ⓔ
17. ⓐ ⓑ ⓒ ⓓ ⓔ
18. ⓐ ⓑ ⓒ ⓓ ⓔ
19. ⓐ ⓑ ⓒ ⓓ ⓔ
20. ⓐ ⓑ ⓒ ⓓ ⓔ

READING COMPREHENSION

1. ⓐ ⓑ ⓒ ⓓ ⓔ
2. ⓐ ⓑ ⓒ ⓓ ⓔ
3. ⓐ ⓑ ⓒ ⓓ ⓔ
4. ⓐ ⓑ ⓒ ⓓ ⓔ
5. ⓐ ⓑ ⓒ ⓓ ⓔ
6. ⓐ ⓑ ⓒ ⓓ ⓔ
7. ⓐ ⓑ ⓒ ⓓ ⓔ
8. ⓐ ⓑ ⓒ ⓓ ⓔ
9. ⓐ ⓑ ⓒ ⓓ ⓔ
10. ⓐ ⓑ ⓒ ⓓ ⓔ
11. ⓐ ⓑ ⓒ ⓓ ⓔ
12. ⓐ ⓑ ⓒ ⓓ ⓔ
13. ⓐ ⓑ ⓒ ⓓ ⓔ
14. ⓐ ⓑ ⓒ ⓓ ⓔ
15. ⓐ ⓑ ⓒ ⓓ ⓔ
16. ⓐ ⓑ ⓒ ⓓ ⓔ
17. ⓐ ⓑ ⓒ ⓓ ⓔ
18. ⓐ ⓑ ⓒ ⓓ ⓔ
19. ⓐ ⓑ ⓒ ⓓ ⓔ
20. ⓐ ⓑ ⓒ ⓓ ⓔ

Analogies

Instructions: In the questions that follow, there will be an initial pair of related words or phrases followed by four answer pairs of words or phrases, identified by letters **a–e**. Choose the answer pair where the relationship of the words or phrases most nearly matches the relationship of the initial pair.

1. SYLLABLE : WORD
   a. heart : card
   b. game : series ✓
   c. iron : ironing board
   d. disc : record
   e. parentheses : brackets

2. EFFICIENT : WASTEFUL
   a. honest : deceptive ✓
   b. facetious : sardonic
   c. hasty : expeditious
   d. churlish : flippant
   e. perceptive : misanthropic

3. PARSLEY : GARNISH
   a. butter : melt
   b. tea : ice
   c. dip : chip ✗
   d. salt : seasoning ✓
   e. flour : cake ✓

4. FUZZY : CLARITY
   a. false : perjury
   b. voluble : constancy
   c. avant-garde : fidelity
   d. mischievous : imbroglio
   e. rigid : flexibility ✓

5. ACRE : LAND
   a. timbre : drum
   b. parcel : sale
   c. slice : cake ✓
   d. coffee : cup
   e. forest : tree

6. SHAFT : SPEAR

    a. neck : guitar

    b. fire : weapon

    c. tie : kerchief

    d. place : hold

    e. grate : poker

7. TRELLIS : GARDEN

    a. till : plant

    b. train : vine

    c. fireplace : house

    d. chancel : choir

    e. reed : basket

8. MANACLE : HANDS

    a. chap : lips

    b. fedora : head

    c. belt : waist

    d. fetter : feet

    e. chew : mouth

9. THRESHER : SHARK

    a. volume : book

    c. plant : factory

    c. chipper : wood

    d. chisel : sculptor

    e. mastiff : dog

10. DOLLY : GRIP

    a. plow : tongue

    b. emphasize : accentuate

    c. bowdlerize : abuse

    d. ticket punch : conductor

    e. broom : handle

11. PARROT : MIMIC

    a. termite : bore

    b. cockatoo : plumage

    c. caribou : hoof

    d. fish : school

    e. owl : wise

12. MANDIBLE : JAW
   a. crucible : trial
   b. socket : shoulder
   c. cartilage : ear
   d. metatarsal : foot
   e. ulna : thigh

13. OVERT : HIDDEN
   a. caustic : sardonic
   b. ebullient : glum
   c. ingenious : fresh
   d. pathetic : pitiful
   e. frank : candid

14. DOLLAR : CENT
   a. general : private
   b. army : battalion
   c. company : regiment
   d. order : command
   e. dime : quarter

15. SCIMITAR : SABER
   a. blade : laser
   b. propeller : jet
   c. mediation : battle
   d. stun : taser
   e. revolver : gun

16. CINEAST : FILM
   a. shaman : medicine
   b. journalist : story
   c. gastronome : food
   d. partisan : treaty
   e. teacher : text

17. LAP : POOL
   a. light-year : space
   b. drink : vessel
   c. gargoyle : edifice
   d. chimera : apparition
   e. lane : track

18. RESIN : VARNISH
   a. sap : tree
   b. preserve : sanctuary
   c. pectin : preserves
   d. couscous : pilaf
   e. candle : wax

19. PAPER : ORIGAMI
   a. china : fragile
   b. syllabus : opus
   c. licorice : fennel
   d. lotion : emollient
   e. osier : baskets

20. MACHIAVELLIAN : DUPLICITOUS
   a. Faustian : pleasant
   b. Orwellian : intrusive
   c. Dickensian : palling
   d. Emersonian : dispiriting
   e. Proustian : succinct

Antonyms

Instructions: In each of the following questions you will be presented with a capitalized word followed by four answer choices lettered **a–e**. Select the answer word or phrase that has a meaning most nearly *opposite* to the initial word.

Some of these questions will require you to discriminate among closely related word choices. Be sure you choose the answer that is most nearly opposed to the capitalized word.

1. AMBIVALENT :
   a. insecure
   b. inconstant
   c. positive
   d. cheerful
   e. insatiable

2. CATASTROPHIC :
   a. bold
   b. pleasurable
   c. salubrious
   d. nihilistic
   e. beneficial

3. PALATIAL :
   a. chintzy
   b. feudal
   c. democratic
   d. decorous
   e. subterranean

4. OMNISCIENT :
   a. resonant
   b. mutable
   c. ignorant
   d. superstitious
   e. phlegmatic

5. CAPITULATE :
   a. embolden
   b. simplify
   c. assuage
   d. persevere
   e. postulate

6. INDEMNIFY :
   a. call for assistance
   b. put at risk
   c. cause to collapse
   d. resist attack
   e. protect from harm

7. PALLIATE :
   a. accumulate
   b. exaggerate
   c. aggravate
   d. extirpate
   e. misconstrue

8. SYCOPHANTIC :
   a. flattering
   b. empathetic
   c. self-serving
   d. self-sufficient
   e. selfless

9. OUST :
   a. veer
   b. ensconce
   c. pacify
   d. purge
   e. enslave

10. ANOMALOUS :
   a. abnormal
   b. confident
   c. reserved
   d. ordinary
   e. careless

11. BRUSQUE :
   a. courteous
   b. diffident
   c. rancorous
   d. jaunty
   e. timely

12. AUDACIOUS :
   a. defiant
   b. daring
   c. timid
   d. simple
   e. possible

13. PALPABLE :
   a. without substance
   b. in lieu of
   c. easily deceived
   d. not forceful
   e. damaging

14. STAID :
   a. serious
   b. weak
   c. climactic
   d. solipsistic
   e. frivolous

15. LOQUACIOUS :
- **a.** meddlesome
- **b.** productive
- **c.** vivacious
- **d.** taciturn
- **e.** piddling

16. PROTRACTED :
- **a.** abridged
- **b.** circumvented
- **c.** excessive
- **d.** tangential
- **e.** monumental

17. OBLIQUE :
- **a.** hearty
- **b.** direct
- **c.** careful
- **d.** superlative
- **e.** insightful

18. DOLOROUS :
- **a.** passive
- **b.** fickle
- **c.** cheerful
- **d.** sincere
- **e.** incredulous

19. MUTABLE :
- **a.** fatuous
- **b.** confusing
- **c.** changeable
- **d.** elemental
- **e.** constant

20. SUPERFLUOUS :
- **a.** insouciant
- **b.** genteel
- **c.** essential
- **d.** obtuse
- **e.** undeserved

Sentence Completion

Instructions: Each of the following sentences contains either one or two blanks. Below each question are answer choices lettered **a–e**. Select the lettered choice that best completes the sentence, bearing in mind its intended meaning.

1. Chemical fingerprints of space debris that has impacted the moon are similar to those found in meteorites that have struck the earth, proving that _____ and _____ impacts derived from analogous sources.
   a. common..extraordinary
   b. lunar..terrestrial
   c. possibility..intergalactic
   d. dangerous..simultaneous
   e. interstellar..other

2. The truth is the truth; neither childish absurdities, nor _____ contradictions, can make it otherwise.
   a. unscrupulous
   b. true
   c. possible
   d. certain
   e. unseemly

3. Humans are necessarily social creatures, for whom _____ is a matter of survival; however, as discrete entities, we often keenly experience yearnings for solitude.
   a. sustenance
   b. entertainment
   c. alienation
   d. encouragement
   e. collectivity

4. The wayfarer, with no companion but his staff, paused to exchange a word with the innkeeper, that the sense of _____ might not utterly overwhelm him before he could reach the first house in the valley.
   a. fatigue
   b. rancor
   c. insufficiency
   d. loneliness
   e. miscalculation

5. In the twentieth century, artists found themselves unshackled from the necessity to faithfully reproduce appearances; and they used their liberation to develop a purely _____ purpose in their _____.

    a. transparent..assertions

    b. commercial..idolatry

    c. aesthetic..oeuvres

    d. benign..portfolios

    e. casual..attire

6. A widely accepted theory of ancient human migration patterns holds that _____ originated in Africa more than 100,000 years ago and from thence _____ the remainder of the world.

    a. music..enchanted

    b. culture..freed

    c. savannahs..dotted

    d. glaciers..covered

    e. homo sapiens..colonized

7. To the writings of the alchemists were almost certainly added spurious elements, which compounded the difficulty of deciphering the _____ from the _____ in an already disconcerting amalgam of fact and allegory.

    a. genuine..apocryphal

    b. gold..silver

    c. Latin..Greek

    d. witchcraft..wizardry

    e. wheat..chaff

8. It is no wonder that insect displays are very popular at zoological parks worldwide; _____ make up over 90 percent of all _____ on earth.

    a. ants..insects

    b. zoos..museums

    c. arthropods..animals

    d. administrators..bureaucrats

    e. curators..people

9. Artistic expression is highly culture-specific; that is to say, the forms art takes and the functions it performs vary radically according to the _____ location and _____ of the artist.

    a. original..temperament

    b. geographic..ethnicity

    c. local..desires

    d. temperate..predilections

    e. possible..opportunities

10. The Industrial Revolution greatly improved physical living conditions for many European inhabitants; however, it also initially fomented _____ working conditions and human rights transgressions such as _____ labor.

   a. radical..intensive

   b. insufficient..malicious

   c. luxurious..inimical

   d. unsafe..child

   e. regressive..hard

11. In literature, a literal image is one that is unambiguously _____ to sensory perception, but a _____ image is subject to wide-ranging interpretation.

   a. apparent..figurative

   b. open..closer

   c. subject..possible

   d. interpretive..retractable

   e. closed..amorphous

12. Voltaire espoused the philosophy that an enlightened monarch would rule with benevolence; such a ruler, he believed, would promote _____ in order to _____ the rights of the populace.

   a. communication..clarify

   b. nutrition..purify

   c. conservation..countermand

   d. iniquity..evince

   e. reforms..enhance

13. Technical shortcomings hindered the advent of polyphonic music until the Renaissance era, when _____ arrangements became increasingly common.

   a. popular

   b. romantic

   c. complex

   d. string

   e. electronic

14. Metacognition is the term for what, why, and how we know what we know; in other words, it is _____ about _____.

   a. much ado..nothing

   b. thinking..thinking

   c. potentially..knowledge

   d. convincing..explanation

   e. presumably..research

15. Science education can be greatly enhanced by the use of interactive videodisc technology; it can be a tremendous _____ to see a scientific principle in action, rather than merely to read about it.
   a. advantage
   b. challenge
   c. tedium
   d. calamity
   e. perception

16. Rarely do we arrive at the summit of truth without running into extremes; in fact, we have frequently to exhaust the part of _____, and even of _____, before we work our way up to the noble goal of tranquil wisdom.
   a. yoga..tai chi
   b. opulence..complacency
   c. parcel..obedience
   d. error..folly
   e. ourselves..others

17. Any grand quest commences with the blind, intuitive calculation that, against all odds, the seeker will inevitably _____.
   a. overreach
   b. commiserate
   c. triumph
   d. dominate
   e. participate

18. Examining the means by which traditional societies living in large groups keep all members supplied with food provides illuminating contrast between the objective material conditions of life and the culture bearers' _____ of those _____.
   a. enchantment..groups
   b. perceptions..conditions
   c. scrutiny..societies
   d. contemplation..proofs
   e. illustrations..objects

19. Let it be remembered that this plan is neither recommended to blind approbation, nor to blind _____, but to a sedate and candid consideration.
   a. idiosyncrasy
   b. pathology
   c. appeasement
   d. uniformity
   e. reprobation

20. Speak not but what may benefit others or yourself; avoid _____ conversation.

    a. trifling

    b. assertive

    c. laudable

    d. dormant

    e. implausible

Reading Comprehension

Instructions: Read the passages that follow. After each passage, answer the content-based questions about it. Each question must be answered using only the information that is either *implied* or *stated* in the passage.

Line   Laughter appears to stand in need of an echo, Listen to it carefully: it is not an articulate, clear, well-defined sound; it is something which would fain be prolonged by reverberating from one to another, something beginning with a crash, to continue in successive rumblings, like thunder in a mountain. Still, this reverberation cannot go on for ever. It can travel within as wide a circle as

(5)   you please: the circle remains, nonetheless, a closed one. Our laughter is always the laughter of a group. It may, perchance, have happened to you, when seated in a railway carriage or at table d'hote, to hear travellers relating to one another stories which must have been comic to them, for they laughed heartily. Had you been one of their company, you would have laughed like them; but, as you were not, you had no desire whatever to do so. A man who was once asked why he did not

(10)   weep at a sermon, when everybody else was shedding tears, replied: "I don't belong to the parish!" What that man thought of tears would be still more true of laughter. However spontaneous it seems, laughter always implies a kind of secret freemasonry, or even complicity, with other laughers, real or imaginary. How often has it been said that the fuller the theatre, the more uncontrolled the laughter of the audience! On the other hand, how often has the remark been made that many

(15)   comic effects are incapable of translation from one language to another, because they refer to the customs and ideas of a particular social group! It is through not understanding the importance of this double fact that the comic has been looked upon as a mere curiosity in which the mind finds amusement, and laughter itself as a strange, isolated phenomenon, without any bearing on the rest of human activity. Hence those definitions which tend to make the comic into an abstract rela-

(20)   tion between ideas: "an intellectual contrast," "a palpable absurdity," etc.,—definitions which, even were they really suitable to every form of the comic, would not in the least explain why the comic makes us laugh. How, indeed, should it come about that this particular logical relation, as soon as it is perceived, contracts, expands and shakes our limbs, whilst all other relations leave the body unaffected? It is not from this point of view that we shall approach the problem. To understand

(25)   laughter, we must put it back into its natural environment, which is society, and above all must we determine the utility of its function, which is a social one. Such, let us say at once, will be the leading idea of all our investigations. Laughter must answer to certain requirements of life in common. It must have a SOCIAL signification.

1. Which of the following titles best describes this passage as a whole?
   a. Comedy: The Misunderstood Art
   b. Observations on the Function of Laughter
   c. The Logical Relation of Comedy to Laughter
   d. Laughter: A Social Function
   e. Echoes of Laughter

2. It can be inferred from the passage that a person would be least likely to laugh in which of the following situations:
   a. a crowded theater
   b. a half-full theater
   c. reading a book
   d. watching a television sitcom
   e. sitting alone in a comedy club

3. According to the passage, an individual may fail to understand the comic because:
   I. it does not mesh with specific customs and ideas of his or her society.
   II. the individual feels apart from the intended audience.
   III. laughter is an isolated phenomenon.
   a. II only
   b. III only
   c. I and II only
   d. II and III only
   e. I, II and III

4. The author supports the assertion in line 1 that laughter is *in need of an echo* by which of the following means?
   a. by comparing it to a storm
   b. by saying it wants to pass from person to person
   c. by relating an anecdote about a parish
   d. by comparing it to thunder in a mountain
   e. by invoking an image of a circle

5. The passage implies that laughter is always contained within a specific group because:
   a. a larger audience portends a larger laugh.
   b. the utility of laughter is a social one.
   c. some people prefer one type of humor over another.
   d. the circle must remain closed.
   e. in social terms, humankind is not universally connected.

Line   Geometry sets out from certain conceptions such as "plane," "point," and "straight line," with which we are able to associate more or less definite ideas, and from certain simple propositions (axioms) which, in virtue of these ideas, we are inclined to accept as "true." Then, on the basis of a logical process, the justification of which we feel ourselves compelled to admit,

(5)   all remaining propositions are shown to follow from those axioms, i.e., they are proven. A proposition is then correct ("true") when it has been derived in the recognized manner from the axioms. The question of "truth" of the individual geometrical propositions is thus reduced to one of the "truth" of the axioms. Now it has long been known that the last question is not only unanswerable by the methods of geometry, but that it is in itself entirely

(10)   without meaning. We cannot ask whether it is true that only one straight line goes through two points. We can only say that Euclidean geometry deals with things called "straight lines," to each of which is ascribed the property of being uniquely determined by two points situated on it. The concept "true" does not tally with the assertions of pure geometry, because by the word "true" we are eventually in the habit of designating always the correspondence with

(15)   a "real" object; geometry, however, is not concerned with the relation of the ideas involved in it to objects of experience, but only with the logical connection of these ideas among themselves.

     It is not difficult to understand why, in spite of this, we feel constrained to call the propositions of geometry "true." Geometrical ideas correspond to more or less exact objects in

(20)   nature, and these last are undoubtedly the exclusive cause of the genesis of those ideas. Geometry ought to refrain from such a course, in order to give to its structure the largest possible logical unity. The practice, for example, of seeing in a "distance" two marked positions on a practically rigid body is something which is lodged deeply in our habit of thought. We are accustomed further to regard three points as being situated on a straight line, if their

(25)   apparent positions can be made to coincide for observation with one eye, under suitable choice of our place of observation.

6. In this passage, the author is chiefly concerned with which of the following topics?
  a. a definition of geometric axioms
  b. the truth, or lack thereof, of geometrical propositions
  c. the reality of geometrical correspondences
  d. the validity of human observations
  e. the exact observation of natural objects

7. The author's assertion in lines 9–10 that *it is in itself entirely without meaning* refers to which of the following?
  a. geometrical propositions
  b. the nature of straight lines
  c. the truth of the axioms of geometry
  d. the methods of geometry
  e. any question of the truth of geometry

8. It can be inferred from the passage that the truth of a geometrical proposition depends on which of the following?

   a. the concept of straight lines

   b. the validity of Euclidean thought

   c. the logical connection of the ideas of geometry

   d. our inclination to accept it as true

   e. the truth of the axioms

9. The author's use of the term *pure geometry* in line 13 refers to which of the following?

   a. the relation of ideas to objects of experience

   b. the logical connection of ideas among themselves

   c. apparent observations of points and planes

   d. more or less exact objects in nature

   e. the existence of straight lines

10. It can be inferred from the passage that our propensity for calling the propositions of geometry *true* is due to which of the following?

   a. The propositions appear to correspond to natural objects.

   b. There is a logical unity to the propositions.

   c. We have been conditioned to believe they are true.

   d. Geometric principles derive from definite ideas.

   e. Observations prove the propositions to be true.

Line   Necessity is the first lawgiver; all the wants which had to be met by this constitution were originally of a commercial nature. Thus the whole constitution was founded on commerce, and the laws of the nation were adapted to its pursuits. The last clause, which excluded foreigners from all offices of trust, was a natural consequence of the preceding articles. So com-

(5)   plicated and artificial a relation between the sovereign and his people, which in many provinces was further modified according to the peculiar wants of each, and frequently of some single city, required for its maintenance the liveliest zeal for the liberties of the country, combined with an intimate acquaintance with them. From a foreigner neither could well be expected. This law, besides, was enforced reciprocally in each particular province; so that in

(10)   Brabant no Fleming, in Zealand no Hollander, could hold office; and it continued in force even after all these provinces were united under one government.

     Above all others, Brabant enjoyed the highest degree of freedom. Its privileges were esteemed so valuable that many mothers from the adjacent provinces removed thither about the time of their accouchment, in order to entitle their children to participate, by birth, in all

(15)   the immunities of that favored country; just as, says Strada, one improves the plants of a rude climate by removing them to the soil of a milder.

11. The author of this passage implies which of the following?
   a. Foreigners are generally not to be trusted.
   b. Crossing borders to give birth is morally suspect.
   c. Laws, as a rule, develop in response to a need for laws.
   d. Unification is a natural tendency for smaller provinces.
   e. No person should be immune to legal restrictions.

12. Which of the following justifications does the author offer for the exclusion of foreigners from all offices of trust?
   I. The laws were extremely complex, necessitating extensive familiarity with their nuances.
   II. Stringent enforcement of the laws was required.
   III. Mutual distrust prevailed at this time among the various provinces.
   a. II only
   b. III only
   c. I and II only
   d. I and III only
   e. I, II and III

13. It is implied in this passage that the first close ties among the mentioned provinces developed as a result of which of the following?
   a. the cooperation required to write a constitution
   b. interprovincial trade
   c. intraprovincial trade
   d. the practice of giving birth in Brabant
   e. the evolution of legal systems within the provinces

14. In this passage the author maintains that which of the following continued after unification of the provinces?
   a. a complex relationship between sovereign and people
   b. a zeal for liberty
   c. the practice of giving birth in Brabant
   d. the pursuit of freedom by residents of Brabant
   e. the exclusion of foreigners from office-holding

15. This passage can best be described as a:
   a. defense of a thesis that increased freedom leads to more vigorous commerce
   b. reconciliation of opposing views of constitutional development
   c. contrast and comparison of vagaries of provincial law, pre-unification
   d. review of similarities and contrasts among pre-unification provincial laws
   e. polemic advocating the desirability of legal reciprocity among neighboring provinces

Line   The discovery which shows, beyond all others, that Hipparchus possessed one of the masterminds of all time was the detection of that remarkable celestial movement known as the precession of the equinoxes. The inquiry which conducted to this discovery involved a most
profound investigation, especially when it is remembered that in the days of Hipparchus the
(5)   means of observation of the heavenly bodies were only of the rudest description, and the
available observations of earlier dates were extremely scanty. We can but look with astonish-
ment on the genius of the man who, in spite of such difficulties, was able to detect such a
phenomenon as the precession, and to exhibit its actual magnitude. I shall endeavour to
explain the nature of this singular celestial movement, for it may be said to offer the first
(10)   instance in the history of science in which we find that combination of accurate observation
with skillful interpretation, of which, in the subsequent development of astronomy, we have
so many splendid examples.

The word equinox implies the condition that the night is equal to the day. To a resident on
the equator the night is no doubt equal to the day at all times in the year, but to one who
(15)   lives on any other part of the earth, in either hemisphere, the night and the day are not generally equal. There is, however, one occasion in spring, and another in autumn, on which the
day and the night are each twelve hours at all places on the earth. When the night and day are
equal in spring, the point which the sun occupies on the heavens is termed the vernal equinox. There is similarly another point in which the sun is situated at the time of the autumnal
(20)   equinox. In any investigation of the celestial movements the positions of these two equinoxes
on the heavens are of primary importance, and Hipparchus, with the instinct of genius, perceived their significance, and commenced to study them. It will be understood that we can
always define the position of a point on the sky with reference to the surrounding stars. No
doubt we do not see the stars near the sun when the sun is shining, but they are there never-
(25)   theless. The ingenuity of Hipparchus enabled him to determine the positions of each of the
two equinoxes relatively to the stars which lie in its immediate vicinity. After examination of
the celestial places of these points at different periods, he was led to the conclusion that each
equinox was moving relatively to the stars, though that movement was so slow that twenty-
five-thousand years would necessarily elapse before a complete circuit of the heavens was
(30)   accomplished. Hipparchus traced out this phenomenon, and established it on an impreg-
nable basis, so that all astronomers have ever since recognized the precession of the
equinoxes as one of the fundamental facts of astronomy. Not until nearly two thousand years
after Hipparchus had made this splendid discovery was the explanation of its cause given by
Newton.

16. It can be inferred from the passage that the way in which Hipparchus contributed most importantly to science was which of the following?

    a. He was the first to observe the heavens.

    b. He was first to perceive the equinoxes.

    c. He was the first to combine observation with skillful interpretation.

    d. He worked primarily with crude instruments of observation.

    e. He was the first to realize stars are merely obscured by the brightness of the sun.

17. According to the passage, the following are all true statements about the vernal and autumnal equinoxes EXCEPT:

    a. Day and night are equivalent in length.

    b. The equinoxes fall on the same day for both northern and southern hemispheres.

    c. It takes 25,000 years for a complete precession to occur.

    d. There are two distinct points each year, one for the vernal equinox and one for the autumnal equinox.

    e. The position of the sun relative to the stars is constant from year to year.

18. According to the passage, Hipparchus used which of the following methods to discover the precession of the equinoxes?

    a. He examined the night sky and compared it to the daytime sky.

    b. He examined historical records and compared them to contemporary measurements.

    c. He consulted with Newton to explain the phenomenon on an impregnable basis.

    d. He measured the positions of the equinoxes and compared them on a periodic basis.

    e. He developed precise instrumentation to facilitate his observations.

19. It can be inferred from the passage that Hipparchus lived and worked in which of the following historical eras?

    a. the early nineteenth century

    b. the second century B.C.

    c. the early Middle Ages

    d. the first part of the sixteenth century

    e. the twentieth century

20. Which of the following statements, if true, most weakens the author's assertion that *Hipparchus possessed one of the masterminds of all time* (lines 1–2)?

    a. In Hipparchus's time, the telescope was commonly employed by observers of the heavens.

    b. Astronomers and astrologers of ancient times routinely noted the occurrence of the vernal and autumnal equinoxes.

    c. The scientific method was formalized by Isaac Newton in the eighteenth century.

    d. It was not until the nineteenth century that nonacademicians were convinced that the earth revolved around the sun.

    e. Hipparchus's observations were routinely dismissed by his contemporaries.

▶ Answers

Analogies

1. b. The relationship in this question is part to whole. A *word* is made up of *syllables*. A *series* is composed of *games*.

2. a. *Efficient* is the opposite of *wasteful*. *Honest* is the opposite of *deceptive*.

3. d. *Parsley* is a type of *garnish*. *Salt* is a type of *seasoning*.

4. e. The concept in this question is one of opposites, though they are different parts of speech. Something that is *fuzzy* lacks *clarity*. Something that is *rigid* lacks *flexibility*.

5. c. *Land* can be divided into *acres*. *Cake* can be divided into *slices*.

6. a. The *shaft* is the long, narrow part of the *spear*. The *neck* is the long, narrow part of the *guitar*.

7. c. You will find a *trellis* in a *garden*. You will find a *fireplace* in a *house*.

8. d. A *manacle* binds the *hands*. A *fetter* binds the *feet*.

9. e. A *thresher* is a type of *shark*. A *mastiff* is a type of *dog*.

10. d. A *grip* in the film industry uses a piece of equipment called a *dolly*. A (train) *conductor* uses a *ticket punch*.

11. a. A *parrot mimics* speech. A *termite bores* wood.

12. d. The *mandible* is the *jaw* bone. The *metatarsal* is a bone in the *foot*.

13. b. *Overt* is the opposite of *hidden*. *Ebullient* is the opposite of *glum*.

14. b. A *dollar* is composed of *cents*. An *army* is composed of *battalions*.

15. e. A *scimitar* is a type of *saber*. A *revolver* is a type of *gun*.

16. c. A *cineaste* loves *film* the way a *gastronome* loves *food*.

17. a. A *lap* is a unit of measurement for a *pool*. A *light-year* is a unit of measurement for *space*.

18. c. *Resin* is an ingredient in *varnish*. *Pectin* is an ingredient in *preserves*.

19. e. *Paper* is used to make *origami*. *Osier* is a willow used to make *baskets*.

20. b. Something *Machiavellian* is *duplicitous*. Something *Orwellian* is *intrusive*.

Antonyms

1. c. To be *ambivalent* is to be uncertain. To be *positive* is to be certain.

2. e. Something which is *catastrophic* is disastrous. That is the opposite of *beneficial*.

3. a. *Palatial* means like a palace. *Chintzy* means cheap and inelegant.

4. c. *Omniscient* means all-knowing (*omni* means all). To be *ignorant* is to know little or nothing.

5. d. To *capitulate* is to give in or give up in the face of opposition. To *persevere* is to continue, usually against opposition or obstacles.

6. b. To *indemnify* is to secure against harm, loss, or damage. To *put at risk* connotes a vulnerability to damage, harm, or loss.

7. c. To *palliate* is to lessen the violence of, to abate something harmful. To *aggravate* is to increase the degree of something harmful.

If you didn't know some of the words in the antonym questions, don't worry about it. Just make a list of the ones you didn't know and learn them. Remember that several short lists are better than one long list. Flash-cards are even easier to work with.

8. e. To be *sycophantic* is to be seeking personal gain, usually by servile flattery. To be *selfless* is to not think of self-gain.

9. b. To *oust* is to eject or remove, usually from property or position. To *ensconce* is to place into power or position.

10. d. To be *anomalous* is to be unusual, out of the ordinary. To be *ordinary* is to be usual or expected.

11. a. To be *brusque* is to be abrupt in a social situation, to the point of being harsh. It is the opposite of being *courteous,* or polite.

12. c. To be *audacious* is to be recklessly bold or daring. To be *timid* is to lack the capacity to be bold or daring.

13. a. To be *palpable* is to be capable of being touched or felt, to be tangible. To be *without substance* is to lack the physical qualities necessary in order to be touched or felt.

14. e. To be *staid* is to be solidly fixed in a serious mode. To be *frivolous* is to lack seriousness.

15. d. To be *loquacious* is to be talkative. To be *taciturn* is to use few words.

16. a. To be *protracted* is to be prolonged or drawn out. To be *abridged* is to be cut short.

17. b. *Oblique* means indirect, not straightforward, with a connotation of underhandedness. *Direct* means straight, either literally or, as here, with a connotation of honesty and lack of deception.

18. c. *Dolorous* means expressive of misery or grief. *Cheerful* is the opposite of that.

19. e. *Mutable* means changeable. *Constant* means unchanging.

20. c. That which is *superfluous* is not required, not essential. That which is *essential* is necessary, or required.

Sentence Completion

1. b. There are two key phrases in this sentence: *are similar to* and *proving that.* It also helps to know the word *analogous,* implying here a correspondence of sources. This sentence can be attacked in sections, based on verbs. The verb phrase *are similar to* refers to *chemical fingerprints of space debris.* That tells you the chemical fingerprints of space debris on the moon are similar to meteorites on earth. Ask yourself what that would prove. Chemical fingerprints, like human fingerprints, are a means of identification. The phrase *proving that* directs you back to the idea of the earth and the moon, referred to in the answers as *lunar* and *terrestrial.*

2. a. The word *and* signifies a restatement of or complement to the statement *the truth is the truth.* Don't be thrown off by the *neither..nor* combination. You are looking for a statement that supports the initial statement. Trying each answer choice in succession will reveal only one that gives the restatement the same meaning as the original statement.

3. e. *For whom* is the phrase that signals support of the statement *humans are necessarily social creatures.* Find the answer choice that supports humans as social beings and try it in the sentence. *Collectivity* means acting collectively, or together.

4. d. In this sentence, the punctuation is your best guide, drawing attention to the word *that. That* carries an implication of *so that* or *in order that.* It tells you to look for a cause and effect. Both bits of information in the sentence up to the blank signal the same cause: the traveller had *no companion but his staff* and he *paused to exchange a word with the innkeeper.* The effect of having no companion is the need to ward off *loneliness,* and that is one of the answer choices.

5. c. The word *and* tells you there is complementarity between the first part of the sentence and the second; in this case it signals cause and effect because of the word *used.* The first part of the sentence tells you artists were freed from the need to *faithfully reproduce appearances.* What they did with their freedom, you learn in the second part of the sentence, was to develop a pure purpose of some sort. You must assume this development had nothing to do with a faithful reproduction of appearances, as that is all the information you have to go on. The words that fit the blanks convey that artists developed a *purely aesthetic purpose* in their *oeuvres,* their work.

6. e. The structure of the sentence is straightforward. You are told immediately that the sentence is about a *theory of ancient human migration patterns.* Knowing that the correct answer choices will have to do with humans and migration patterns, you can eliminate choices **a** and **c.** Choice **b,** while having to do with humans, has nothing to do with migration patterns, nor does it make sense when placed in the blanks (freed whom from what?). Choice **d** does not relate to the subject of the sentence.

7. a. This sentence is about the *writings of the alchemists. Spurious elements* is a key phrase, which means doubtful or false components. The answer must somehow address the issue of *spurious elements* in the *writings of the alchemists.* Therefore, you can eliminate choices **b** and **d.** Choice **c** has to do with *writing* but nothing to do with *spurious elements.* Choice **e** works only if you disregard the subject of the sentence.

8. c. Remember to stick to the information introduced in the sentence. The lack of any word or phrase signaling another type of relationship means this is a restatement of or elaboration on the first unit of the sentence. In this case, only insects (arthropods) and a rising type of zoo displays have been mentioned. Choice **c** is the only one that logically follows from the first sentence unit.

9. b. The phrase *that is to say* signals a restatement of the first sentence unit, *artistic expression is highly culture-specific.* The only answer choice that mentions culture in any way is **b,** *geographic..ethnicity.*

10. d. In this sentence *however* signals a relationship of contrast between the first sentence unit and that which follows. The sentence starts by talking about the *greatly improved..living conditions* of the *Industrial Revolution.* The second unit, therefore, must contrast conceptually with that idea, so you can eliminate choices **a, c,** and **e.** *Malicious labor* is not necessarily a *human rights transgression,* but *child labor* is.

11. a. The word *but* signals a contrast between the two units of the sentence. The first unit is about the definition of a *literal image,* which is something that can actually be perceived. The second unit of the sentence is contrasting some type of image with a *literal image.* In literature, *literal* contrasts most clearly with *figurative. Apparent* also works well in the first blank.

12. e. The first unit of the sentence is about Voltaire's philosophy concerning an *enlightened monarch.* The second unit elaborates on the first, as signaled by the phrase *he believed,* a variation on *espoused.* You are looking for positive words to fit with the concept of a benevolent, enlightened ruler. Only *reforms..enhance* work well in the sentence.

13. c. The key word here is *polyphonic.* If you don't know the word, separate it into *poly* (meaning several or many) and *phonic* (having to do with sound). That will lead you to the correct answer, *complex.*

14. b. The first unit of the sentence defines the word *metacognition.* The second unit restates the definition, as cued by the phrase *in other words.*

15. a. The lack of a word or phrase signaling contrast or any other relationship means that the second unit is a restatement of the first. Something that is an *enhance*ment is also an *advantage.*

16. d. In the first unit of this sentence there are two pairs of words that set up the meaning of the sentence. *Rarely* is paired with *without,* and *truth* is paired with *extremes.* The first two cancel each other out in the same way double negatives would, leaving the meaning that we usually get to *the summit of truth* by way of *extremes.* The phrase *in fact* signals a restatement or even amplification of the first unit. The answer choice that fits with the concept of extremes is **d,** *error..folly.*

17. c. The key phrases in this sentence are *grand quest* and *against all odds.* The answer choice that contrasts with *against all odds* and completes the thought is **c,** *triumph.*

18. b. This sentence has no punctuation to guide you, but it does contain the phrase *contrast between,* which leads you to look at the next phrase, *the objective material conditions of life.* The word that contrasts most clearly with *objective,* meaning factual, is subjective, referring to personal perception. That leads to **b** as the correct answer.

19. e. This sentence has three units. Each unit is referring to a *plan.* The first unit does not recommend *blind approbation* (approval). The second unit uses the word *nor* to signal a contrast (disapproval), and the final unit recommends consideration. The answer choice that means disapproval is **e,** *reprobation.*

20. a. The two words *not but* juxtaposed in this sentence mean *only,* when taken together. The second unit of the sentence contrasts with the first, because it is an imperative sentence, giving advice. The word *avoid* signals the contrast, and **a,** *trifling,* is the word that contrasts with the advice given in the first unit.

Reading Comprehension

1. d. Although the author makes several points within the article, each one supports the main thesis that laughter is a social function.

2. c. In lines 5–8, in particular, the author clearly discusses the point that we are most likely to laugh in the company of others with whom we share the laughter. Even a sitcom has a laugh track, which reminds us that others find it amusing.

3. c. The author supports assertion I in lines 15–16 and assertion II in lines 9–10. Assertion III is contradicted throughout the passage.

4. b. The phrase *would fain be prolonged by reverberating from one to another* in lines 2–3 refers to the method by which a laugh, like an echo, bounces successively off surfaces (people). *Fain* is an archaic word meaning *willingly*.

5. e. The author uses several examples to make this point. If one is not a member of a group, of a social circle that is sharing a laugh, one is not inclined to laugh along with the others. Groups can be variously defined and may vary in size, but it is safe to say that no social group includes all of humankind.

6. b. The author repeatedly refers to *truth* in relation to geometrical propositions. See, for example, lines 3, 6, 7, 8, 13, 14, and 19. The author (Albert Einstein) is laying the groundwork for an argument that the principles of geometry are only apparently true.

7. c. To answer this question, you have to find the antecedent of *it*. First, you discover that *it* refers to *the last question*. Then you must trace back to realize that *the last question* itself refers to *the "truth" of the axioms* in the previous sentence.

8. e. This question deals with the same two sentences as the previous question and adds the previous sentence. Lines 4–8 contain the statements that argue that the truth of the propositions depends on the truth of the axioms.

9. b. The sentence that begins on line 13 and goes through line 17 is the one that contains the assertion about *pure geometry*.

10. a. In order to answer this question correctly, you must tie together the first sentence of the passage and the series of sentences that begin on line 18.

11. c. This assertion is contained in the first sentence of the passage and further supported in the second sentence.

12. c. Lines 3–9 contain the sentences that set up and support the discussion of the exclusion of foreigners from office.

13. b. The answer to this question requires you to extrapolate from the author's opening two sentences, stating that the first constitution was written in response to the necessities of trade among the provinces. The prefix *inter* more clearly denotes interaction among the provinces than does the prefix *intra*, which has a connotation of internal interaction.

14. e. Lines 9–11 state that the exclusion of foreigners continued after unification.

15. d. The choice of **d** as the correct answer (as opposed to **c**) requires you to know the meaning of the word *vagaries*, which connotes capriciousness and does not apply to the author's discussion of legal development in the provinces.

16. c. Lines 6–8 discuss Hipparchus's most important contribution to science. The first two statements are not supported by the passage. The last statement is not a contribution.

17. e. The sentence that begins on line 28 is the one that most clearly states that *each equinox was moving relatively to the stars . . . .* That is the phenomenon called the precession of the equinoxes.

18. d. The sentence that begins on line 25 sets up Hipparchus's method. The next sentence, beginning on line 26, most clearly states that he made periodic comparisons.

19. b. The last sentence of the passage is the key to the correct answer. You have to know roughly when Newton lived and subtract two thousand years.

20. a. The author devotes much of the first paragraph to a discussion of the limited means and methods available to Hipparchus. Choice **b** is correct but does not diminish Hipparchus's achievements. Neither choice **c** nor **d** would have any bearing whatsoever on something that happened two thousand years earlier. Even if choice **e** were true, it would in no way detract from Hipparchus's work.

► What Now?

Go back and assess your performance on each of the three sections. Why did you miss the questions you missed? Are there strategies that would help you if you practice them? Were there many words you didn't know?

Whatever your weaknesses are, it's much better to learn about them now and spend the time between now and the GRE test turning them into strengths than it is to pretend they don't exist. It can be hard to focus on your weaknesses. The human tendency is to want to ignore them, nevertheless, if you focus on this task—doing well on the GRE test—your effort will repay you many times over. You will go to the school you want and enjoy the career you want, and it will have all started with the relatively few hours you devoted to preparing for a standardized test. What are you waiting for?

► Finally

One last consideration about the Verbal section of the GRE test is the effect of good time management during the exam. The basic rule is a minute a question, but some questions (analogies and antonyms) will take less time, and others will take more time. Don't hold yourself to a strict schedule, but learn to be aware of the time you are taking.

If you can eliminate one or more answers on a tough question, go ahead and make a guess. Don't leave any questions blank and don't spend too much time on any one question.

These time management strategies apply to the Verbal section of the GRE test; they also will serve you well on the Quantitative portion of the test. The Quantitative review in this book will provide you with additional powerful strategies for that section of the exam.

5 ▶ The GRE Quantitative Section

This chapter will help you prepare for the Quantitative section of the GRE test. The Quantitative section of the GRE test contains 28 total questions:

- 14 quantitative comparison questions
- 14 problem solving questions

You will have 45 minutes to complete these questions. This section of the GRE test assesses general high school mathematical knowledge. More information regarding the type and content of the questions is reviewed in this chapter.

It is important to remember that a computer-adaptive test (CAT) is tailored to your performance level. The test will begin with a question of medium difficulty. Each question that follows is based on how you responded to earlier questions. If you answer a question correctly, the next question will be more difficult. If you answer a question incorrectly, the next question will be easier. The test is designed to analyze every answer you give as you take the test in order to determine the next question that will be presented. This is done to ascertain a precise measure of your quantitative abilities using fewer test questions than traditional paper tests would use.

▶ Introduction to the Quantitative Section

The Quantitative section measures your general understanding of basic high school mathematical concepts. You will not need to know any advanced mathematics. This test is a simple measure of your ability to reason clearly in a quantitative setting. Therefore, you will not be allowed to use a calculator on this exam. Many of the questions are posed as word problems relating to real-life situations. The quantitative information is given in the text of the questions, in tables and graphs, or in coordinate systems.

It is important to know that all of the questions are based on real numbers. In terms of measurement, units of measure are used from both the English and metric systems. Although conversion will be given between English and metric systems when needed, simple conversions will not be given. (Examples of simple conversions are minutes to hours or centimeters to millimeters.)

Most of the geometric figures on the exam are not drawn to scale. For this reason, do not attempt to estimate answers by sight. These answers should be calculated by using geometric reasoning. In addition, on a CAT, some geometric figures may appear a bit jagged on the computer screen. Ignore these minor irregularities in lines and curves. They will not affect your answers.

There are eight symbols listed below with their meanings. It is important to become familiar with these symbols before proceeding further.

$<$	$x < y$ x is less than y
$>$	$x > y$ x is greater than y
$\leq$	$x \leq y$ x is less than or equal to y
$\geq$	$x \geq y$ x is greater than or equal to y
$\neq$	$x \neq y$ x is not equal to y
$\parallel$	$x \parallel y$ x is parallel to y
$\perp$	$x \perp y$ x is perpendicular to y
$\llcorner$	 angle A is a right angle

The Quantitative section covers four types of math: arithmetic, algebra, geometry, and data analysis.

Arithmetic

The types of arithmetic concepts you should be prepared to face in the Quantitative section include the following:

- arithmetic operations—addition, subtraction, multiplication, division, and powers of real numbers
- operations with radical expressions
- the real number line and its applications
- estimation, percent, and absolute value
- properties of integers (divisibility, factoring, prime numbers, and odd and even integers)

Algebra

The types of algebra concepts you should be prepared to face in the Quantitative section include the following:

- rules of exponents
- factoring and simplifying of algebraic expressions
- concepts of relations and functions
- equations and inequalities
- solving linear and quadratic equations and inequalities
- reading word problems and writing equations from assigned variables
- applying basic algebra skills to solve problems

Geometry

The types of geometry concepts you should be prepared to face in the Quantitative section include the following:

- properties associated with parallel lines, circles, triangles, rectangles, and other polygons
- calculating area, volume, and perimeter
- the Pythagorean theorem and angle measure

There will be no questions regarding geometric proofs.

Data Analysis

The type of data analysis concepts you should be prepared to face in the Quantitative section include the following:

- general statistical operations such as mean, mode, median, range, standard deviation, and percentages
- interpretation of data given in graphs and tables
- simple probability
- synthesizing information about and selecting appropriate data for answering questions

▶ The Two Types of Quantitative Section Questions

As stated earlier, the quantitative questions on the GRE test will be either quantitative comparison or problem solving questions. Quantitative comparison questions measure your ability to compare the relative sizes of two quantities or to determine that there is not enough information given to make a decision. Problem solving questions measure your ability to solve a problem using general mathematical knowledge. This knowledge is applied to reading and understanding the question, as well as to making the needed calculations.

Quantitative Comparison Questions

Each of the quantitative comparison questions contains two quantities, one in column A and one in column B. Based on the information given, you are to decide between the following answer choices:

    a. The quantity in Column A is greater.
    b. The quantity in Column B is greater.
    c. The two quantities are equal.
    d. The relationship cannot be determined from the information given.

Problem Solving Questions

These questions are essentially standard, multiple-choice questions. Every problem solving question has one correct answer and four incorrect ones. Although the answer choices in this book are labeled **a**, **b**, **c**, **d**, and **e**, keep in mind that on the computer test, they will appear as blank ovals in front of each answer choice. Specific tips and strategies for each question type are given directly before the practice problems later in the book. This will help keep them fresh in your mind during the test.

▶ About the Pretest

The following pretest will help you figure out what skills you have already mastered and what skills you need to improve. After you check your answers, read through the skills sections and concentrate on the topics that gave you trouble on the pretest. The skills section is followed by 80 practice problems that mirror those found on the GRE test. Make sure to look over the explanations, as well as the answers, when you check to see how you did. When you complete the practice problems, you will have a better idea of how to focus on your studying for the GRE test.

ANSWER SHEET

1. ⓐ ⓑ ⓒ ⓓ
2. ⓐ ⓑ ⓒ ⓓ
3. ⓐ ⓑ ⓒ ⓓ
4. ⓐ ⓑ ⓒ ⓓ
5. ⓐ ⓑ ⓒ ⓓ
6. ⓐ ⓑ ⓒ ⓓ
7. ⓐ ⓑ ⓒ ⓓ

8. ⓐ ⓑ ⓒ ⓓ
9. ⓐ ⓑ ⓒ ⓓ
10. ⓐ ⓑ ⓒ ⓓ
11. ⓐ ⓑ ⓒ ⓓ ⓔ
12. ⓐ ⓑ ⓒ ⓓ ⓔ
13. ⓐ ⓑ ⓒ ⓓ ⓔ
14. ⓐ ⓑ ⓒ ⓓ ⓔ

15. ⓐ ⓑ ⓒ ⓓ ⓔ
16. ⓐ ⓑ ⓒ ⓓ ⓔ
17. ⓐ ⓑ ⓒ ⓓ ⓔ
18. ⓐ ⓑ ⓒ ⓓ ⓔ
19. ⓐ ⓑ ⓒ ⓓ ⓔ
20. ⓐ ⓑ ⓒ ⓓ ⓔ

▶ Pretest

Directions: In each of the questions 1–10, compare the two quantities given. Select the appropriate choice for each one according to the following:

Select   **a.** if the quantity in Column A is greater
        b. if the quantity in Column B is greater
        c. if the two quantities are equal
        d. if there is not enough information given to determine the relationship of the two quantities.

Column A　　　　　　　　　　　　　　　　　　　　　　　　　　**Column B**

1.
$$z + w = 13$$
$$z + 3 = 8$$

z 　　　　　　　　　　　　　　　　　　　　　　　　　　w

2. Ida spent \$75 on a skateboard and an additional
\$27 to buy new wheels for it. She then sold the
skateboard for \$120.

the money Ida received in excess
of the total amount she spent 　　　　　　　　　　　　　　\$20

3.

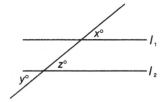

x 　　　　　　　　　　　　　　　　　　　　　　　　　　y

4. $-2(-2)(-5)$ 　　　　　　　　　　　　　　　　　　　$(0)(3)(9)$

5.   11 $10 + x$

6. $\frac{1}{2} + \frac{3}{5}$ $\frac{1+3}{2+5}$

7.

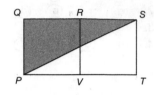

Squares PQRV and VRST
have sides of length 6.

the area of shaded   36
region *PQS*

8. R, S, and T are three consecutive odd
                           integers and $R < S < T$.

   $R + S + 1$ $S + T - 1$

9.

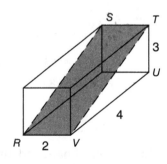

the area of the shaded   9
rectangular region

10. $x^2 y > 0$
                                 $xy^2 < 0$

         x y

Directions: For each question, select the best answer choice given.

11. $\sqrt{(42 - 6)(25 + 11)}$

    a. 6

    b. 18

    c. 36

    d. 120

    e. 1,296

12. What is the remainder when 6^3 is divided by 8?

    a. 5

    b. 3

    c. 2

    d. 1

    e. 0

13.

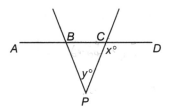

In the figure above, $BP = CP$. If $x = 120°$, then $y =$

    a. 30°

    b. 60°

    c. 75°

    d. 90°

    e. 120°

14. If $y = 3x$ and $z = 2y$, then in terms of x, $x + y + z =$

    a. $10x$.

    b. $9x$.

    c. $8x$.

    d. $6x$.

    e. $5x$.

15.

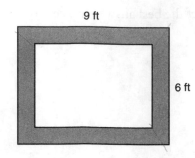

9 ft

6 ft

The rectangular rug shown in the figure above has a floral border 1 foot wide on all sides. What is the area, in square feet, of the portion of the rug that excludes the border?

a. 28
b. 40
c. 45
d. 48
e. 54

16. If $\frac{d - 3n}{7n - d} = 1$, which of the following must be true about the relationship between d and n?

a. n is 4 more than d
b. d is 4 more than n
c. n is $\frac{7}{3}$ of d
d. d is 5 times n
e. d is 2 times n

17. How many positive whole numbers less than 81 are NOT equal to squares of whole numbers?

a. 9
b. 70
c. 71
d. 72
e. 73

18. Of the following, which could be the graph of $2 - 5x \leq \frac{6x - 5}{-3}$?

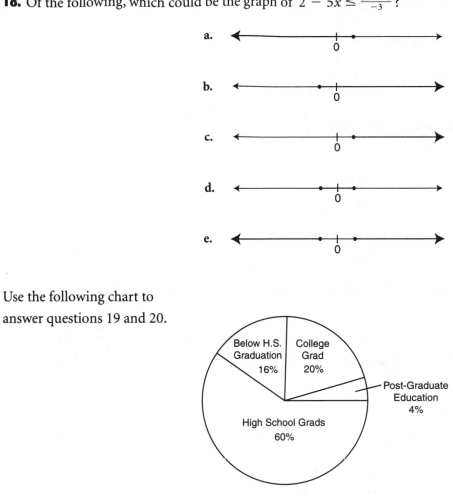

a.

b.

c.

d.

e.

Use the following chart to answer questions 19 and 20.

19. If the chart is drawn accurately, how many degrees should there be in the central angle of the sector indicating the number of college graduates?

   a. 20

   b. 40

   c. 60

   d. 72

   e. more than 72

20. If the total number of students in the study was 250,000, what is the number of students who graduated from college?

   a. 6,000

   b. 10,000

   c. 50,000

   d. 60,000

   e. more than 60,000

► Answer Explanations for Pretest

1. b. Since $z + 3 = 8$, z must be 5. Since $z + w = 5 + w = 13$, w must be 8.

2. b. Ida spent \$102 on her skateboard (\$75 + \$27). Therefore, in selling the skateboard for \$120, she got \$18 in excess of what she spent.

3. c. In the figure, $y = z$ because they are vertical angles. Also, since $l_1 \parallel l_2$, $z = x$ because they are corresponding angles. Therefore, $y = x$.

4. b. $(-2)(-2)(-5)$ is less than zero because multiplying an odd number of negative numbers results in a negative value. Since $(0)(3)(9) = 0$, column B is greater.

5. d. The value of $10 + x$ is unknown because the value of x is not given, nor can it be found. Therefore, it is impossible to know if the sum of this expression is greater than or equal to 11.

6. a. By looking at the first value, you know that $\frac{1}{2} + \frac{3}{5} > 1$. Since, $\frac{1+3}{2+5} = \frac{4}{7}$ and $\frac{4}{7}$ is < 1, you know that column A is greater.

7. c. In the figure, the two squares have a common side, RV, so that $PQST$ is a 12 by 6 rectangle. Its area is therefore 72. You are asked to compare the area of region PQS with 36. Since diagonal PS splits region $PQST$ in half, the area of region PQS is $\frac{1}{2}$ of 72, or 36.

8. b. It is given that R, S, and T are consecutive odd integers, with $R < S < T$. This means that S is two more than R, and T is two more than S. You can rewrite each of the expressions to be compared as follows:

$$R + S + 1 = R + 1R + 22 + 1 = 2R + 3$$
$$S + T - 1 = 1R + 22 + 1R + 42 - 1 = 2R + 5$$

Since $5 > 3$, then $2R + 5 > 2R + 3$. You might also notice that both expressions to be compared contain S: $S + (R + 1)$ and $S + (T - 1)$. Therefore, the difference in the two expressions depends on the difference in value of $R + 1$ and $T - 1$. Since T is four more than R, $T - 1 > R + 1$.

9. a. You need to determine the area of the shaded rectangular region. It is given that $VR = 2$, but the length of VT is not given. However, $UV = 4$ and $TU = 3$, and VTU is a right triangle, so by the Pythagorean theorem, $VT = 5$. Thus, the area of $RVTS$ (the shaded region) is 5×2, or 10, which is greater than 9.

10. b. It is given that $x^2y > 0$ and $xy^2 < 0$, so neither x nor y can be 0. If neither x nor y can be 0, then both x^2 and y^2 are positive. By the first equation, y must also be positive; by the second equation, x must be negative. That is, $x < 0 < y$.

11. c. $\sqrt{(42 - 6)(25 + 11)} = \sqrt{(36)(36)} = \sqrt{36} \times \sqrt{36} = 6 \times 6 = 36$

12. e. You can solve this problem by calculation, but you might notice that $8 = 2^3$, so if you think of writing it this way,

$$\frac{6^3}{8} = \frac{6^3}{2^3} = \left(\frac{6}{2}\right)^3$$

you can see that 6^3 is divisible by 8; that is, the remainder is 0.

13. b. You are given that $x = 120$, so the measure of $\angle PBC$ must be 60°. You are also given $BP = CP$, so $\angle PBC$ has the same measure as $\angle PBC$. Since the sum of the measures of the angles of $\angle BPC$ is 180°, y must also be 60.

14. a. Since $z = 2y$ and $y = 3x$, then $z = 2(3x) = 6x$. Thus, $x + y + z = x + (3x) + (6x)$
$= (1 + 3 + 6)x = 10x$.

15. a. The rug is 9 feet by 6 feet. The border is 1 foot wide. This means that the portion of the rug that excludes the border is 7 feet by 4 feet. Its area is therefore 7×4, or 28.

16. d. $\frac{d - 3n}{7n - d} = 1$ means that $d - 3n = 7n - d$. Then, $d - 3n = 7n - d$ means that $d = 10n - d$ or $2d = 10n$ or $d = 5n$.

17. d. There are 80 positive whole numbers that are less than 81. They include the squares of only the whole numbers 1 through 8. That is, there are 8 positive whole numbers less than 81 that are squares of whole numbers, and $80 - 8 = 72$ that are NOT squares of whole numbers.

18. c. If $2 - 5x \le \frac{6x - 5}{-3}$, you should notice that $(-3)(2 - 5x) \ge 6x - 5$, because multiplying an inequality by a negative number reverses the direction of the inequality.

19. d. 20% or $\frac{1}{5}$ of 360° = 72°.

20. d. 20% of college graduates + 4% of post graduate education students = 24%, therefore $(24\%)(250,000) = 60,000$.

▶ Arithmetic Review

This section is a review of basic mathematical skills. To do well on the GRE test, it is important that you master these skills. Because the GRE test measures your ability to reason rather than calculate, most of this section is devoted to concepts rather than arithmetic drills. Be sure to review all of the topics before moving on to the algebra section.

Absolute Value

The *absolute value* of a number or expression is always positive because it is the distance a number is away from zero on a number line.

Example:

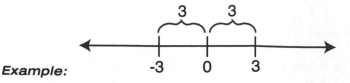

Number Lines and Signed Numbers

You have surely dealt with number lines in your distinguished career as a math student. The concept of the number line is simple: *Less than* is to the left and *greater than* is to the right.

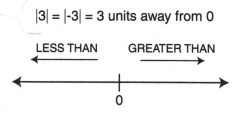

$|3| = |-3| = 3$ units away from 0

Sometimes, however, it is easy to get confused about the values of negative numbers. To keep things simple, remember this rule: If $a > b$, then $-b > -a$.

> *Example:*
> If $7 > 5$, then $-5 > -7$.

Integers

Integers are the set of whole numbers and their opposites.

The set of integers $= \{ \ldots, -3, -2, -1, 0, 1, 2, 3, \ldots \}$

Integers in a sequence such as 47, 48, 49, 50 or $-1, -2, -3, -4$ are called consecutive integers, because they appear in order, one after the other. The following explains rules for working with integers.

MULTIPLYING AND DIVIDING

The multiplication of two integers results in a third integer. The first two integers are called *factors* and the third integer, the answer, is called the *product*. In division, the number being divided is called the *dividend* and the number doing the dividing is called the *divisor*. The answer that results from a division problem is called the *quotient*. Here are some patterns that apply to multiplying and dividing integers:

$$(+) \times (+) = + \qquad (+)/(+) = +$$
$$(+) \times (-) = - \qquad (+)/(-) = -$$
$$(-) \times (-) = + \qquad (-)/(-) = +$$

A simple rule for remembering the above is that if the signs are the same when multiplying or dividing, the answer will be positive and if the signs are different, the answer will be negative.

ADDING

Adding two numbers with the same sign results in a sum of the same sign:

$$(+) + (+) = + \qquad \text{and} \qquad (-) + (-) = -$$

When adding numbers of different signs, follow this two-step process:

1. Subtract the absolute values of the numbers.
2. Keep the sign of the larger number.

Examples:

$$-2 + 3 =$$

Subtract the absolute values of the numbers: $3 - 2 = 1$. The sign of the larger number (3) was originally positive, so the answer is positive.

$$8 + -11 =$$

Subtract the absolute values of the numbers: $11 - 8 = 3$
The sign of the larger number (11) was originally negative, so the answer is -3.

SUBTRACTING

When subtracting integers, change all subtraction signs to addition and change the sign of the number being subtracted to its opposite. Then follow the rules for addition.

Examples:

$$(+10) - (+12) = (+10) + (-12) = -2$$
$$(-5) - (-7) = (-5) + (+7) = +2$$

REMAINDERS

The division of one integer by another will result in a remainder of either zero or a positive integer. For example:

$$
\begin{array}{r}
1\,\text{R}1 \\
4\,\overline{)\,5} \\
\underline{-4} \\
1
\end{array}
$$

If there is no remainder, the integer is said to be "divided evenly" by the number.

When it is said that an integer *n* is divided evenly by an integer *x*, it is meant that *n* divided by *x* results in an answer with a remainder of 0. In other words, there is nothing left over.

ODD AND EVEN NUMBERS

An *even* number is a number that can be divided evenly by the number 2, for example, 2, 4, 6, 8, 10, 12, 14, and so on. An *odd* number cannot be divided evenly by the number 2, for example, 1, 3, 5, 7, 9, 11, 13, and so on. The even and odd numbers listed are also examples of consecutive even numbers and consecutive odd numbers because they differ by two.

Here are some helpful rules for how even and odd numbers behave when added or multiplied:

even + even = even	and	even × even = even
odd + odd = even	and	odd × odd = odd
odd + even = odd	and	even × odd = even

FACTORS AND MULTIPLES

Factors are numbers that can be divided into a larger number without a remainder.

> ***Example:***
>
> $12 \times 3 = 4$
>
> The number 3 is, therefore, a factor of the number 12. Other factors of 12 are 1, 2, 4, 6, and 12.

The *common factors* of two numbers are the factors that are the same for both numbers.

> ***Example:***
>
> The factors of 24 = 1, 2, 3, 4, 6, 8, 12, and 24.
> The factors of 18 = 1, 2, 3, 6, 9, and 18.

From the previous example, you can see that the common factors of 24 and 18 are 1, 2, 3, and 6. This list also shows that we can determine that the *greatest common factor* of 24 and 18 is 6. Determining the greatest common factor is useful for reducing fractions.

Any number that can be obtained by multiplying a number *x* by a positive integer is called a *multiple* of *x*.

> ***Example:***
>
> Some multiples of 5 are: 5, 10, 15, 20, 25, 30, 35, 40 . . .
> Some multiples of 7 are: 7, 14, 21, 28, 35, 42, 49, 56 . . .

From this example, you can also determine that the *least common multiple* of the numbers 5 and 7 is 35. The least common multiple, or LCM, is used when performing various operations with fractions such as finding a common denominator.

PRIME AND COMPOSITE NUMBERS

A positive integer that is greater than the number 1 is either prime or composite, but not both. A factor is an integer that divides evenly into a number.

- A prime number has only itself and the number 1 as factors.

    Examples:

    2, 3, 5, 7, 11, 13, 17, 19, 23 . . .

- A composite number is a number that has more than two factors.

    Examples:

    4, 6, 8, 9, 10, 12, 14, 15, 16 . . .

    The number 1 is neither prime nor composite.

Variables

In a mathematical sentence, a variable is a letter that represents a number. Consider this sentence: $x + 4 = 10$. It is easy to figure out that x represents 6. However, problems with variables on the GRE test will become much more complex than that, and there are many rules and procedures that need to be learned. Before you learn to solve equations with variables, you need to learn how they operate in formulas. The next section on fractions will give you some examples.

Fractions

A fraction is a number of the form $\frac{a}{b}$, where a and b are integers and $b \neq 0$. In $\frac{a}{b}$ the a is called the numerator, and the b is called the denominator. Since the fraction $\frac{a}{b}$ means a ÷ b, b cannot be equal to zero. To do well when working with fractions, it is necessary to understand some basic concepts. The following math rules for fractions with variables are found below:

$$\frac{a}{b} \times \frac{c}{d} = \frac{a \times c}{b \times d} \qquad \frac{a}{b} + \frac{c}{b} = \frac{a+c}{b}$$

$$\frac{a}{b} \div \frac{c}{d} = \frac{a}{b} \times \frac{d}{c} = \frac{a \times d}{b \times c} \qquad \frac{a}{b} + \frac{c}{d} = \frac{ad+bc}{bd}$$

Dividing by Zero

Dividing by zero is not possible. This is important when solving for a variable in the denominator of a fraction.

> *Example:* $\frac{6}{a-3}$
>
> $a - 3 = 0$
>
> $a \neq 3$

In this problem, we know that *a* cannot be equal to 3 because that would yield a zero in the denominator.

Multiplication of Fractions

Multiplying fractions is one of the easiest operations to perform. To multiply fractions, simply multiply the numerators and the denominators, writing each in the respective place over or under the fraction bar.

Example:

$$\frac{4}{5} \times \frac{6}{7} = \frac{24}{35}$$

Division of Fractions

Dividing by a fraction is the same thing as multiplying by the *reciprocal* of the fraction. To find the reciprocal of any number, switch its numerator and denominator. For example, the reciprocals of the following numbers are:

$$\frac{1}{3} \Rightarrow \frac{3}{1} = 3 \qquad x \Rightarrow \frac{1}{x} \qquad \frac{4}{5} \Rightarrow \frac{5}{4} \qquad 5 \Rightarrow \frac{1}{5}$$

When dividing fractions, simply multiply the dividend by the divisor's reciprocal to get the answer. For example:

$$\frac{12}{21} \div \frac{3}{4} = \frac{12}{21} \times \frac{4}{3} = \frac{48}{63} = \frac{16}{21}$$

Adding and Subtracting Fractions

- To add or subtract fractions with like denominators, just add or subtract the numerators and leave the denominator as it is. For example:

$$\frac{1}{7} + \frac{5}{7} = \frac{6}{7} \qquad \text{and} \qquad \frac{5}{8} - \frac{2}{8} = \frac{3}{8}$$

- To add or subtract fractions with unlike denominators, you must find the *least common denominator* or LCD. In other words, if given the denominators 8 and 12, 24 would be the LCD because $8 \times 3 = 24$, and $12 \times 2 = 24$. So, the LCD is the smallest number divisible by each of the original denominators.
  Once you know the LCD, convert each fraction to its new form by multiplying both the numerator and denominator by the necessary number to get the LCD, and then add or subtract the new numerators.

  For example:

$$\frac{1}{3} + \frac{2}{5} = \frac{5(1)}{5(3)} + \frac{3(2)}{3(5)} = \frac{5}{15} + \frac{6}{15} = \frac{11}{15}$$

Mixed Numbers and Improper Fractions

A *mixed number* is a fraction that contains both a whole number and a fraction. For example, $4\frac{1}{2}$ is a mixed number. To multiply or divide a mixed number, simply convert it to an improper fraction. An *improper fraction* is a fraction that has a numerator greater than or equal to its denominator. The mixed number $4\frac{1}{2}$ can be expressed as the improper fraction $\frac{9}{2}$. This is done by multiplying the denominator by the whole number and then adding the numerator. The denominator remains the same in the improper fraction.

For example, convert $5\frac{1}{3}$ to an improper fraction.

1. Start by multiplying the denominator by the whole number: $5 \times 3 = 15$.

2. Now add the numerator to the product: $15 + 1 = 16$.

3. Write the sum over the denominator (which stays the same): $\frac{16}{3}$.

Therefore, $5\frac{1}{3}$ can be converted to the improper fraction $\frac{16}{3}$.

Decimals

The most important thing to remember about decimals is that the first place value to the right is tenths. The place values are as follows:

1	2	6	8	.	3	4	5	7
THOUSANDS	HUNDREDS	TENS	ONES	DECIMAL POINT	TENTHS	HUNDREDTHS	THOUSANDTHS	TEN THOUSANDTHS

In expanded form, this number can also be expressed as:

$$1268.3457 = (1 \times 1{,}000) + (2 \times 100) + (6 \times 10) + (8 \times 1) + (3 \times .1) + (4 \times .01)$$
$$+ (5 \times .001) + (7 \times .0001)$$

Comparing Decimals

Comparing decimals is actually quite simple. Just line up the decimal points and fill in any zeroes needed to have an equal number of digits.

Example: Compare .5 and .005

Line up decimal points and add zeros: **.500**

                  .005

Then ignore the decimal point and ask, which is bigger: 500 or 5?

500 is definitely bigger than 5, so .5 is larger than .005

Operations with Decimals

To add and subtract decimals, you must always remember to line up the decimal points:

356.7	3.456	8.9347
+34.9854	+.333	−0.24
391.6854	3.789	8.9107

To multiply decimals, it is not necessary to align decimal points. Simply perform the multiplication as if there is no decimal point. Then, to determine the placement of the decimal point in the answer, count the numbers located to the right of the decimal point in the decimals being multiplied. The total numbers to the right of the decimal point in the original problem is the number of places the decimal point is moved in the product.

For example:

$$
\begin{array}{r}
1\,2.3\,4 \\
\times\ .5\,6 \\
\hline
7\,4\,0\,4 \\
6\,1\,7\,0\,0 \\
\hline
6.9\,1\,0\,4
\end{array}
$$

= TOTAL #'S TO THE RIGHT OF THE DECIMAL POINT = 4

To divide a decimal by another, such as $13.916 \div 2.45$, or $2.45\sqrt{13.916}$, move the decimal point in the divisor to the right until the divisor becomes a whole number. Next, move the decimal point in the dividend the same number of places;

$$245\overline{)1391.6}$$

This process results in the correct position of the decimal point in the quotient. The problem can now be solved by performing simple long division.

$$
\begin{array}{r}
5.68 \\
245\overline{)1391.6} \\
-1225 \\
\hline
166\,6 \\
-1470 \\
\hline
1960
\end{array}
$$

Percents

A percent is a measure of a part to a whole, with the whole being equal to 100.

- To change a decimal to a percentage, move the decimal point two units to the right and add a percentage symbol.

Examples:

$.45 = 45\%$ $.07 = 7\%$ $.9 = 90\%$

- To change a fraction to a percentage, first change the fraction to a decimal. To do this, divide the numerator by the denominator. Then change the decimal to a percentage by moving the decimal two places to the right.

   Examples:

   $\frac{4}{5} = .80 = 80\%$ $\frac{2}{5} = .4 = 40\%$ $\frac{1}{8} = .125 = 12.5\%$

- To change a percentage to a decimal, simply move the decimal point two places to the left and eliminate the percentage symbol.

   Examples:

   $64\% = .64$ $87\% = .87$ $7\% = .07$

- To change a percentage to a fraction, divide by 100 and reduce.

   Examples:

   $64\% = \frac{64}{100} = \frac{16}{25}$ $75\% = \frac{75}{100} = \frac{3}{4}$ $82\% = \frac{82}{100} = \frac{41}{50}$

- Keep in mind that any percentage that is 100 or greater will need to reflect a whole number or mixed number when converted.

   Examples:

   $125\% = 1.25$ or $1\frac{1}{4}$
   $350\% = 3.5$ or $3\frac{1}{2}$

Here are some conversions with which you should be familiar:

FRACTION	DECIMAL	PERCENTAGE
$\frac{1}{2}$	.5	50%
$\frac{1}{4}$	.25	25%
$\frac{1}{3}$	.333 . . .	33.$\overline{3}$%
$\frac{2}{3}$	.666 . . .	66.$\overline{6}$%
$\frac{1}{10}$	.1	10%
$\frac{1}{8}$	.125	12.5%
$\frac{1}{6}$	.1666 . . .	16.$\overline{6}$%
$\frac{1}{5}$	.2	20%

Order of Operations

There is an order for doing every mathematical operation. That order is illustrated by the following acronym: _Please Excuse My Dear Aunt Sally_. Here is what it means mathematically:

P: Parentheses. Perform all operations within parentheses first.
E: Exponents. Evaluate exponents.
M/D: Multiply/Divide. Work from left to right in your division.
A/S: Add/Subtract. Work from left to right in your subtraction.

Example:

$$5 + \frac{20}{(3-2)^2} = 5 + \frac{20}{(1)^2}$$

$$= 5 + \frac{20}{1}$$

$$= 5 + 20$$

$$= 25$$

Exponents

An exponent tells you how many times the number, called the _base_, is a factor in the product.

Example:

$$2^{5-\text{exponent}} = 2 \times 2 \times 2 \times 2 \times 2 = 32$$
$$\Uparrow$$
base

Sometimes you will see an exponent with a variable: b^n. The b represents a number that will be multiplied by itself n times.

Example:

b^n where $b = 5$ and $n = 3$
$b^n = 5^3 = 5 \times 5 \times 5 = 125$

Don't let the variables fool you. Most expressions are very easy once you substitute in numbers.

Laws of Exponents

- Any nonzero base to the zero power is always 1.

Examples:

$5^0 = 1 \qquad 70^0 = 1 \qquad 29874^0 = 1$

- When multiplying identical bases, you add the exponents.

    Examples:
    $$2^2 \times 2^4 \times 2^6 = 2^{12} \qquad a^2 \times a^3 \times a^5 = a^{10}$$

- When dividing identical bases, you subtract the exponents.

    Examples:
    $$\frac{2^5}{2^3} = 2^2 \qquad \frac{a^7}{a^4} = a^3$$

    Here is another method of illustrating multiplication and division of exponents:

    $$b^m \times b^n = b^{m+n}$$
    $$\frac{b^m}{b^n} = b^{m-n}$$

- If an exponent appears outside of parentheses, you multiply the exponents together.

    Examples:
    $$(3^3)^7 = 3^{21} \qquad (g^4)^3 = g^{12}$$

- Exponents can be negative also. The following rules for negative exponents are listed below:

    $$m^{-1} = \frac{1}{m} \qquad\qquad 5^{-1} = \frac{1}{5^1} = \frac{1}{5}$$

    $$m^{-2} = \frac{1}{m^2} \qquad\qquad 5^{-2} = \frac{1}{5^2} = \frac{1}{25}$$

    $$m^{-3} = \frac{1}{m^3} \qquad\qquad 5^{-3} = \frac{1}{5^3} = \frac{1}{125}$$

    $$m^{-n} = \frac{1}{m^n}$$ for all integers n.

    If $m = 0$, then these expressions are undefined.

Squares and Square Roots

The square of a number is the product of a number and itself. For example, in the expression $3^2 = 3 \times 3 = 9$, the number 9 is the *square* of the number 3. If we reverse the process we can say that the number 3 is the *square root* of the number 9. The symbol for square root is $\sqrt{}$ and is called the *radical*. The number inside of the radical is called the *radicand*.

    Example:
    $5^2 = 25$; therefore, $\sqrt{25} = 5$

    Since 25 is the square of 5, we also know that 5 is the square root of 25.

Perfect Squares

The square root of a number might not be a whole number.

For example, the square root of 7 is 2.645751311 . . . It is not possible to find a whole number that can be multiplied by itself to equal 7. A whole number is a *perfect square* if its square root is also a whole number.

Examples of perfect squares: 1, 4, 9, 16, 25, 36, 49, 64, 81, 100 . . .

Properties of Square Root Radicals

- The product of the square roots of two numbers is the same as the square root of their product.

    Example:

    $$\sqrt{a} \times \sqrt{b} = \sqrt{a \times b}$$

    $$\sqrt{5} \times \sqrt{3} = \sqrt{15}$$

- The quotient of the square roots of two numbers is the square root of the quotient.

    Example:

    $$\frac{\sqrt{a}}{\sqrt{b}} = \sqrt{\frac{a}{b}} \quad (b \neq 0)$$

    $$\frac{\sqrt{15}}{\sqrt{3}} = \sqrt{\frac{15}{3}} = \sqrt{5}$$

- The square of a square root radical is the radicand.

    Example:

    $$(\sqrt{N})^2 = N$$

    $$(\sqrt{3})^2 = \sqrt{3} \cdot \sqrt{3} = \sqrt{9} = 3$$

- To combine square root radicals with the same radicands, combine their coefficients and keep the same radical factor. You may add or subtract radicals with the same radicand.

    Example:

    $$a\sqrt{b} + c\sqrt{b} = (a + c)\sqrt{b}$$

    $$4\sqrt{3} + 2\sqrt{3} = 6\sqrt{3}$$

- Radicals cannot be combined using addition and subtraction.

    Example:

    $$\sqrt{a + b} \neq \sqrt{a} + \sqrt{b}$$

    $$\sqrt{4 + 11} \neq \sqrt{4} + \sqrt{11}$$

- To simplify a square root radical, write the radicand as the product of two factors, with one number being the largest perfect square factor. Then write the radical over each factor and simplify.

> ***Example:***
>
> $$\sqrt{8} = \sqrt{4} \cdot \sqrt{2} = 2\sqrt{2}$$

Ratio

The ratio of the numbers 10 to 30 can be expressed in several ways; for example:

> 10 to 30 or
>
> 10 : 30 or
>
> $\frac{10}{30}$

Since a ratio is also an implied division, it can be reduced to lowest terms. Therefore, since both 10 and 30 are multiples of 10, the above ratio can be written as:

> 1 to 3 or
>
> 1 : 3 or
>
> $\frac{1}{3}$

▶ Algebra Review

Congratulations on making it through the arithmetic section. Fortunately, you will need to know only a small portion of the algebra normally taught in a high school algebra course for the GRE test. The following section outlines only the essential concepts and skills you will need to be successful on the GRE Quantitative section.

Equations

An equation is solved by finding a number that is equal to a certain variable.

SIMPLE RULES FOR WORKING WITH EQUATIONS

1. The equal sign separates an equation into two sides.
2. Whenever an operation is performed on one side, the same operation must be performed on the other side.
3. Your first goal is to get all of the variables on one side and all of the numbers on the other.
4. The final step often will be to divide each side by the coefficient, leaving the variable equal to a number.

Example of solving an equation:

$$3x + 5 = 20$$
$$\underline{-5 = -5}$$
$$3x = 15$$
$$\frac{3x}{3} = \frac{15}{3}$$
$$x = 5$$

Now replace the x with the answer 5:

$3x + 5 = 20$ becomes $3(5) + 5 = 20$

$15 + 5 = 20$

$20 = 20$

Therefore, since $20 = 20$, you know that the answer $x = 5$ is correct.

Cross Multiplying

You can solve an equation that sets one fraction equal to another by *cross multiplication*. Cross multiplication involves setting the products of opposite pairs of numerators and denominators equal.

Example:

$\frac{x}{6} = \frac{x+10}{12}$ becomes

$$12x = 6(x) + 6(10)$$
$$12x = 6x + 60$$
$$12x - 6x = 6x - 6x + 60$$
$$6x = 60$$
$$\frac{6x}{6} = \frac{60}{6}$$
$$x = 10$$

Checking Equations

To check an equation, substitute the number equal to the variable in the original equation.

Example:

To check the equation from the previous page, substitute the number 10 for the variable x.

$$\frac{x}{6} = \frac{x+10}{12}$$
$$\frac{10}{6} = \frac{10+10}{12}$$
$$\frac{10}{6} = \frac{20}{12} = \frac{10}{6}$$

Because this statement is true, you know the answer $x = 10$ must be correct.

Special Tips for Checking Equations

1. If time permits, be sure to check all equations.

2. If you get stuck on a problem with an equation, check each answer, beginning with choice **c**. If choice **c** is not correct, pick an answer choice that is either larger or smaller. This process will be further explained in the strategies for answering five-choice questions.

3. Be careful to answer the question that is being asked. Sometimes, this involves solving for a variable and then performing another operation.

> *Example:*
>
> If the question asks the value of $x - 2$, and you find $x = 2$, the answer is not 2, but $2 - 2$.
> Thus, the answer is 0.

Equations with More than One Variable

Many equations have more than one variable. To find the solution, solve for one variable in terms of the other(s). To do this, follow the rule regarding variables and numbers on opposite sides of the equal sign. Isolate only one variable.

> *Example:*
> Solve for x:

$2x + 4y = 12$	To isolate the x variable, move the $4y$ to the other side.
$\underline{\quad - 4y = -4y\quad}$	
$2x = 12 - 4y$	Then divide both sides by the coefficient of 2.
$\frac{2x}{2} = \frac{12 - 4y}{2}$	The last step is to simplify your answer.
$x = 6 - 2y$	This expression for x is written in terms of y

Polynomials

A *polynomial* is the sum or difference of two or more unlike terms. Like terms have exactly the same variable(s).

> *Example:*
> $2x + 3y - z$

The above expression represents the sum of three unlike terms $2x$, $3y$, and $-z$.

Three Kinds of Polynomials

- A *monomial* is a polynomial with one term, as in $2b^3$.
- A *binomial* is a polynomial with two unlike terms, as in $5x + 3y$.
- A *trinomial* is a polynomial with three unlike terms, as in $y^2 + 2z - 6$.

Operations with Polynomials

- To add polynomials, be sure to change all subtraction to addition and change the sign of the number that is being subtracted. Then simply combine like terms.

    Example:

$(3y^3 - 5y + 10) + (y^3 + 10y - 9)$	Begin with a polynomial.
$3y^3 + -5y + 10 + y^3 + 10y + -9$	Change all subtraction to addition and change the sign of the number being subtracted.
$3y^3 + y^3 + -5y + 10y + 10 + -9 = 4y^3 + 5y + 1$	Combine like terms.

- If an entire polynomial is being subtracted, change all of the subtraction to addition within the parentheses and then add the opposite of each term in the polynomial being subtracted.

    Example:

$(8x - 7y + 9z) - (15x + 10y - 8z)$	Begin with a polynomial.
$(8x + -7y + 9z) - (15x + 10y + -8z)$	Change all subtraction within the parentheses first.
$(8x + -7y + 9z) + (-15x + - 10y + 8z)$	Then change the subtraction sign outside of the parentheses to addition and the sign of each polynomial being subtracted. (*Note that the sign of the term 8z changes twice because it is being subtracted twice.*)
$8x + -15x + -7y + - 10y + 9z + 8z$	All that is left to do is combine like terms.
$-7x + -17y + 17z$	This is your answer.

- To multiply monomials, multiply their coefficients and multiply like variables by adding their exponents.

    Example:
    $$(-5x^3y)(2x^2y^3) = (-5)(2)(x^3)(x^2)(y)(y^3) = -10x^5y^4$$

- To divide monomials, divide their coefficients and divide like variables by subtracting their exponents.

    Example:

    $$\frac{16x^4y^5}{24x^3y^2} = \frac{(16)}{(24)} \frac{(x^4)}{(x^3)} \frac{(y^5)}{(y^2)} = \frac{2}{3}xy^3$$

- To multiply a polynomial by a monomial, multiply each term of the polynomial by the monomial and add the products.

Example:

$$6x \times \left(10x - 5y + 7\right)$$

Change subtraction to addition: $\quad 6x \times \left(10x + -5y + 7\right)$

Multiply: $\quad (6x)(10x) + (6x)(-5y) + (6x)(7)$

Your answer is: $\quad 60x^2 + -30xy + 42x$

- To divide a polynomial by a monomial, divide each term of the polynomial by the monomial and add the quotients.

Example:

$$\frac{5x - 10y + 20}{5} = \frac{5x}{5} - \frac{10y}{5} + \frac{20}{5} = x - 2y + 4$$

FOIL

The FOIL method is used when multiplying two binomials. FOIL stands for the order used to multiply the terms: First, Outer, Inner, and Last. To multiply binomials, you multiply according to the FOIL order and then add the products.

Example:

$(3x + 1)(7x + 10) =$

$3x$ and $7x$ are the first pair of terms,

$3x$ and 10 are the outermost pair of terms,

1 and $7x$ are the innermost pair of terms, and

1 and 10 are the last pair of terms.

Therefore, $(3x)(7x) + (3x)(10) + (1)(7x) + (1)(10) = 21x^2 + 30x + 7x + 10$.

After we combine like terms, we are left with the answer: $21x^2 + 37x + 10$.

Factoring

Factoring is the reverse of multiplication:

$2(x + y) = 2x + 2y \qquad$ Multiplication

$2x + 2y = 2(x + y) \qquad$ Factoring

Three Basic Types of Factoring

There are three basic types of factoring:

- Factoring out a common monomial:

$10x^2 - 5x = 5x(2x - 1) \qquad$ and $\qquad xy - zy = y(x - z)$

- Factoring a quadratic trinomial using the reverse of FOIL:

$y^2 - y - 12 = (y - 4)(y + 3) \qquad$ and $\qquad z^2 - 2z + 1 = (z - 1)(z - 1) = (z - 1)^2$

- Factoring the difference between two squares using the rule:

$a^2 - b^2 = (a + b)(a - b) \qquad$ and $\qquad x^2 - 25 = (x + 5)(x - 5)$

Removing a Common Factor

If a polynomial contains terms that have common factors, the polynomial can be factored by using the reverse of the distributive law.

> ### Example:
>
> In the binomial $49x^3 + 21x$, $7x$ is the greatest common factor of both terms. Therefore, you can divide $49x^3 + 21x$ by $7x$ to get the other factor.
>
> $$\frac{49x^3 + 21x}{7x} = \frac{49x^3}{7x} + \frac{21x}{7x} = 7x^2 + 3$$
>
> Thus, factoring $49x^3 + 21x$ results in $7x(7x^2 + 3)$.

Isolating Variables Using Fractions

It may be necessary to use factoring in order to isolate a variable in an equation.

> ### Example:
>
> If $ax - c = bx + d$, what is x in terms of a, b, c, and d?

- The first step is to get the "x" terms on the same side of the equation:
  $$ax - bx = c + d$$

- Now you can factor out the common "x" term on the left side:
  $$x(a - b) = c + d$$

- To finish, divide both sides by $a - b$ to isolate the variable of x:
  $$\frac{x(a - b)}{a - b} = \frac{c + d}{a - b}$$

- The $a - b$ binomial cancels out on the left, resulting in the answer:
  $$x = \frac{c + d}{a - b}$$

Quadratic Trinomials

A *quadratic trinomial* contains an x^2 term as well as an x term; $x^2 - 5x + 6$ is an example of a quadratic trinomial. It can be factored by reversing the FOIL method.

- Start by looking at the last term in the trinomial, the number 6. Ask yourself, "What two integers, when multiplied together, have a product of positive 6?"
- Make a mental list of these integers:
  $$1 \times 6, \qquad -1 \times -6, \qquad 2 \times 3, \qquad \text{and} \qquad -2 \times -3$$
- Next, look at the middle term of the trinomial, in this case, the negative $5x$. Choose the two factors from the above list that also add up to negative 5. Those two factors are: -2 and -3.
- Thus, the trinomial $x^2 - 5x + 6$ can be factored as $(x - 3)(x - 2)$.
- Be sure to use the FOIL method to double check your answer. The correct answer is:
  $$(x - 3)(x - 2) = x^2 - 2x - 3x + 6 = x^2 - 5x + 6$$

Algebraic Fractions

Algebraic fractions are very similar to fractions in arithmetic.

Example:

Write $\frac{x}{5} - \frac{x}{10}$ as a single fraction.

Solution:

Just like in arithmetic, you need to find the LCD of 5 and 10, which is 10. Then change each fraction into an equivalent fraction that has 10 as a denominator:

$$\frac{x}{5} - \frac{x}{10} = \frac{x(2)}{5(2)} - \frac{x}{10}$$

$$= \frac{2x}{10} - \frac{x}{10}$$

$$= \frac{x}{10}$$

Reciprocal Rules

There are special rules for the sum and difference of reciprocals. Memorizing this formula might help you be more efficient when taking the GRE test.

- If x and y are not 0, then $\frac{1}{x} + \frac{1}{y} = \frac{x+y}{xy}$

- If x and y are not 0, then $\frac{1}{x} - \frac{1}{y} = \frac{y-x}{xy}$

Quadratic Equations

A *quadratic equation* is an equation in which the greatest exponent of the variable is 2, as in $x^2 + 2x - 15 = 0$. A quadratic equation has two roots, which can be found by breaking down the quadratic equation into two simple equations. You can do this by factoring or by using the quadratic formula to find the roots.

Zero-Product Rule

The *zero-product rule* states that if the product of two or more numbers is 0, then at least one of the numbers is 0.

Example:

Solve for x:
$(x + 5)(x - 3) = 0$

Using the zero−product rule, it can be determined that either $x + 5 = 0$ or that $x - 3 = 0$.

$$\frac{x + 5}{-5} = \frac{0}{-5} \quad \text{or} \quad \frac{x - 3}{+3} = \frac{0}{+3}$$

$$x = -5 \quad \text{or} \quad x = 3$$

Thus, the possible values of x are -5 and 3.

Solving Quadratic Equations by Factoring

- If a quadratic equation is not equal to zero, you need to rewrite it.

> *Example:*
> Given $x^2 - 5x = 14$, you will need to subtract 14 from both sides to form
> $x^2 - 5x - 14 = 0$. This quadratic equation can now be factored by using the zero-product
> rule. Therefore, $x^2 - 5x - 14 = 0$ becomes $(x - 7)(x + 2) = 0$ and, using the zero-product
> rule, you can set the two equations equal to zero.

$$
\begin{array}{ccc}
x - 7 = 0 & \text{and} & x + 2 = 0 \\
\underline{+7 +7} & & \underline{-2 -2} \\
x = 7 & & x = -2
\end{array}
$$

- It may be necessary to factor a quadratic equation before solving it and therefore to use the zero-product rule.

> *Example:*
> $x^2 + 4x = 0$ must first be factored, before it can be solved: $x(x + 4) = 0$ and
> the equation $x(x + 4) = 0$ becomes $x = 0$ and $x + 4 = 0$

$$
\begin{array}{c}
\underline{-4 = -4} \\
x = 0 \quad \text{and} \quad x = -4
\end{array}
$$

Solving Quadratic Equations Using the Quadratic Formula

The standard form of a quadratic equation is $ax^2 + bx + c = 0$, where a, b, and c are real numbers ($a \neq 0$). In order to use the quadratic formula to solve a quadratic equation, first put the equation into standard form and identify a, b, and c. Then substitute those values into the formula:

$$
x = \frac{-b \pm \sqrt{b^2 - 4ac}}{2a}
$$

For example, in the quadratic equation $2x^2 - x - 6 = 0$, $a = 2$, $b = -1$, and $c = -6$. When these values are substituted into the formula, two answers will result:

$$
x = \frac{-(-1) \pm \sqrt{(-1)^2 - 4(2)(-6)}}{2(2)}
$$

$$
x = \frac{1 \pm \sqrt{49}}{4}
$$

$$
x = \frac{1 \pm 7}{4}
$$

$$
x = \frac{1 + 7}{4} \text{ or } \frac{1 - 7}{4}
$$

$$
x = 2 \quad \text{or} \quad x = \frac{-6}{4} \text{ or } \frac{-3}{2}
$$

Quadratic equations can have two real solutions, as in the previous example. Therefore, it is important to check each solution to see if it satisfies the equation. Keep in mind that some quadratic equations may have only one solution or no solution at all.

Check:

$$2x^2 - x - 6 = 0$$

$$2(2^2) - 2 - 6 = 0 \qquad \text{or} \qquad 2(\tfrac{-3}{2})^2 - \tfrac{-3}{2} - 6 = 0$$

$$2(4) - 8 = 0 \qquad\qquad\qquad\qquad 2(\tfrac{9}{4}) - 4\tfrac{1}{2} = 0$$

$$8 - 8 = 0 \qquad\qquad\qquad\qquad\qquad 4\tfrac{1}{2} - 4\tfrac{1}{2} = 0$$

Therefore, both solutions are correct.

Systems of Equations

A system of equations is a set of 2 or more equations with the same solution. Two methods for solving a system of equations are *substitution* and *linear combination*.

Substitution

Substitution involves solving for one variable in terms of another and then substituting that expression into the second equation.

Example:

$2p + q = 11$ and $p + 2q = 13$

- First, choose an equation and rewrite it, isolating one variable in terms of the other. It does not matter which variable you choose.

$2p + q = 11$ becomes $q = 11 - 2p$

- Second, substitute $11 - 2p$ for q in the other equation and solve:

$$p + 2(11 - 2p) = 13$$
$$p + 22 - 4p = 13$$
$$22 - 3p = 13$$
$$22 = 13 + 3p$$
$$9 = 3p$$
$$p = 3$$

- Now substitute this answer into either original equation for p to find q.

$$2p + q = 11$$
$$2(3) + q = 11$$
$$6 + q = 11$$
$$q = 5$$

Thus, $p = 3$ and $q = 5$.

Linear Combination

Linear combination involves writing one equation over another and then adding or subtracting the like terms so that one letter is eliminated.

> ***Example:***
> $x - 9 = 2y$ and $x - 3 = 5y$

- Rewrite each equation in the form $ax + by = c$.

    $x - 9 = 2y$ becomes $x - 2y = 9$ and $x - 3 = 5y$ becomes $x - 5y = 3$.

- If you subtract the two equations, the "x" terms will be eliminated, leaving only one variable:

    Subtract:

    $$-\frac{x - 2y = 9}{(x - 5y = 3)}$$

    $$\frac{3y}{3} = \frac{6}{3}$$

    $y = 2$ is the answer.

- Substitute 2 for y in one of the original equations and solve for x.
$$x - 9 = 2y$$
$$x - 9 = 2(2)$$
$$x - 9 = 4$$
$$x - 9 + 9 = 4 + 9$$
$$x = 13$$

- The answer to the system of equations is $y = 2$ and $x = 13$.

Inequalities

Linear inequalities are solved in much the same way as simple equations. The most important difference is that when an inequality is multiplied or divided by a negative number, the inequality symbol changes direction.

Example:

$$10 > 5 \qquad \text{so} \qquad (10)(-3) < (5)(-3)$$
$$-30 < -15$$

Solving Linear Inequalities

To solve a linear inequality, isolate the letter and solve the same as you would in a first-degree equation. Remember to reverse the direction of the inequality sign if you divide or multiply both sides of the equation by a negative number.

Example:

If $7 - 2x > 21$, find x.

■ Isolate the variable.

$$\frac{7 - 2x}{-7} > \frac{21}{-7}$$

$$-2x > 14$$

■ Because you are dividing by a negative number, the inequality symbol changes direction.

$$\frac{-2x}{-2} > \frac{14}{-2}$$
$$x < -7$$

■ The answer consists of all real numbers less than -7.

Solving Combined (or Compound) Inequalities

To solve an inequality that has the form $c < ax + b < d$, isolate the letter by performing the same operation on each member of the equation.

Example:

If $-10 < -5y - 5 < 15$, find y.

■ Add five to each member of the inequality.

$$-10 + 5 < -5y - 5 + 5 < 15 + 5$$
$$-5 < -5y < 20$$

■ Divide each term by -5, changing the direction of both inequality symbols:

$$\frac{-5}{-5} < \frac{-5y}{-5} < \frac{20}{-5} = 1 > y > -4$$

■ The solution consists of all real numbers less than 1 and greater than -4.

Translating Words into Numbers

The most important skill needed for word problems is being able to translate words into mathematical operations. The following list will assist you in this by giving you some common examples of English phrases and their mathematical equivalents.

- "Increase" means add.

    Example:

    A number increased by five = $x + 5$.

- "Less than" means subtract.

    Example:

    10 less than a number = $x - 10$.

- "Times" or "product" means multiply

    Example:

    Three times a number = $3x$.

- "Times the sum" means to multiply a number by a quantity.

    Example:

    Five times the sum of a number and three = $5 (x + 3)$.

- Two variables are sometimes used together.

    Example:

    A number y exceeds five times a number x by ten.
    $y = 5x + 10$

- Inequality signs are used for "at least" and "at most," as well as "less than" and "more than."

    Examples:

    The product of x and 6 is greater than 2.
    $x \times 6 > 2$
    When 14 is added to a number x, the sum is less than 21.
    $x + 14 < 21$
    The sum of a number x and four is at least nine.
    $x + 4 > 9$
    When seven is subtracted from a number x, the difference is at most four.
    $x - 7 < 4$

Assigning Variables in Word Problems

It may be necessary to create and assign variables in a word problem. To do this, first identify an unknown and a known. You may not actually know the exact value of the "known," but you will know at least something about its value.

Examples:

- Max is three years older than Ricky.

    Unknown = Ricky's age = x.

    Known = Max's age is three years older.

    Therefore, Ricky's age = x and Max's age = $x + 3$.

- Siobhan made twice as many cookies as Rebecca.

    Unknown = number of cookies Rebecca made = x.

    Known = number of cookies Siobhan made = $2x$.

- Cordelia has five more than three times the number of books that Becky has.

    Unknown = the number of books Becky has = x.

    Known = the number of books Cordelia has = $3x + 5$.

Algebraic Functions

Another way to think of algebraic expressions is to think of them as "machines" or *functions*. Just like you would a machine, you can input material into an equation that expels a finished product, an output or solution. In an equation the input is a value of a variable x. For example, in the expression $\frac{3x}{x-1}$, the input $x = 2$ yields an output of $\frac{3(2)}{2-1} = \frac{6}{1}$ or 6. In function notation, the expression $\frac{3x}{x-1}$ is deemed a function and is indicated by a letter, usually the letter f:

$$f(x) = \frac{3x}{x-1}$$

It is said that the equation $\frac{3x}{x-1}$ defines the function $f(x)$. For this example with input $x = 2$ and output 6, you write $f(2) = 6$. The output 6 is called the *value of the function* with an input $x = 2$. The value of the same function corresponding to $x = 4$ is 4, since $\frac{2b}{b+a}$.

Furthermore, any real number x can be used as an input value for the function $f(x)$, except for $x = 1$, as this substitution results in a 0 denominator. Thus, it is said that $f(x)$ is undefined for $x = 1$. Also keep in mind that when you encounter an input value that yields the square root of a negative number, it is not defined under the set of real numbers. It is not possible to square two numbers to get a negative number. For example, in the function $f(x) = x^2 + \sqrt{x} + 10$, $f(x)$ is undefined for $x = -10$, since one of the terms would be $\sqrt{-10}$.

▶ Geometry Review

About one-third of the questions on the Quantitative section of the GRE test have to do with geometry. However, there are only a small number of facts you will need to know to master these questions. The geometrical concepts tested on the GRE test are far fewer than those that would be tested in a high school geometry class. Fortunately, it will not be necessary for you to be familiar with those dreaded geometric proofs! All you will need to know to do well on the geometry questions is contained within this section.

Lines

The *line* is a basic building block of geometry. A line is understood to be straight and infinitely long. In the figure below, *A* and *B* are points on line *l*.

The portion of the line from *A* to *B* is called a *line segment* with *A* and *B* as the endpoints, meaning that a line segment is finite in length.

PARALLEL AND PERPENDICULAR LINES

Parallel lines are lines that have equal slopes. Slope will be explained later in this section, so for now, simply know that parallel lines are lines that never intersect even though they continue in both directions forever.

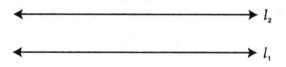

Perpendicular lines are lines that intersect at a 90 degree angle.

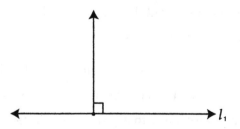

Angles

An *angle* is formed by an endpoint, or vertex, and two rays.

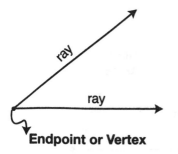

NAMING ANGLES

There are three ways to name an angle.

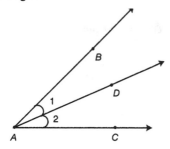

1. An angle can be named by the vertex when no other angles share the same vertex: ∠A

2. An angle can be represented by a number written in the interior of the angle near the vertex: ∠1

3. When more than one angle has the same vertex, three letters are used, with the vertex always being the middle letter: ∠1 can be written as ∠BAD or as ∠DAB; ∠2 can be written as ∠DAC or as ∠CAD.

CLASSIFYING ANGLES

Angles can be classified into the following categories: acute, right, obtuse, and straight.

- An *acute* angle is an angle that measures less than 90 degrees.

Acute Angle

- A *right* angle is an angle that measures exactly 90 degrees. A right angle is symbolized by a square at the vertex.

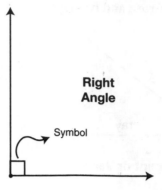

Right Angle

Symbol

- An *obtuse* angle is an angle that measures more than 90 degrees, but less then 180 degrees.

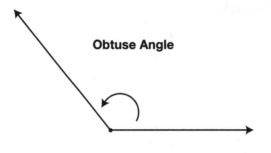

Obtuse Angle

- A *straight* angle is an angle that measures 180 degrees. Thus, both of its sides form a line.

Straight Angle

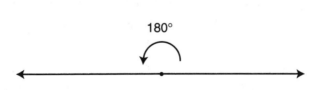

180°

COMPLEMENTARY ANGLES

Two angles are *complementary* if the sum of their measures is equal to 90 degrees.

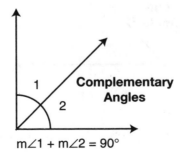

Complementary Angles

1

2

$m\angle 1 + m\angle 2 = 90°$

SUPPLEMENTARY ANGLES

Two angles are *supplementary* if the sum of their measures is equal to 180 degrees.

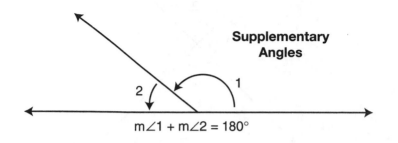

Supplementary Angles

$m\angle 1 + m\angle 2 = 180°$

ADJACENT ANGLES

Adjacent angles have the same vertex, share a side, and do not overlap.

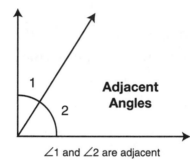

Adjacent Angles

$\angle 1$ and $\angle 2$ are adjacent

The sum of all possible adjacent angles around the same vertex is equal to 360 degrees.

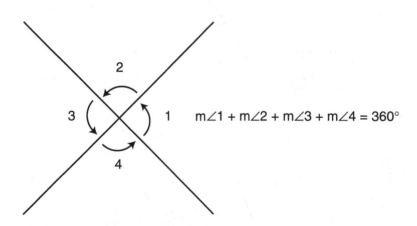

$m\angle 1 + m\angle 2 + m\angle 3 + m\angle 4 = 360°$

ANGLES OF INTERSECTING LINES

When two lines intersect, vertical angles are formed. Vertical angles have equal measures and are supplementary to adjacent angles.

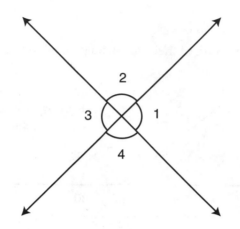

- m∠1 = m∠3 and m∠2 = m∠4
- m∠1 + m∠2 = 180 and m∠2 + m∠3 = 180
- m∠3 + m∠4 = 180 and m∠1 + m∠4 = 180

BISECTING ANGLES AND LINE SEGMENTS

Both angles and lines are said to be bisected when divided into two parts with equal measures.

Example:

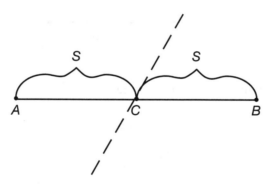

Therefore, line segment AB is bisected at point C.

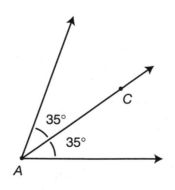

According to the figure, ∠A is bisected by ray AC.

ANGLES FORMED BY PARALLEL LINES

When two parallel lines are intersected by a third line, or transversal, vertical angles are formed.

- Of these vertical angles, four will be equal and acute, and four will be equal and obtuse. The exception to this is if the transversal is perpendicular to the parallel lines. In this case, each of the angles formed measures 90 degrees.
- Any combination of an acute and obtuse angle will be supplementary.

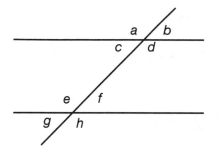

In the above figure:
- $\angle b$, $\angle c$, $\angle f$, and $\angle g$ are all acute and equal.
- $\angle a$, $\angle d$, $\angle e$, and $\angle h$ are all obtuse and equal.
- Also, any acute angle added to an any obtuse angle will be supplementary.

Some examples:

$$m\angle b + m\angle d = 180°$$
$$m\angle c + m\angle e = 180°$$
$$m\angle f + m\angle h = 180°$$
$$m\angle g + m\angle a = 180°$$

Example:

In the figure below, if $m \parallel n$ and $a \parallel b$, what is the value of x?

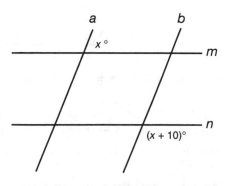

Solution:

Because $\angle x$ is acute, you know that it can be added to $x + 10$ to equal 180. The equation is thus, $x + x + 10 = 180$.

Solve for x: $\frac{2x}{-10} + \frac{10}{-10} = 180$

$$\frac{2x}{2} = \frac{170}{2}$$

$$x = 85$$

Therefore, $m\angle x = 85$ and the obtuse angle is equal to $180 - 85 = 95$.

ANGLES OF A TRIANGLE

The measures of the three angles in a triangle always equal 180 degrees.

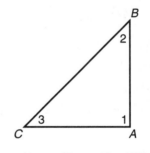

$m\angle 1 + m\angle 2 + m\angle 3 = 180°$

EXTERIOR ANGLES

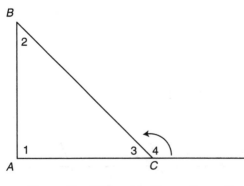

$m\angle 4 + m\angle 3 = 180°$ and $m\angle 4 = m\angle 2 + m\angle 1$

An *exterior angle* can be formed by extending a side from any of the three vertices of a triangle. Here are some rules for working with exterior angles:

- An exterior angle and interior angle that share the same vertex are supplementary.
- An exterior angle is equal to the sum of the nonadjacent interior angles.

Example:

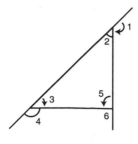

$$m\angle 1 = m\angle 3 + m\angle 5$$
$$m\angle 4 = m\angle 2 + m\angle 5$$
$$m\angle 6 = m\angle 3 + m\angle 2$$

- The sum of the exterior angles of a triangle equal 360 degrees.

Triangles

More geometry questions on the GRE test pertain to triangles than to any other topic. The following topics cover the information you will need to apply when solving triangle problems.

CLASSIFYING TRIANGLES

It is possible to classify triangles into three categories based on the number of equal sides:

Scalene Triangle: no equal sides
Isosceles Triangle: two equal sides
Equilateral Triangle: all sides equal

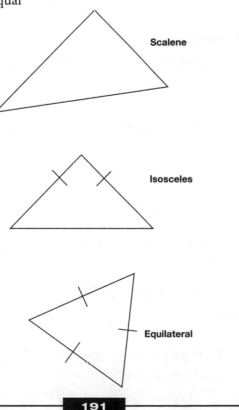

It is also possible to classify triangles into three categories based on the measure of the greatest angle:

Acute Triangle: greatest angle is acute
Right Triangle: greatest angle is 90 degrees
Obtuse Triangle: greatest angle is obtuse

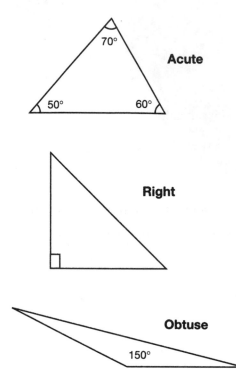

Acute

Right

Obtuse

ANGLE-SIDE RELATIONSHIPS

Knowing the angle-side relationships in isosceles, equilateral, and right triangles will be useful when you take the GRE test.

■ In isosceles triangles, equal angles are opposite equal sides.

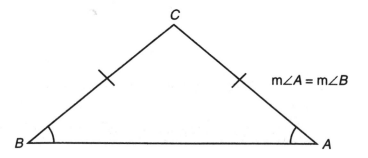

$m\angle A = m\angle B$

- In equilateral triangles, all sides are equal and all angles are equal.

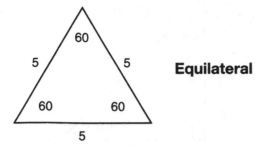

- In a right triangle, the side opposite the right angle is called the hypotenuse. The hypotenuse is the longest side of the triangle.

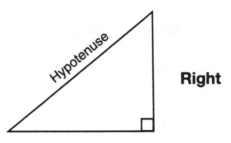

PYTHAGOREAN THEOREM

The *Pythagorean theorem* is an important tool for working with right triangles.

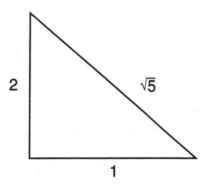

It states: $a^2 + b^2 = c^2$, where a and b represent the length of the legs and c represents the length of the hypotenuse.

This theorem allows you to find the length of any side as along as you know the measure of the other two.

$$a^2 + b^2 = c^2$$
$$1^2 + 2^2 = c^2$$
$$1 + 4 = c^2$$
$$5 = c^2$$
$$\sqrt{5} = c$$

45-45-90 RIGHT TRIANGLES

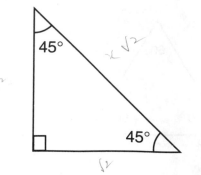

A right triangle with two angles each measuring 45 degrees is called an *isosceles right triangle*. In an isosceles right triangle:

- The length of the hypotenuse is $\sqrt{2}$ multiplied by the length of one of the legs of the triangle.

- The length of each leg is $\frac{\sqrt{2}}{2}$ multiplied by the length of the hypotenuse.

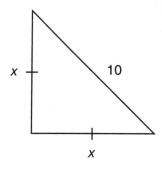

$$x = \frac{\sqrt{2}}{2} \times \frac{10}{1} = \frac{\sqrt{2}}{2} = 5\sqrt{2}$$

30-60-90 RIGHT TRIANGLES

In a right triangle with the other angles measuring 30 and 60 degrees:

- The leg opposite the 30 degree angle is half of the length of the hypotenuse. (And, therefore, the hypotenuse is two times the length of the leg opposite the 30 degree angle.)
- The leg opposite the 60 degree angle is $\sqrt{3}$ times the length of the other leg.

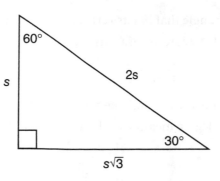

Example:

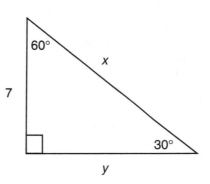

$x = 2 \times 7 = 14$ and $y = 7\sqrt{3}$

Circles

A *circle* is a closed figure in which each point of the circle is the same distance from a fixed point called the center of the circle.

ANGLES AND ARCS OF A CIRCLE

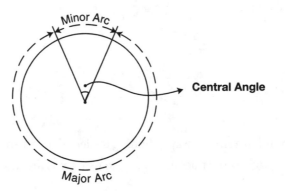

- An arc is a curved section of a circle. A *minor arc* is smaller than a semicircle and a *major arc* is larger than a semicircle.

- A *central angle* of a circle is an angle that has its vertex at the center and that has sides that are radii.
- Central angles have the same degree measure as the arc it forms.

LENGTH OF ARC

To find the length of an arc, multiply the circumference of the circle, $2\pi r$, where r = the radius of the circle, by the fraction $\frac{x}{360}$, where x is the degree measure of the arc or central angle of the arc.

> ### Example:
> Find the length of the arc if $x = 36$ and $r = 70$.

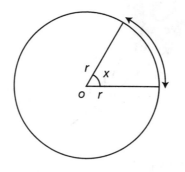

$L = \frac{36}{360} \times 2(\pi)70$

$L = \frac{1}{10} \times 140\pi$

$L = 14\pi$

AREA OF A SECTOR

A *sector* of a circle is a region contained within the interior of a central angle and arc.

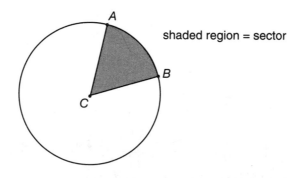

shaded region = sector

The area of a sector is found in a similar way to finding the length of an arc. To find the area of a sector, simply multiply the area of a circle, πr^2, by the fraction $\frac{x}{360}$, again using x as the degree measure of the central angle.

Example:

Given $x = 60$ and $r = 8$, find the area of the sector:

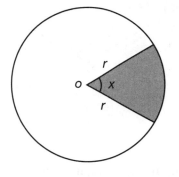

$A = \frac{60}{360} \times (\pi)8^2$

$A = \frac{1}{6} \times 64(\pi)$

$A = \frac{64}{6}(\pi)$

$A = \frac{32}{3}(\pi)$

Polygons and Parallelograms

A polygon is a figure with three or more sides.

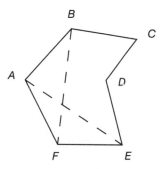

TERMS RELATED TO POLYGONS

- *Vertices* are corner points, also called endpoints, of a polygon. The vertices in the previous polygon are *A*, *B*, *C*, *D*, *E*, and *F*.
- A *diagonal* of a polygon is a line segment between two nonadjacent vertices. The two diagonals indicated in the previous polygon are line segments *BF* and *AE*.
- A *regular* (or *equilateral*) polygon has sides that are all equal.
- An *equiangular* polygon has angles that are all equal.

ANGLES OF A QUADRILATERAL

A *quadrilateral* is a four-sided polygon. Since a quadrilateral can be divided by a diagonal into two triangles, the sum of its angles will equal $180 + 180 = 360$ degrees.

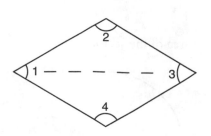

$$m\angle 1 + m\angle 2 + m\angle 3 + m\angle 4 = 360°$$

INTERIOR ANGLES

To find the sum of the interior angles of any polygon, use this formula:

$$S = 180(x - 2)$$

where x is the number of polygon sides.

Example:

Find the sum of the angles in the polygon below:

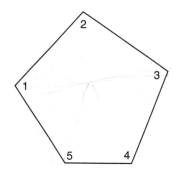

$$S = (5 - 2) \times 180$$
$$S = 3 \times 180$$
$$S = 540$$

EXTERIOR ANGLES

Similar to the exterior angles of a triangle, the sum of the exterior angles of *any* polygon equals 360 degrees.

SIMILAR POLYGONS

If two polygons are similar, their corresponding angles are equal and the ratio of the corresponding sides is in proportion. The sides of the first polygon are twice the size of the second polygon.

Example:

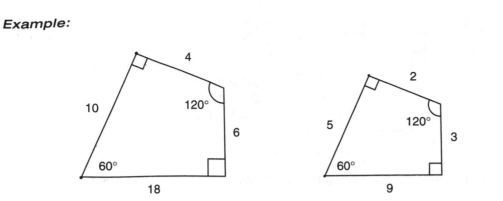

These two polygons are similar because their angles are equal and the ratio of the corresponding sides is in proportion.

Parallelograms

A *parallelogram* is a quadrilateral with two pairs of parallel sides.

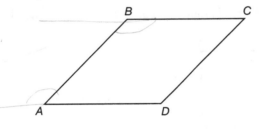

In this figure, line $\overline{AB} \parallel \overline{CD}$ and $\overline{BC} \parallel \overline{AD}$.

A parallelogram has the following characteristics:

- opposite sides that are equal ($AB = CD$ and $BC = AD$)
- opposite angles that are equal ($m\angle A = m\angle C$ and $m\angle B = m\angle D$)
- consecutive angles that are supplementary ($m\angle A + m\angle B = 180°$, $m\angle B + m\angle C = 180°$, $m\angle C + m\angle D = 180°$, $m\angle D + m\angle A = 180°$)

SPECIAL TYPES OF PARALLELOGRAMS

There are three types of parallelograms:

- A *rectangle* is a parallelogram that has four right angles.

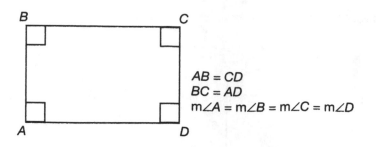

$AB = CD$
$BC = AD$
$m\angle A = m\angle B = m\angle C = m\angle D$

- A *rhombus* is a parallelogram that has four equal sides.

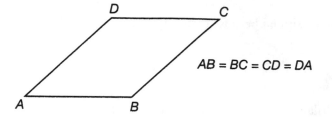

$AB = BC = CD = DA$

- A *square* is a parallelogram in which all angles are equal to 90 degrees and all sides are equal to each other.

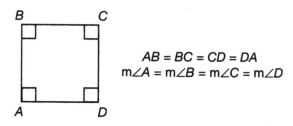

$AB = BC = CD = DA$
$m\angle A = m\angle B = m\angle C = m\angle D$

DIAGONALS

In all parallelograms, diagonals cut each other in two equal halves.

- In a rectangle, diagonals are the same length.

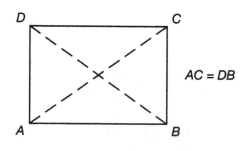

$AC = DB$

■ In a rhombus, diagonals intersect to form 90 degree angles.

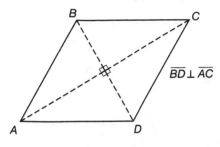

$$\overline{BD} \perp \overline{AC}$$

■ In a square, diagonals have both the same length and intersect at 90 degree angles.

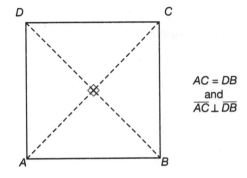

$$AC = DB$$
$$\text{and}$$
$$\overline{AC} \perp \overline{DB}$$

Solid Figures, Perimeter, and Area

You will need to know some basic formulas for finding area, perimeter, and volume on the GRE test. It is important that you be able to recognize the figures by their names and to understand when to use which formula. To begin, it is necessary to explain five kinds of measurement:

PERIMETER

The perimeter of an object is simply the sum of the lengths of all of its sides.

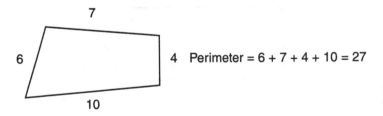

Perimeter = 6 + 7 + 4 + 10 = 27

AREA

Area is the space inside of the lines defining the shape.

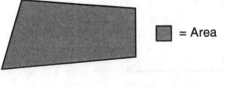

= Area

You will need to know how to find the area of several geometric shapes and figures. The formulas needed for each are listed here:

- To find the area of a triangle, use the formula $A = \frac{1}{2}bh$.

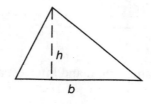

- To find the area of a circle, use the formula $A = \pi r^2$.

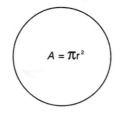

- To find the area of a parallelogram, use the formula $A = bh$.

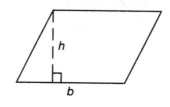

- To find the area of a rectangle, use the formula $A = lw$.

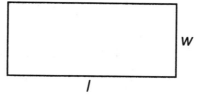

- To find the area of a square, use the formula $A = s^2$ or $A = \frac{1}{2}d^2$

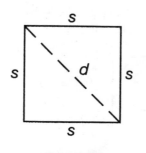

- To find the area of a trapezoid, use the formula $A = \frac{1}{2}(b_1 + b_2)h$

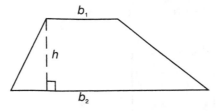

VOLUME

Volume is a measurement of a three-dimensional object such as a cube or a rectangular solid. An easy way to envision volume is to think about filling an object with water. The volume measures how much water can fit inside.

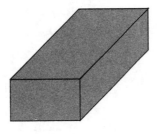

- To find the volume of a rectangular solid, use the formula $V = lwh$.

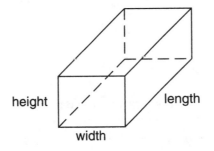

- To find the volume of a cube, use the formula $V = e^3$.

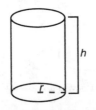

- To find the volume of a cylinder, use the formula $V = \pi r^2 h$.

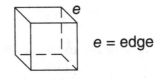

SURFACE AREA

The surface area of an object measures the combined areas of each of its faces. The total surface area of a rectangular solid is double the sum of the areas of the three faces. For a cube, simply multiply the surface area of one of its sides by 6.

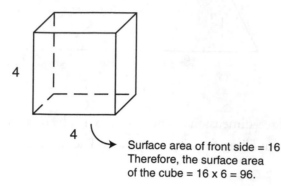

4

4

Surface area of front side = 16
Therefore, the surface area
of the cube = 16 × 6 = 96.

- To find the surface area of a rectangular solid, use the formula $A = 2(lw + lh + wh)$.

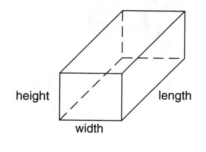

height   length

width

$$V = lwh$$

- To find the surface area of a cube, use the formula $A = 6e^2$.

e

e = edge

- To find the surface area of a right circular cylinder, use the formula $A = 2\pi r^2 + 2\pi rh$.

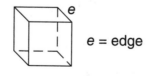

CIRCUMFERENCE

Circumference is the measure of the distance around a circle.

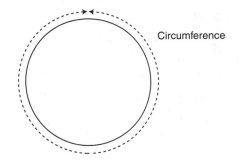

Circumference

- To find the circumference of a circle, use the formula $C = 2\pi r$.

Coordinate Geometry

Coordinate geometry is a form of geometrical operations in relation to a coordinate plane. A *coordinate plane* is a grid of square boxes divided into four quadrants by both a horizontal (x) axis and a vertical (y) axis. These two axes intersect at one coordinate point—(0,0)—the origin. A *coordinate pair*, also called an ordered pair, is a specific point on the coordinate plane with the first number representing the horizontal placement and the second number representing the vertical. Coordinate points are given in the form of (x,y).

GRAPHING ORDERED PAIRS

To graph ordered pairs, follow these guidelines:

- The *x-coordinate* is listed first in the ordered pair and tells you how many units to move either to the left or to the right. If the *x*-coordinate is positive, move to the right. If the *x*-coordinate is negative, move to the left.
- The *y-coordinate* is listed second and tells you how many units to move up or down. If the *y*-coordinate is positive, move up. If the *y*-coordinate is negative, move down.

> **Example:**
> Graph the following points: (2,3), (3,−2), (−2,3), and (−3,−2).

II						I
	(−2,3)			(2,3)		
	(−3,−2)			(3,−2)		
III						IV

■ Notice that the graph is broken into four quadrants with one point plotted in each one. Here is a chart to indicate which quadrants contain which ordered pairs, based on their signs:

Points	Sign of Coordinates	Quadrant
(2,3)	(+,+)	I
(-2,3)	(-,+)	II
(-3,-2)	(-,-)	III
(3,-2)	(+,-)	IV

LENGTHS OF HORIZONTAL AND VERTICAL SEGMENTS

Two points with the same y-coordinate lie on the same horizontal line and two points with the same x-coordinate lie on the same vertical line. The distance between a horizontal or vertical segment can be found by taking the absolute value of the difference of the two points.

Example:

Find the length of the line AB and the line BC.

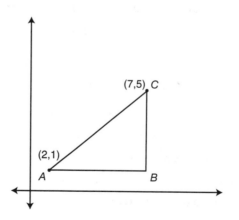

Solution:

$| 2 - 7 | = 5 = AB$

$| 1 - 5 | = 4 = BC$

DISTANCE OF COORDINATE POINTS

To find the distance between two points, use this variation of the Pythagorean theorem:

$$d = \sqrt{(x_2 - x_1)^2 + (y_2 - y_1)^2}$$

Example:

Find the distance between points (2,3) and (1,–2).

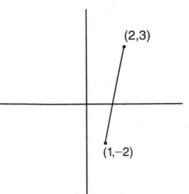

Solution:

$$d = \sqrt{(1-2)^2 + (-2-3)^2}$$
$$d = \sqrt{(1+-2)^2 + (-2+-3)^2}$$
$$d = \sqrt{(-1)^2 + (-5)^2}$$
$$d = \sqrt{1 + 25}$$
$$d = \sqrt{26}$$

MIDPOINT

To find the midpoint of a segment, use the following formula:

$$\text{Midpoint } x = \frac{x_1 + x_2}{2} \qquad \text{Midpoint } y = \frac{y_1 + y_2}{2}$$

Example:

Find the midpoint of the segment *AB*.

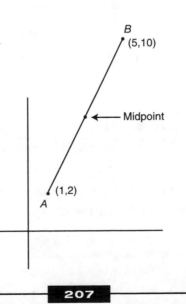

Solution:

Midpoint $x = \frac{1+5}{2} = \frac{6}{2} = 3$ Midpoint $y = \frac{2+10}{2} = \frac{12}{2} = 6$

Therefore the midpoint of $\overline{AB}$ is (3,6).

Slope

The *slope* of a line measures its steepness. It is found by writing the change in *y*-coordinates of any two points on the line, over the change of the corresponding *x*-coordinates. (This is also known as the *rise* over the *run.*) The last step is to simplify the fraction that results.

Example:

Find the slope of a line containing the points (3,2) and (8,9).

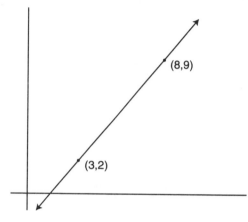

Solution:

$\frac{9-2}{8-3} = \frac{7}{5}$

Therefore, the slope of the line is $\frac{7}{5}$.

NOTE: If you know the slope and at least one point on a line, you can find the coordinate point of other points on the line. Simply move the required units determined by the slope. In the example above, from (8,9), given the slope $\frac{7}{5}$, move up seven units and to the right five units. Another point on the line, thus, is (13,16).

IMPORTANT INFORMATION ABOUT SLOPE

The following are a few rules about slope that you should keep in mind:

- A line that rises to the right has a positive slope and a line that falls to the right has a negative slope.
- A horizontal line has a slope of 0 and a vertical line does not have a slope at all—it is undefined.
- Parallel lines have equal slopes.
- Perpendicular lines have slopes that are negative reciprocals.

▶ Data Analysis Review

Many questions on the GRE test will test your ability to analyze data. Analyzing data can be in the form of statistical analysis (as in using measures of central location), finding probability, reading charts and graphs. All of these topics, followed by a few more, are covered in the following section. Don't worry, you are almost done! This is the last review section before the practice problems. Sharpen your pencil and brush off your eraser one more time before the fun begins. Next stop . . . statistical analysis!

Measures of Central Location

Three important measures of central location will be tested on the GRE test. The central location of a set of numeric values is defined by the value that appears most frequently (the mode), the number that represents the middle value (the median), and/or the average of all of the values (the mean).

MEAN AND MEDIAN

To find the average, or the *mean*, of a set of numbers, add all of the numbers together and divide by the quantity of numbers in the set.

$$\text{Average} = \frac{\text{number set}}{\text{quantity of set}}$$

Example:
Find the average of 9, 4, 7, 6, and 4.

$$\frac{9 + 4 + 7 + 6 + 4}{5} = \frac{30}{5} = 6$$

The denominator is 5 because there are 5 numbers in the set.

To find the *median* of a set of numbers, arrange the numbers in ascending order and find the middle value.

- If the set contains an odd number of elements, then simply choose the middle value.

  Example:
  Find the median of the number set: 1, 5, 3, 7, 2.
  First arrange the set in ascending order: 1, 2, 3, 5, 7.
  Then choose the middle value: 3.
  The answer is 3.

- If the set contains an even number of elements, simply average the two middle values.

  Example:
  Find the median of the number set: 1, 5, 3, 7, 2, 8.
  First arrange the set in ascending order: 1, 2, 3, 5, 7, 8.
  Then choose the middle values 3 and 5.
  Find the average of the numbers $\frac{3 + 5}{2} = 4$.
  The answer is 4.

MODE

The *mode* of a set of numbers is the number that occurs the greatest number of times.

> ### Example:
> For the number set 1, 2, 5, 3, 4, 2, 3, 6, 3, 7, the number 3 is the mode because it occurs the most number of times.

Measures of Dispersion

Measures of dispersion, or the spread of a number set, can be in many different forms. The two forms covered on the GRE test are *range* and *standard deviation*.

RANGE

The range of a data set is the greatest measurement minus the least measurement. For example, given the following values: 5, 9, 14, 16, and 11. The range would be $16 - 5 = 11$.

STANDARD DEVIATION

As you can see, the range is affected by only the two most extreme values in the data set. Standard deviation is a measure of dispersion that is affected by every measurement. To find the standard deviation of *n* measurements, follow these steps:

1. First, find the mean of the measurements.
2. Subtract the mean from each measurement.
3. Square each of the differences.
4. Sum the square values.
5. Divide the sum by *n*.
6. Choose the nonnegative square root of the quotient.

For example:

x	$x - 10$	$(x - 10)^2$
6	−4	16
7	−3	9
7	−3	9
9	−1	1
15	5	25
16	6	36
		96

In the first column, the mean is 10.

$$\text{STANDARD DEVIATION} = \sqrt{\frac{96}{6}} = 4$$

When you find the standard deviation of a data set, you are finding the average distance from the mean for the *n* measurements. It cannot be negative, and when two sets of measurements are compared, the larger the standard deviation, the larger the dispersion.

FREQUENCY DISTRIBUTION

The frequency distribution is essentially the number of times, or how frequently, a measurement appears in a data set. It is represented by a chart like the one below. The *x* represents a measurement, and the *f* represents the number of times that measurement occurs.

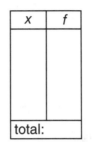

To use the chart, simply list each measurement only once in the *x* column and then write how many times it occurs in the *f* column.

For example, show the frequency distribution of the following data set that represents the number of students enrolled in 15 classes at Middleton Technical Institute:

12, 10, 15, 10, 7, 13, 15, 12, 7, 13, 10, 10, 12, 7, 12

x	f
7	3
10	4
12	4
13	2
15	2
total:	15

Be sure that the total number of measurements taken is equal to the total at the bottom of the frequency distribution chart.

DATA REPRESENTATION AND INTERPRETATION

The GRE test will test your ability to analyze graphs and tables. It is important to read each graph or table very carefully before reading the question. This will help you to process the information that is presented. It is extremely important to read all of the information presented, paying special attention to headings and units of measure. Here is an overview of the types of graphs you will encounter.

Circle Graphs or Pie Charts

This type of graph is representative of a whole and is usually divided into percentages. Each section of the chart represents a portion of the whole, and all of these sections added together will equal 100% of the whole.

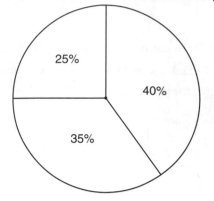

Bar Graphs

Bar graphs compare similar things by using different length bars to represent different values. On the GRE test, these graphs frequently contain differently shaded bars used to represent different elements. Therefore, it is important to pay attention to both the size and shading of the graph.

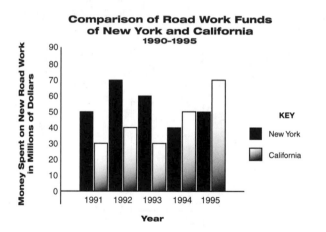

Broken-Line Graphs

Broken-line graphs illustrate a measurable change over time. If a line is slanted up, it represents an increase, whereas a line sloping down represents a decrease. A flat line indicates no change as time elapses.

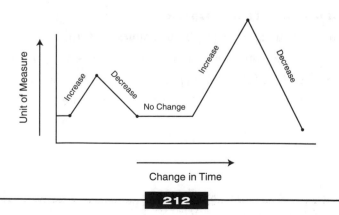

Percentage and Probability

Part of data analysis is being able to calculate and apply percentages and probability. Further review and examples of these two concepts are covered further in the following sections.

PERCENTAGE PROBLEMS

There is one formula that is useful for solving the three types of percentage problems:

$$\frac{\#}{} = \frac{\%}{100}$$

When reading a percentage problem, substitute the necessary information into the previous formula based on the following:

- 100 is always written in the denominator of the percentage-sign column.
- If given a percentage, write it in the numerator position of the number column. If you are not given a percentage, then the variable should be placed there.
- The denominator of the number column represents the number that is equal to the whole, or 100%. This number always follows the word *of* in a word problem. For example: " . . . 13 of 20 apples . . . "
- The numerator of the number column represents the number that is the percent.
- In the formula, the equal sign can be interchanged with the word *is*.

> **Example:**
> Finding a percentage of a given number:
> What number is equal to 40% of 50?

$$\frac{\#}{\underset{50}{x}} = \frac{\%}{\underset{100}{40}}$$

Solve by cross multiplying.

$$100(x) = (40)(50)$$

$$100x = 2,000$$

$$\frac{100x}{100} = \frac{2,000}{100}$$

$$x = 20$$

Therefore, 20 is 40% of 50.

Example:

Finding a number when a percentage is given:

40% of what number is 24?

$$\frac{\overset{\#}{24}}{x} = \frac{\overset{\%}{40}}{100}$$

Cross multiply:

$$(24)(100) = 40x$$

$$2{,}400 = 40x$$

$$\frac{2{,}400}{40} = \frac{40x}{40}$$

$$60 = x$$

Therefore, 40% of 60 is 24.

Example:

Finding what percentage one number is of another:

What percentage of 75 is 15?

$$\frac{\overset{\#}{15}}{75} = \frac{\overset{\%}{x}}{100}$$

Cross multiply:

$$15(100) = (75)(x)$$

$$1{,}500 = 75x$$

$$\frac{1{,}500}{75} = \frac{75x}{75}$$

$$20 = x$$

Therefore, 20% of 75 is 15.

Probability

Probability is expressed as a fraction; it measures the likelihood that a specific event will occur. To find the probability of a specific outcome, use this formula:

$$\text{Probability of an event} = \frac{\text{Number of specific outcomes}}{\text{Total number of possible outcomes}}$$

Example:

If a bag contains 5 blue marbles, 3 red marbles, and 6 green marbles, find the probability of selecting a red marble:

$$\text{Probability of an event} = \frac{\text{Number of specific outcomes}}{\text{Total number of possible outcomes}} = \frac{3}{5+3+6}$$

Therefore, the probability of selecting a red marble is $\frac{3}{14}$.

MULTIPLE PROBABILITIES

To find the probability that two or more events will occur, add the probabilities of each. For example, in the problem above, if we wanted to find the probability of drawing either a red or blue marble, we would add the probabilities together.

The probability of drawing a red marble $= \frac{3}{14}$. And the probability of drawing a blue marble $= \frac{5}{14}$. Add the two together: $\frac{3}{14} + \frac{5}{14} = \frac{8}{14} = \frac{4}{7}$.

So the probability for selecting either a blue or a red would be 8 in 14, or 4 in 7.

Helpful Hints about Probability

- If an event is certain to occur the probability is 1.
- If an event is certain not to occur, the probability is 0.
- If you know the probability an event will occur, you can find the probability of the event *not* occurring by subtracting the probability that the event will occur from 1.

Special Symbols Problems

The last topic to be covered is the concept of special symbol problems. The GRE test will sometimes invent a new arithmetic operation symbol. Don't let this confuse you. These problems are generally very easy. Just pay attention to the placement of the variables and operations being performed.

Example:

Given $a \Delta b = (a \times b + 3)^2$, find the value of $1 \Delta 2$.

Solution:

Fill in the formula with 1 being equal to a and 2 being equal to b.

$(1 \times 2 + 3)^2 = (2 + 3)^2 = (5)^2 = 25.$ So, $1 \Delta 2 = 25$.

Example:

If
$$\triangle = \frac{a-b}{c} + \frac{a-c}{b} + \frac{b-c}{a}$$
(with b at top, a at bottom left, c at bottom right)

Then what is the value of . . .

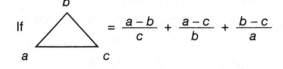

Solution:

Fill in variables according to the placement of number in the triangular figure. $a = 1$, $b = 2$, and $c = 3$.

$$\frac{1-2}{3} + \frac{1-3}{2} + \frac{2-3}{1} = \frac{-1}{3} + -1 + -1 = -2\frac{1}{3}$$

▶ Tips and Strategies for the Official Test

You are almost ready to begin practicing. But before you begin the practice problems, read through this section to learn some tips and strategies for working with each problem type.

Quantitative Comparison Questions

- It is not necessary to find the exact value of the two variables, and often, it is important **not** to waste time doing so. It is important to use estimating, rounding, and the eliminating unnecessary information to determine the relationship.

- Attempt to make the two columns look as similar as possible. For example, make sure all units are equal. This is similar to a strategy given in the problem solving section, and it is even more applicable here. This is also true if one of the answer choices is a fraction or a decimal. If this is the case, make the other answer into an improper fraction or a decimal, which ever is going to make the choices the most similar.

- Eliminate any information the two columns share. This will leave you with an easier comparison. For example, if you are given the two quantities: $5(x + 1)$ and $3(x + 1)$, and told that x is positive, you would select the first quantity because you can eliminate the $(x + 1)$ from both. That leaves you to decide which is greater, 5 or 3. This has become a very easy problem resulting from eliminating information the two quantities shared.

- Substitute real values for unknowns or variables. If you can do so quickly, many of the comparisons will be straightforward and clear. The process of substituting numbers should be used in most QC questions when given a variable. However, be sure to simplify the equation or expression as much as possible before plugging in.

- The QC section tests how quick, creative, and accurate you can be. Do not get stuck doing complex computations. If you feel yourself doing a lot of computations, stop and try another method. There is often more than one way to solve a problem. Try to pick the easiest way.

- Make no assumptions about the information listed in the columns. If the question requires you to make assumptions, then choose answer **d**. For example, if one of the questions asks for the root of x^2, you cannot assume that the answer is a positive root. Remember that x^2 will have two roots, one positive and one negative. Do not let the test fool you. Be aware of the possibility of multiple answers.

- If one or both of the expressions being compared have parentheses, be sure to evaluate the expression(s) to remove the parentheses before proceeding. This is a simple technique that can make a large difference in the similarity of the two comparisons. For example, if you are comparing the binomial $(x - 2)(x - 2)$ with the trinomial $x^2 - 4x + 4$, first remove the parentheses from the product of $(x - 2)(x - 2)$ by multiplying the two binomials. The product will be the trinomial $x^2 - 4x + 4$. You can clearly see that they are equal.

- Perform the same operation to both columns. This is especially useful when working with fractions. Often, finding an LCD and multiplying both columns by that number helps to make the comparison easier. Just keep in mind that, like working in an equation, the operation must be performed exactly the same in each column.

Problem Solving Questions

Problem solving questions test your mathematical reasoning skills. This means that you will be required to apply several basic math techniques for each problem. Here are some helpful strategies to help you improve your math score on the problem solving questions:

- Read questions carefully and know the answer being sought. In many problems you will be asked to solve an equation and then perform an operation with the resulting variable to get an answer. In this situation, it is easy to solve the equation and feel like you have the answer. Paying special attention to what each question is asking, and then double-checking that your answer satisfies this, is an important technique for performing well on the GRE test.

- Sometimes it may be best to try one of the answers. Many times it is quicker to pick an answer and check to see if it is a solution. When you do this, use response **c**. It will be the middle number and you can adjust the outcome to the problem as needed by choosing **b** or **d** next, depending on whether you need a larger or smaller answer. This is also a good strategy when you are unfamiliar with the information the problem is asking.

- When solving word problems, look at each phrase individually, then rewrite each in math language. This is very similar to creating and assigning variables, as addressed earlier in the word-problem section. In addition to identifying what is "known" and "unknown," also take time to translate operation words into actual symbols. It is best when working with a word problem to represent every part of it, phrase by phrase, in mathematical language.

- Make sure all the units are equal before you begin. This will save a great deal of time doing conversions. This is a very effective way to save time. Almost all conversions are easier to make at the beginning of a problem rather than at the end. Sometimes a person can get so excited about getting an answer that they forget to make the conversion at all, resulting in an incorrect answer. Making the conversions at the start of the problem is definitely more advantageous for this reason.

- Draw pictures when solving word problems if needed. Pictures are always helpful when a word problem doesn't have one already, especially when the problem is dealing with a geometrical figure or location. Many students are also better at solving problems when they see a visual representation. Do not make the drawings too elaborate; unfortunately, the GRE test does not give points for artistic flair. A simple drawing, labeled correctly, is usually all it takes.

- Avoid lengthy calculations. It is seldom, if ever, necessary to spend a great deal of time doing calculations. This is a test of mathematical concepts, not calculations. If you find yourself doing a very complex, lengthy calculation—stop! Either you are not doing the problem correctly or you are missing a much easier solution.

- Be careful when solving Roman numeral problems. Roman numeral problems will give you several answer possibilities that list a few different combinations of solutions. You will have five options: **a, b, c, d,** and **e**. To solve a Roman numeral problem, treat each Roman numeral as a true or false statement. Mark each Roman numeral with a "T" or "F" on scrap paper, then select the answer that matches your "T's" and "F's."

These strategies will help you to do well on the GRE test, but simply reading them will not. You must practice, practice, and practice. That is why there are 80 problems in the following section for you to solve. Keep in mind that on the actual GRE test you will only have 28 problems in the Quantitative section. By doing 80 problems now, it will seem easy to do only 28 questions on the test. Keep this in mind as you work through the practice problems.

Now the time has come for all of your studying to be applied; the practice problems are next. Good luck!

ANSWER SHEET

1. ⓐ ⓑ ⓒ ⓓ	28. ⓐ ⓑ ⓒ ⓓ	55. ⓐ ⓑ ⓒ ⓓ ⓔ
2. ⓐ ⓑ ⓒ ⓓ	29. ⓐ ⓑ ⓒ ⓓ	56. ⓐ ⓑ ⓒ ⓓ ⓔ
3. ⓐ ⓑ ⓒ ⓓ	30. ⓐ ⓑ ⓒ ⓓ	57. ⓐ ⓑ ⓒ ⓓ ⓔ
4. ⓐ ⓑ ⓒ ⓓ	31. ⓐ ⓑ ⓒ ⓓ	58. ⓐ ⓑ ⓒ ⓓ ⓔ
5. ⓐ ⓑ ⓒ ⓓ	32. ⓐ ⓑ ⓒ ⓓ	59. ⓐ ⓑ ⓒ ⓓ ⓔ
6. ⓐ ⓑ ⓒ ⓓ	33. ⓐ ⓑ ⓒ ⓓ	60. ⓐ ⓑ ⓒ ⓓ ⓔ
7. ⓐ ⓑ ⓒ ⓓ	34. ⓐ ⓑ ⓒ ⓓ	61. ⓐ ⓑ ⓒ ⓓ ⓔ
8. ⓐ ⓑ ⓒ ⓓ	35. ⓐ ⓑ ⓒ ⓓ	62. ⓐ ⓑ ⓒ ⓓ ⓔ
9. ⓐ ⓑ ⓒ ⓓ	36. ⓐ ⓑ ⓒ ⓓ	63. ⓐ ⓑ ⓒ ⓓ ⓔ
10. ⓐ ⓑ ⓒ ⓓ	37. ⓐ ⓑ ⓒ ⓓ	64. ⓐ ⓑ ⓒ ⓓ ⓔ
11. ⓐ ⓑ ⓒ ⓓ	38. ⓐ ⓑ ⓒ ⓓ	65. ⓐ ⓑ ⓒ ⓓ ⓔ
12. ⓐ ⓑ ⓒ ⓓ	39. ⓐ ⓑ ⓒ ⓓ	66. ⓐ ⓑ ⓒ ⓓ ⓔ
13. ⓐ ⓑ ⓒ ⓓ	40. ⓐ ⓑ ⓒ ⓓ	67. ⓐ ⓑ ⓒ ⓓ ⓔ
14. ⓐ ⓑ ⓒ ⓓ	41. ⓐ ⓑ ⓒ ⓓ ⓔ	68. ⓐ ⓑ ⓒ ⓓ ⓔ
15. ⓐ ⓑ ⓒ ⓓ	42. ⓐ ⓑ ⓒ ⓓ ⓔ	69. ⓐ ⓑ ⓒ ⓓ ⓔ
16. ⓐ ⓑ ⓒ ⓓ	43. ⓐ ⓑ ⓒ ⓓ ⓔ	70. ⓐ ⓑ ⓒ ⓓ ⓔ
17. ⓐ ⓑ ⓒ ⓓ	44. ⓐ ⓑ ⓒ ⓓ ⓔ	71. ⓐ ⓑ ⓒ ⓓ ⓔ
18. ⓐ ⓑ ⓒ ⓓ	45. ⓐ ⓑ ⓒ ⓓ ⓔ	72. ⓐ ⓑ ⓒ ⓓ ⓔ
19. ⓐ ⓑ ⓒ ⓓ	46. ⓐ ⓑ ⓒ ⓓ ⓔ	73. ⓐ ⓑ ⓒ ⓓ ⓔ
20. ⓐ ⓑ ⓒ ⓓ	47. ⓐ ⓑ ⓒ ⓓ ⓔ	74. ⓐ ⓑ ⓒ ⓓ ⓔ
21. ⓐ ⓑ ⓒ ⓓ	48. ⓐ ⓑ ⓒ ⓓ ⓔ	75. ⓐ ⓑ ⓒ ⓓ ⓔ
22. ⓐ ⓑ ⓒ ⓓ	49. ⓐ ⓑ ⓒ ⓓ ⓔ	76. ⓐ ⓑ ⓒ ⓓ ⓔ
23. ⓐ ⓑ ⓒ ⓓ	50. ⓐ ⓑ ⓒ ⓓ ⓔ	77. ⓐ ⓑ ⓒ ⓓ ⓔ
24. ⓐ ⓑ ⓒ ⓓ	51. ⓐ ⓑ ⓒ ⓓ ⓔ	78. ⓐ ⓑ ⓒ ⓓ ⓔ
25. ⓐ ⓑ ⓒ ⓓ	52. ⓐ ⓑ ⓒ ⓓ ⓔ	79. ⓐ ⓑ ⓒ ⓓ ⓔ
26. ⓐ ⓑ ⓒ ⓓ	53. ⓐ ⓑ ⓒ ⓓ ⓔ	80. ⓐ ⓑ ⓒ ⓓ ⓔ
27. ⓐ ⓑ ⓒ ⓓ	54. ⓐ ⓑ ⓒ ⓓ ⓔ	

▶ Practice

Directions: In each of the questions 1–40, compare the two quantities given. Select the appropriate choice for each one according to the following:

    a. if the quantity in Column A is greater,
    b. if the quantity in Column B is greater,
    c. if the two quantities are equal, or
    d. if there is not enough information given to determine the relationship of the two quantities.

	Column A		**Column B**

1. $n > 1$

Column A: $\dfrac{n + 7}{3} + \dfrac{n - 3}{4}$

Column B: $\dfrac{7n + 19}{7}$

2. $0.1y + 0.01y = 2.2$

Column A: $0.1y$

Column B: 20

3. Column A: the reciprocal of 4

Column B: $\sqrt{\dfrac{1}{16}}$

4. Column A: 3 feet, 5 inches

Column B: 1.5 yards

5.
$$x = 6 + 7 + 8 + 9 + 10$$
$$y = 5 + 6 + 7 + 8 + 9$$

Column A: $5(15)$

Column B: $x + y$

6.
$$
\begin{array}{r}
5678 \\
\times\ 73 \\
\hline
170\blacktriangle4 \\
3974\square0 \\
\hline
414494
\end{array}
$$

Column A: value of $\blacktriangle$

Column B: value of $\square$

7. $4x = 4(14) - 4$

Column A: x

Column B: 14

8.

Cindy covered 36 miles in 45 minutes.

Cindy's average speed
(in miles/hour)

48 miles/hour

9.

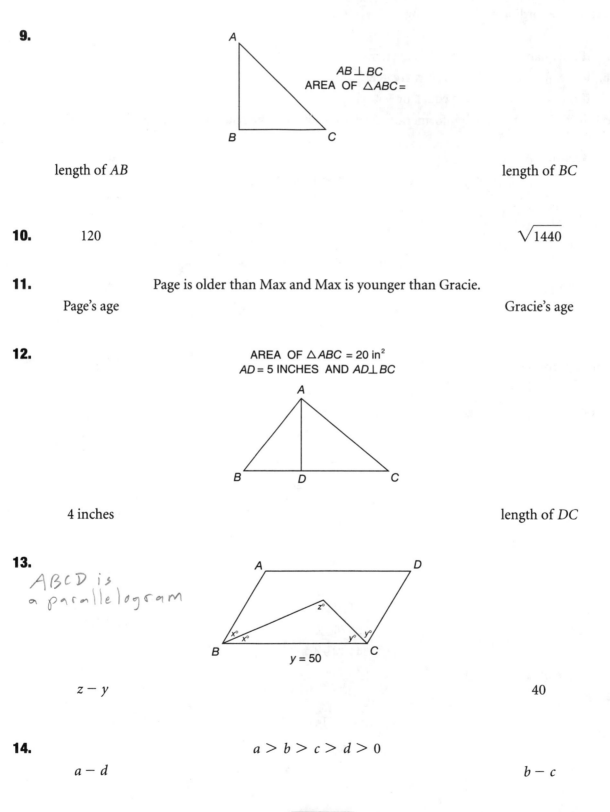

$AB \perp BC$
AREA OF $\triangle ABC =$

length of AB

length of BC

10.   120

$\sqrt{1440}$

11.

Page is older than Max and Max is younger than Gracie.

Page's age

Gracie's age

12.

AREA OF $\triangle ABC = 20$ in^2
$AD = 5$ INCHES AND $AD \perp BC$

4 inches

length of DC

13.

ABCD is
a parallelogram

$y = 50$

$z - y$

40

14.

$a > b > c > d > 0$

$a - d$

$b - c$

15.

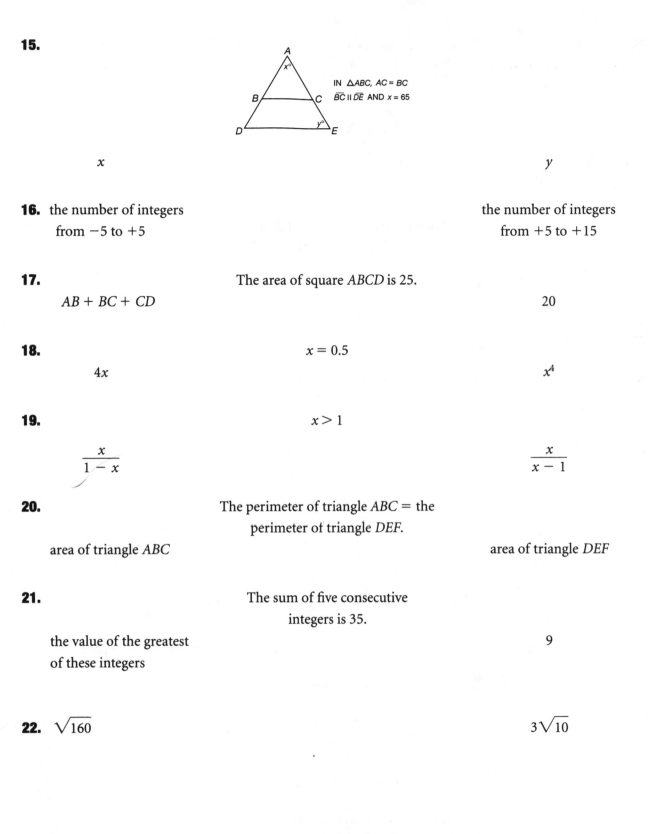

IN △ABC, AC = BC
$\overline{BC} \parallel \overline{DE}$ AND x = 65

x y

16. the number of integers
from -5 to $+5$

the number of integers
from $+5$ to $+15$

17.   The area of square *ABCD* is 25.

$AB + BC + CD$ 20

18. $x = 0.5$

$4x$ x^4

19. $x > 1$

$\dfrac{x}{1-x}$ $\dfrac{x}{x-1}$

20.   The perimeter of triangle *ABC* = the
perimeter of triangle *DEF*.

area of triangle *ABC*   area of triangle *DEF*

21.   The sum of five consecutive
integers is 35.

the value of the greatest
of these integers   9

22. $\sqrt{160}$ $3\sqrt{10}$

23.

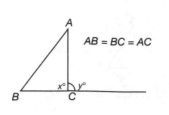

$$AB = BC = AC$$

$2x$ y

24.

The water tank is two-thirds full with
12 gallons of water.

the capacity of this tank   20 gallons

25.

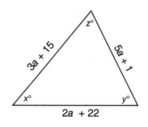

a 7

26. $$x - y = 7$$

$x + y$ 14

27. The area of isosceles right triangle *ABC* is 18.

the length of leg *AB*   the length of hypotenuse *AC*

Questions 28 and 29 refer to the following diagram:

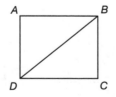

ABCD IS A SQUARE.
DIAGONAL $BD = 6\sqrt{2}$.

28. perimeter of *ABCD*   24

29. area of *ABD*   18

30.   In triangle *ABC*, *AB* = *BC*, and the measure of angle
                           B = the measure of angle *C*.

the measure of angle *B* +   the measure of angle *B* +
   the measure of angle *C*   the measure of angle *A*

31. $a < b < c$
                                     $d < e < f$

            a   *f*

32. $64 < x < 81$

            x   65

33.

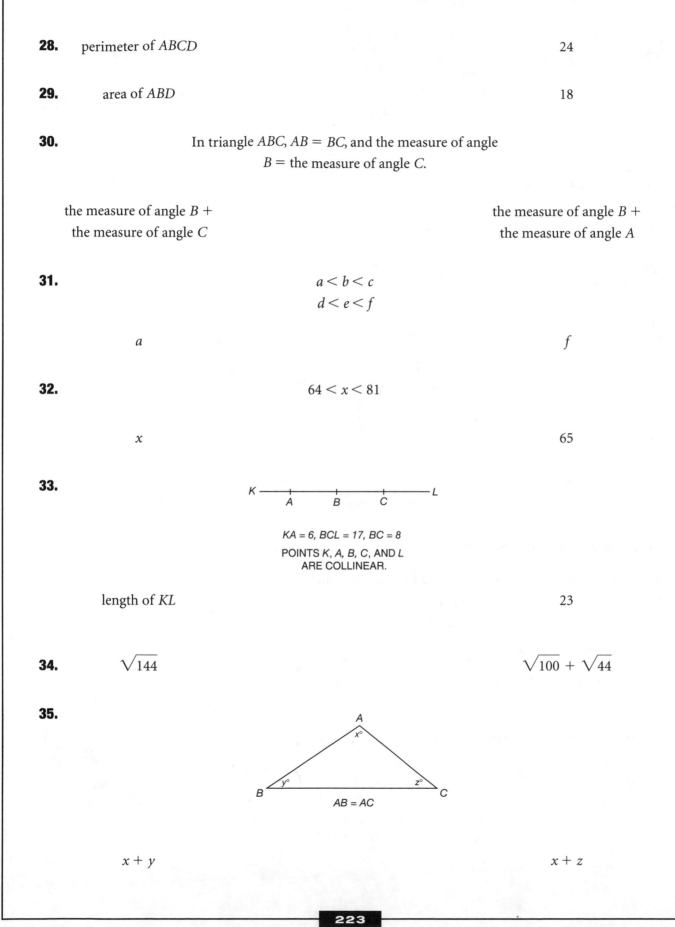

KA = 6, *BCL* = 17, *BC* = 8

POINTS *K*, *A*, *B*, *C*, AND *L*
ARE COLLINEAR.

length of *KL*   23

34. $\sqrt{144}$ $\sqrt{100} + \sqrt{44}$

35.

AB = *AC*

            $x + y$ $x + z$

36. $\dfrac{3\sqrt{48}}{\sqrt{3}}$ 12

37. $\dfrac{x}{4} + \dfrac{x}{3} = \dfrac{7}{12}$

       x -1

38. 0.003%   0.0003

39. $\dfrac{k}{400}$ $\dfrac{k}{4}\%$

40.

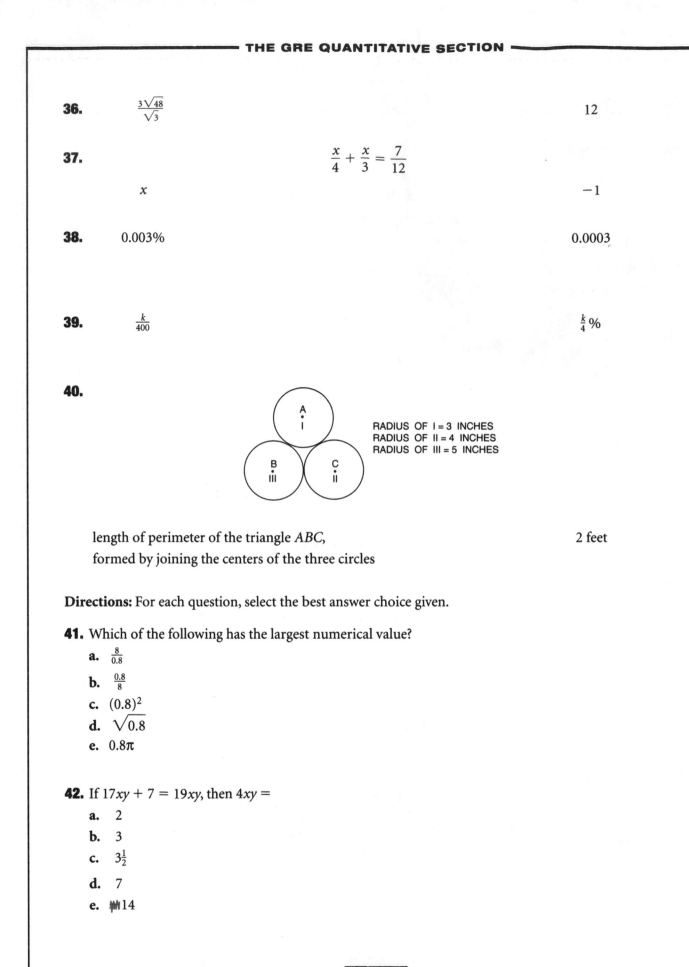

RADIUS OF I = 3 INCHES
RADIUS OF II = 4 INCHES
RADIUS OF III = 5 INCHES

length of perimeter of the triangle *ABC*,   2 feet
formed by joining the centers of the three circles

Directions: For each question, select the best answer choice given.

41. Which of the following has the largest numerical value?

   a. $\dfrac{8}{0.8}$

   b. $\dfrac{0.8}{8}$

   c. $(0.8)^2$

   d. $\sqrt{0.8}$

   e. 0.8π

42. If $17xy + 7 = 19xy$, then $4xy =$

   a. 2

   b. 3

   c. $3\frac{1}{2}$

   d. 7

   e. 14

43. The average of two numbers is *xy*. If one number is equal to *x*, the other number is equal to

   a. y

   b. $2y$

   c. $xy - x$

   d. $2xy - x$

   e. $xy - 2x$

44. A snapshot $1\frac{7}{8}$ inches $\times$ $2\frac{1}{2}$ inches is to be enlarged so that the longer dimension will be 4 inches. What will be the length (in inches) of the shorter dimension?

   a. $2\frac{3}{8}$

   b. $2\frac{1}{2}$

   c. 3

   d. $3\frac{3}{8}$

   e. $3\frac{1}{2}$

45. The length and width of rectangle *AEFG* are each $\frac{2}{3}$ of the corresponding parts of *ABCD*. *AEB* = 12; *AGD* = 6.

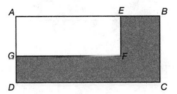

The area of the shaded part is

   a. 24

   b. 32

   c. 36

   d. 40

   e. 48

Questions 46–50 refer to the following chart and graph.

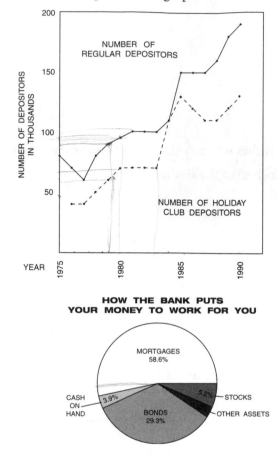

46. How many thousands of regular depositors did the bank have in 1980?

   a. 70

   b. 85

   c. 95

   d. 100

   e. 950

47. In 1979 what was the ratio of the number of Holiday Club depositors to the number of regular depositors?

   a. 2:3

   b. 2:1

   c. 1:2

   d. 7:9

   e. 3:2

48. Which of the following can be inferred from the graphs?

   I. Interest rates were static in the 1980–1983 period.

   II. The greatest increase in the number of Holiday Club depositors over a previous year occurred in 1984.

   III. Alameda Savings Bank invested most of its assets in stocks and bounds.

a. I only

b. II only

c. III only

d. I and III

e. II and III

49. About how many degrees (to the nearest degree) are in the angle of the sector representing mortgages?

a. 59

b. 106

c. 211

d. 246

e. 318

50. The average annual interest on mortgage investments is m percent and the average annual interest on the bond investment is b percent. If the annual interest on the bond investment is x dollars, how many dollars are invested in mortgages?

a. $\frac{xm}{b}$

b. $\frac{xb}{m}$

c. $\frac{100xb}{m}$

d. $\frac{bx}{100m}$

e. $\frac{200x}{b}$

51. What is the area of *ABCD*?

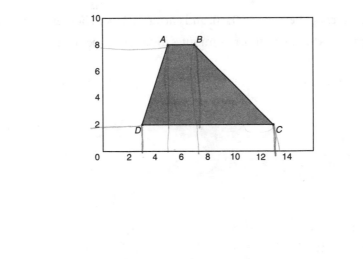

a. 24

b. 30

c. 35

d. 36

e. 48

52. If $x^2 + 2x - 8 = 0$, then x is either -4 or

   a. -2
   b. -1
   c. 0
   d. 2
   e. 8

53. Weight distribution in average adult; total average body weight is 70,000 grams.

Elements of the Body	Weight (in grams)
Muscles	30,000
Water	18,800
Skeleton	10,000
Blood	5,000
Gastrointestinal Tract	2,000
Liver	1,700
Brain	1,500
Lungs	1,000

If the weight of an adult's skeleton is represented as g grams, his or her total body weight can be represented as

   a. $7g$
   b. $g + 6$
   c. $60g$
   d. $g + 60$
   e. $70,000g$

54. The afternoon classes in a school begin at 1:00 P.M. and end at 3:52 P.M. There are four afternoon class periods with 4 minutes between periods. The number of minutes in each class period is

   a. 39
   b. 40
   c. 43
   d. 45
   e. 59

55. The average of P numbers is x, and the average of N numbers is y. What is the average of the total numbers $(P + N)$?

    a. $\dfrac{x + y}{2}$

    b. $x + y$

    c. $\dfrac{Py + Nx}{xy(P + N)}$

    d. $\dfrac{x + y}{P + N}$

    e. $\dfrac{Px + Ny}{P + N}$

56. For which of the values of n and d is $\dfrac{n}{d} > 1$?

    a. $n = 5$ and $d = 6$
    b. $n = 3$ and $d = 2$
    c. $n = 1$ and $d = 2$
    d. $n = 1$ and $d = 1$
    e. $n = 0$ and $d = 1$

57.

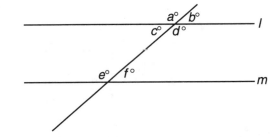

In the figure above, $l \parallel m$. All of the following are true EXCEPT:
    a. $m\angle c = m\angle d$
    b. $m\angle a = m\angle d$
    c. $m\angle a = m\angle e$
    d. $m\angle f = m\angle b$
    e. $m\angle f = m\angle c$

58. If 0.6 is the average of the four quantities 0.2, 0.8, 1.0, and x, what is the numerical value of x?
    a. 0.2
    b. 0.4
    c. 0.67
    d. 1.3
    e. 2.4

59. $\frac{a^2 - b^2}{(a - b)}$ is equal to

  a. $a + b$

  b. $a - b$

  c. $\frac{a + b}{a - b}$

  d. $\frac{a - b}{a + b}$

  e. 1

60. The area of square *EFGH* is equal to the area of rectangle *ABCD*. If *GH* = 6 feet and *AD* = 4 feet, the perimeter (in feet) of the rectangle is

  a. 9

  b. 13

  c. 24

  d. 26

  e. 36

Questions 61–65 refer to the following chart and graph.

CALORIES

COMPOSITION OF AVERAGE DIET

	GRAMS	CALORIES
CARBOHYDRATES	500	2,050
PROTEIN	100	410
FAT	100	930

**CALORIES REQUIRED PER DAY
BY BOYS AND GIRLS**

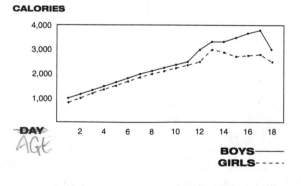

BOYS ———
GIRLS - - - - -

61. How many calories are there in 1 gram of carbohydrates?

   a. 0.2

   b. 2

   c. 4.1

   d. 10.25

   e. 1.025

62. What percent (to the nearest whole number) of the total calories in the average diet is derived from proteins?

   a. 12

   b. 14

   c. 22

   d. 27

   e. 32

63. Approximately how many more calories per day are required by boys than girls at age 17?

   a. 500

   b. 1,000

   c. 2,500

   d. 3,500

   e. 4,000

64. Which of the following can be inferred from the graphs?

  I. Calorie requirements for boys and girls have similar rates of increase until age 11.

  II. From ages 4 to 12 calorie requirements for boys and girls are wholly dissimilar.

  III. Calorie requirements for boys and girls reach their peaks at different ages.

   a. I only

   b. II only

   c. III only

   d. I and III

   e. II and III

65. How many grams of carbohydrates (to the nearest gram) are needed to yield as many calories as 1,000 grams of fat?

   a. 1,110

   b. 2,050

   c. 2,268

   d. 4,100

   e. 4,536

66. The radius of a circular pool is twice the radius of a circular flowerbed. The area of the pool is how many times the area of the flowerbed?

   a. $\frac{1}{4}$

   b. $\frac{1}{2}$

   c. 2

   d. 4

   e. 8

67.

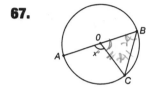

In the figure above, AB is the diameter and $OC = BC$. What is the value of $\frac{x}{2}$?

   a. 20

   b. 30

   c. 60

   d. 90

   e. 120

68. One-half of a number is 17 more than one-third of that number. What is the number?

   a. 51

   b. 84

   c. 102

   d. 112

   e. 204

69. Patricia and Ed together have $100.00. After giving Ed $10.00, Patricia finds that she has $4.00 more than $\frac{1}{5}$ the amount Ed now has. How much does Patricia now have?

   a. $18.67

   b. $20.00

   c. $21.00

   d. $27.50

   e. $30.00

70. If two items cost c cents, how many items can be purchased for x cents?

 a. $\frac{x}{2c}$

 b. $\frac{2c}{x}$

 c. $\frac{2x}{c}$

 d. $\frac{cx}{2}$

 e. $2cx$

71. If four cows produce 4 cans of milk in 4 days, how many days does it take eight cows to produce 8 cans of milk?

 a. 1
 b. 2
 c. 4
 d. 8
 e. 16

72. A quart of alcohol containing $\frac{1}{2}$ pint of pure alcohol is diluted by the addition of $1\frac{1}{2}$ pints of distilled water. How much pure alcohol is contained in the diluted alcohol?

 a. $\frac{1}{2}$ pint
 b. $1\frac{1}{2}$ pints
 c. 2 pints
 d. 3 pints
 e. $3\frac{1}{2}$ pints

73. If 20 teachers out of a faculty of 80 are transferred, what percentage of the original faculty remains?

 a. 4
 b. 16
 c. 25
 d. 60
 e. 75

74. The total weight of three children is 152 pounds and 4 ounces. The average weight is 50 pounds and

    a. $\frac{1}{3}$ pound.

    b. $\frac{1}{2}$ pound.

    c. $1\frac{1}{3}$ ounces.

    d. 9 ounces.

    e. 12 ounces.

75. Thirty prizes were distributed to 5% of the original entrants in a contest. Assuming one prize per person, the number of entrants in this contest was

    a. 15

    b. 60

    c. 150

    d. 300

    e. 600

76. To ride a ferry, the total cost T is 50 cents for the car and driver and c cents for each additional passenger in the car. What is the total cost for a car with n persons in the automobile?

    a. $T = n + c$

    b. $T = 50 + nc$

    c. $T = cn$

    d. $T = 50 + c(n - 1)$

    e. $T = 50 + (n + 1)c$

77. Julie wants to make some candy using a recipe that calls for $1\frac{1}{2}$ cups of sugar, $\frac{1}{2}$ cup of boiling water and several other ingredients. She finds that she has only 1 cup of sugar. If she adjusts the recipe for 1 cup of sugar, how much water should she use?

    a. $\frac{1}{6}$ cup

    b. $\frac{1}{4}$ cup

    c. $\frac{1}{3}$ cup

    d. $\frac{3}{4}$ cup

    e. 1 cup

78. How many pounds of baggage are allowed for a plane passenger if the European regulations permit 20 kilograms per passenger? (1 kg = 2.2 lbs)

   a. 11
   b. 44
   c. 88
   d. 91
   e. 440

79. Which of the following statements is (are) always true? (Assume a, b, and c are not equal to zero.)

   I. $\frac{1}{a}$ is less than a.

   II. $\frac{a + b}{2a}$ equals $\frac{2b}{b + a}$ when a equals b.

   III. $\frac{a + c}{b + c}$ is more than $\frac{a}{b}$.

   a. II only
   b. I and II only
   c. I and III only
   d. II and III only
   e. I, II, and III

80. If $bx - 2 = k$, then x equals

   a. $\frac{k}{b} + 2$
   b. $k - \frac{2}{b}$
   c. $2 - \frac{k}{b}$
   d. $\frac{k + 2}{b}$
   e. $k - 2$

▶ Answers

1. b. $\frac{n + 7}{3} + \frac{n - 3}{4}$

$\frac{4n + 28 + 3n - 9}{12}$

$\frac{7n + 19}{12}$

The numerators are the same but the fraction in Column B has a smaller denominator, denoting a larger quantity.

2. b.

$$1y + 0.01y = 2.2$$

$$10y + 1y = 220 \quad \text{Multiply each term by 100}$$

$$11y = 220$$

$$y = 20$$

$$0.1y = 2 \quad \text{Divide by 10 on each side}$$

3. c. The reciprocal of 4 is $\frac{1}{4}$; $\sqrt{\frac{1}{16}} = \frac{1}{4}$.

4. b. 1 yard = 3 feet and (0.5) or $\frac{1}{2}$ yard = 1 foot 6 inches. Therefore, (1.5) or $1\frac{1}{2}$ yards = 4 feet 6 inches.

5. c. Add: $5 + 6 + 7 + 8 + 9 = 35$; $6 + 7 + 8 + 9 + 10 = 40$; so $x + y = 75$; $5 \times 15 = 75$ so the two quantities are equal.

6. b.

$$8 \times 3 = 24 \text{ and } 7 \times 3 = 21 + 2 + 23.$$

$$\text{Therefore, } \blacktriangle = 3. \text{ Since } 8 \times 7 = 56, \square = 6.$$

7. b.

$$4x = 4(14) - 4$$
$$4x = 56 - 4$$
$$4x = 52$$
$$x = 13$$

8. c.

$$\text{Rate} = \text{Distance} \div \text{Time}$$
$$\text{Rate} = 36 \text{ miles} \div \frac{3}{4} \text{ hour}$$
$$(36)\tfrac{4}{3} = 48 \text{ miles/hour}$$

9. d.

$\frac{BC \times AB}{2} = 18$, but any of the following may be true: $BC > AB$, $BC < AB$, or $BC = AB$

10. a. $\sqrt{1440}$ is a two-digit number, so you know that it is less than 120.

11. d. Since Gracie is older than Max, she may be older or younger than Page.

12. d. Since $AD = 5$ and the area is 20 square inches, we can find the value of base BC but not the value of DC. BC equals 8 inches but BD will be equal to DC only if $AB = AC$.

13. c. Since $y = 50$, the measure of angle DCB is 100° and the measure of angle ABC is 80° since $ABCD$ is a parallelogram. Since $x = 40$,

$$z = 180 - 90 = 90$$
$$z - y = 90 - 50 = 40$$

14. a. In Column A, d, the smallest integer, is subtracted from a, the integer with the largest value.

15. a. Since $x = 65$ and $AC = BC$, then the measure of angle ABC is 65°, and the measure of angle ACB is 50°. Since $BC \| DE$, then $y = 50°$ and $x > y$.

16. c. From -5 to $+5$ there are 11 integers. Also, from $+5$ to $+15$ there are 11 integers.

17. b. Since the area $= 25$, each side $= 5$. The sum of three sides of the square $= 15$.

18. a. $x = 0.5$
$$4x = (0.5)(4) = 2.0$$
$$x^4 = (0.5)(0.5)(0.5)(0.5) = 0.0625$$

19. b. The fraction in Column A has a denominator with a negative value, which will make the entire fraction negative.

20. d. The area of a triangle is one-half the product of the lengths of the base and the altitude, and cannot be determined using only the values of the sides without more information.

21. c. Let $x =$ the first of the integers. Then:
$$\text{sum} = x + x + 1 + x + 2 + x + 3 + x + 4$$
$$= 5x + 10$$
$5x + 10 = 35$ (given), then $5x = 25$.
$$x = 5 \text{ and the largest integer, } x + 4 = 9.$$

22. a. $\sqrt{160} = \sqrt{16}\,\sqrt{10} = 4\sqrt{10}$

23. c. Since the triangle is equilateral, $x = 60$ and exterior angle $y = 120$. Therefore, $2x = y$.

24. b. If $\frac{2}{3}$ corresponds to 12 gallons, then $\frac{1}{3}$ corresponds to 6 gallons. Therefore, $\frac{3}{3}$ corresponds to 18 gallons, which is the value of Column A.

25. c. Since the triangle has three congruent angles, the triangle is equilateral and each side is also equal.
$$3a + 15 = 5a + 1 = 2a + 22$$
$$3a + 15 = 5a + 1$$
$$14 = 2a$$
$$7 = a$$

26. d. Since $x - y = 7$, then $x = y + 7$; x and y have many possible values, and, therefore, $x + y$ cannot be determined.

27. b. $\frac{x^2}{2} = 18$
$$x^2 = 36$$
$$x = 6$$

Therefore $AC = 6\sqrt{2}$ and $6\sqrt{2} > 6$. In addition, the hypotenuse is always the longest side of a right triangle, so the length of AC would automatically be larger than a leg.

28. c. Since the diagonal of the square measures $6\sqrt{2}$, the length of each side of the square is 6. Therefore, $AB = 6$ and thus the perimeter $= 24$.

29. c. Area $= \frac{1}{2}(6)(6) = 18$.

30. c. $AB = BC$ (given)
Since the measure of angle B equals the measure of angle C, $AB = AC$. Therefore, ABC is equilateral and $m\angle A = m\angle B = m\angle C = m\angle B + m\angle C = m\angle B = + m\angle A$.

31. d. There is no relationship between a and f given.

32. d. The variable x may have any value between 64 and 81. This value could be smaller, larger, or equal to 65.

33. a. $KL = 23 +$ length of AB and $KL > 23$.

34. b. $\sqrt{144} = 12$ and $\sqrt{100} + \sqrt{44} = 10 + \approx 6.6 > 12$

35. c. Because $y = z$ and $AB = AC$, then $x + y = x + z$ (if equal values are added to equal values, the results are also equal.)

36. c. $\frac{3\sqrt{48}}{\sqrt{3}} \times \frac{\sqrt{3}}{\sqrt{3}} = \frac{3\sqrt{144}}{3} = \frac{(3)(12)}{3} = 12$

37. a. $\frac{x}{4} + \frac{x}{3} = \frac{7}{12}$

$\frac{3x}{12} + \frac{4x}{12} = \frac{7}{12}$

$3x + 4x = 7$

$x = 1$

$1 > -1$

38. b. $0.003\% = 0.00003$

$0.0003 > 0.00003$

39. c. $\frac{k}{4}\% = \frac{k}{4} \div 100 = \frac{k}{4} \times \frac{1}{100} = \frac{k}{400}$

40. c. $AB = 3$ inches $+ 5$ inches $= 8$ inches
$BC = 5$ inches $+ 4$ inches $= 9$ inches
$AC = 4$ inches $+ 3$ inches $= 7$ inches
Total $= 24$ inches $= 2$ feet

41. a. $\frac{8}{0.8} = \frac{80}{8} = 10$

$\frac{0.8}{8} = \frac{8}{80} = \frac{1}{10}$

$(0.8)^2 = 0.64$

$\sqrt{0.8} = 0.89$

$0.8\pi = (0.8)(3.14) = 2.5$

42. e. $17xy + 7 = 19xy$
$$7 = 2xy$$
$$14 = 4xy$$

43. d. Average $= xy$
Sum $\div 2 = xy$
Sum $= 2xy$
$2xy = x + ?$
$? = 2xy - x$

44. c. This is a direct proportion. Let $x =$ length of the shorter dimension of enlargement

$$\frac{\text{longer dimension}}{\text{shorter dimension}} = \frac{2\frac{1}{2}}{1\frac{7}{8}} = \frac{4}{x}$$

$$2\tfrac{1}{2}x = (4)(1\tfrac{7}{8})$$

$$\frac{5x}{2} = \frac{60}{8}$$

$$x = 3$$

45. d. $AEB = 12 \quad AE = 8$
$AGD = 6 \quad AG = 4$
Area $AEFG = 32$
Area $ABCD = 72$
Area of Shaded part $= 72 - 32 = 40$

46. c. Be careful to read the proper line (regular depositors). The point is midway between 90 and 100.

47. a. Number of Holiday Club depositors $= 60,000$
Number of regular depositors $= 90,000$
The ratio 60,000:90,000 reduces to 2:3.

48. b. I is not true; although the number of depositors remained the same, one may not assume that interest rates were the cause. II is true; in 1984 there were 110,000 depositors. Observe the largest angle of inclination for this period. III is not true; the circle graph indicates that more than half of the bank's assets went into mortgages.

49. c. (58.6%) of $360° = (0.586)(360°) = 210.9°$

50. e. $(\text{Amount invested}) \times (\text{Rate of interest}) = \text{Interest}$

or

$$\text{Amount invested} = \frac{\text{Interest}}{\text{Rate of interest}}$$

$$\text{Amount invested in bonds} = \frac{x\,\text{dollars}}{b\%} \text{ or } \frac{x\,\text{dollars}}{b\%}$$

$$\text{or } x \div \frac{b}{100} \text{ or } x\left(\frac{100}{b}\right) \text{ or } (x)\left(\frac{100}{b}\right) \text{ or } \frac{100x}{b}$$

Since the amount invested in bonds $= \frac{100x}{b}$, the amount invested in mortgages must be $2\left(\frac{100x}{b}\right)$ dollars or $\frac{200x}{b}$ since the chart indicates that twice as much (58.6%) is invested in mortgages as is invested in bonds (28.3%).

51. d. Draw altitudes of AE and BF.

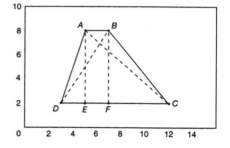

$$\triangle AED + \triangle BFC + \square AEFB$$

$$\text{Area of } \triangle AED = \frac{BH}{2} = \frac{(2)(6)}{2} = 6 \text{ square units}$$

$$\text{Area of figure} = \text{Area of } \triangle BCF = \frac{(6)(6)}{2} =$$

$$\text{Area of } \square AEFB = lw = (2)(6) = 12 \text{ square units}$$

$$\text{Sum} = 36 \text{ square units}$$

52. d. Factor $x^2 + 2x - 8$ into $(x + 4)(x - 2)$. If x is either -4 or 2, then $x^2 + 2x - 8 = 0$.

53. a. Set up a proportion. Let $x =$ the total body weight in terms of g.

$$\frac{\text{weight of skeleton}}{\text{total body weight}} = \frac{10,000 \text{ grams}}{70,000 \text{ grams}} = \frac{g}{x}$$

$$\frac{1}{7} = \frac{g}{x}$$

$$x = 7g$$

54. b. Between 1 P.M. and 3:52 P.M., there are 172 minutes. There are three intervals between the classes. Therefore, 3×4 minutes, or 12 minutes, is the time spent in passing to classes. That leaves a total of $172 - 12$, or 160, minutes for instruction, or 40 minutes for each class period.

55. e. (Average)(Number of items) = sum

$$(x)(P) = Px$$
$$(y)(N) = Ny$$

$$\frac{\text{Sum}}{\text{Number of items}} = \text{Average}$$

$$\frac{Px + Ny}{P + N} = \text{Average}$$

56. b. Select the choice in which the value of n is greater than the value of d in order to yield a value of $\frac{n}{d}$ greater than 1.

57. a. $m\angle c + m\angle d = 180°$ but $m\angle c \neq m\angle d$.

$m\angle a = m\angle d$ (vertical angles)

$m\angle a = m\angle e$ (corresponding angles)

$m\angle f = m\angle b$ (corresponding angles)

$m\angle f = m\angle c$ (alternate interior angles)

58. b. Sum = (0.6)(4) or 2.4

$0.2 + 0.8 + 1 = 2$

$x = 2.4 - 2$ or 0.4

59. a. $\frac{a^2 - b^2}{(a - b)} = \frac{a + b(a - b)}{(a + b)(a - b)} = \frac{a + b}{a + b}$

60. d. Area of square $EFGH$ = 36 square feet and area of rectangle $ABCD$ = 36 square feet. Since $AD = 4$, then $DC = 9$ feet. The perimeter of $ABCD$ is $4 + 9 + 4 + 9 = 26$ feet.

61. c. 500 grams of carbohydrates = 2,050 calories

100 grams of carbohydrates = 410 calories

1 gram of carbohydrates = 4.1 calories

62. a. Total calories = 3,390

Calories from protein = 410

$\frac{410}{3,390} = \frac{41}{339} = 12\%$

63. b. Boys at 17 require 3,750 calories per day.

Girls at 17 require 2,750 calories per day.

Difference = $3,750 - 2,750 = 1,000$.

64. d. I is true; observe the regular increase for both sexes up to age 11. II is not true; from age 4 to 12, calorie requirements are generally similar for boys and girls. Note that the broken line and the solid line are almost parallel. III is true; boys reach their peak at 17, while girls reach their peak at 13.

65. c. 100 grams of fat = 930 calories

1,000 grams of fat = 9,300 calories

To obtain 9,300 calories from carbohydrates, set up a proportion, letting x = number of grams of carbohydrates needed.

$$\frac{500 \text{ grams}}{2{,}050 \text{ calories}} = \frac{x}{9{,}300 \text{ calories}}$$

$$2{,}050x = (9{,}300)(500)$$

$$x = 2{,}268 \text{ (to the nearest gram)}$$

66. d. Since the formula for the area of a circle is πr^2, any change in r will affect the area by the square of the amount of the change. Since the radius is doubled, the area will be four times as much $(2)^2$.

67. c. Since $OC = BC$ and OC and OB are radii, triangle BOC is equilateral and the measure of angle BOC = 60°. Therefore, $x = 120$ and $\frac{1}{2}x = 60$.

68. c. Let x = the number and multiply both sides by 6 to eliminate the fractions.

$$\frac{x}{2} = \frac{x}{3} + 17$$

$$3x = 2x + 102$$

$$x = 102$$

69. b.   Let x = amount Ed had.

Let y = amount Patricia had.

$x + \$10$ = amount Ed now has.

$y - \$10$ = amount Patricia now has.

$$\frac{x + \$10}{5} + \$4 = y - 10$$

$$x + \$10 + \$20 = 5y - \$50$$

$$x - 5y = -\$80$$

$$x - y = \$100$$

$$-x - y = -100 \text{ (multiply by } -1)$$

$$x - 5y = -\$80$$

$$-6y = -180 \text{ (subtraction)}$$

$$y = \$30 \text{ (amount Patricia had)}$$

$$\$30 - \$10 = \$20 \text{ (amount Patricia now has)}$$

70. c. This is a ratio problem.

$$\frac{\text{number of items}}{\text{cost in cents}} = \frac{2}{c} = \frac{?}{x}$$

$$c(?) = 2x$$

$$(?) = \frac{2x}{c}$$

71. c. Four cows produce 1 can of milk in 1 day. Therefore, eight cows could produce 2 cans of milk in 1 day. In 4 days, eight cows will be able to produce 8 cans of milk.

72. a. Visualize the situation. The *amount* of pure alcohol remains the same after the dilution with water.

73. e. Note that the question gives information about the transfer of teachers, but asks about the remaining teachers. If there are 20 teachers that are transferred, then there are 60 teachers remaining.

$$\frac{60}{80} = \frac{3}{4} = 75\%$$

74. e. 152 pounds and 4 ounces = 152.25 pounds. $152.25 \div 3 = 50.75$ pounds. Therefore, 0.75 pounds = 12 ounces.

75. e. Let x = number of contestants.

$$0.05x = 30$$
$$5x = 3,000$$
$$x = 600$$

76. d. Since the driver's fee is paid with the car, the charge for $n - 1$ person = $c(n - 1)$ cents; cost of car and driver = 50 cents. Therefore, $T = 50 + c(n - 1)$.

77. c. This is a direct proportion.

$$\frac{\text{cups of sugar}}{\text{cups of water}} = \frac{1.5}{0.5} = \frac{1}{x}$$

$$1.5x = 0.5$$
$$15x = 5$$
$$x = \frac{1}{3}$$

78. b. If 1 kg = 2.2 lb, then 20 kg = 44 lb ($2.2 \times 20 = 44$).

79. a. I is not correct because $\frac{1}{a}$ is not less than a if a is 1 or a fraction less than 1. II is correct because $\frac{a + b}{2a} = \frac{2b}{b + a}$ reduces to $\frac{2b}{2b} = \frac{2b}{2b}$ when $a = b$. III is incorrect when a is greater than b or when c is negative and a is less than b. Therefore, II is the only correct answer.

80. ~~a.~~ d. $bx - 2 = k$

$$\underline{+2 \quad +2}$$

$$bx = k + 2$$

$$\frac{bx}{b} = \frac{k + 2}{b}$$

$$x = \frac{k + 2}{b}$$

Appendix: Additional Resources

This book has given you a good start on studying for the GRE test. However, one book is seldom enough—it is best to be equipped with several resources, from general to specific.

▶ GRE General Test

Bader, William and Thomas H. Martinson. *Master the GRE CAT.* (Princeton, NJ: Peterson's, 2001).

Bobrow, Jerry. *Cliff's TestPrep GRE General Test.* (New York: Hungry Minds, 2002).

GRE: Practicing to Take the General Test. (Princeton, NJ: Educational Testing Service, 2000).

Kaplan. *Kaplan GRE 2003 with CD-ROM.* (New York: Kaplan, 2002).

Lurie, Karen, Magda Pecsenye, and Adam Robinson. *Cracking the GRE, 2003 Edition.* (New York: Random House, 2002).

Orton, Peter Z., and Rajiv Rimal. *30 Days to the GRE CAT: Teacher-Tested Strategies for Scoring High.* (New York: ARCO, 2002).

Vlk, Suzee. *The GRE Test for Dummies, 5th Edition.* (New York: Wiley, 2002).

▶ GRE Verbal Test

Cornog, Mary Wood. *Merriam-Webster's Vocabulary Builder.* (New York: Merriam Webster Mass Market, 1999).

Kaplan. *Kaplan GRE Exam Verbal Workbook.* (New York: Kaplan, 2002).

Ogden, James. *Verbal Builder: An Excellent Review for Standardized Tests.* (Piscataway, NJ: REA, 1998).

Rosenstein, Amy, David Stuart, and Stanley H. Kaplan Educational Center. *GRE Exam Verbal Workbook.* (New York: Kaplan, 1999).

LearningExpress. *Vocabulary and Spelling Success in 20 Minutes a Day, 3rd edition.* (New York: LearningExpress, 2002).

Wu, Yung Yee. *GRE Verbal Workout.* (Princeton, NJ: Princeton Review, 1997).

▶ GRE Analytical Writing Test

Biggs, Emily D. and Jean Eggenschwiler. *Cliffs Quick Review*[TM] *Writing : Grammar, Usage, and Style.* (New York: Wiley, 2001).

Barrass, Robert. *Students Must Write: A Guide to Better Writing in Coursework and Examinations.* (New York: Routledge, 2003).

Flesch, Rudolph, and A.H. Lass. *The Classic Guide to Better Writing.* (New York: HarperCollins, 1996).

Kaplan. *Writing Power.* (New York: Kaplan, 2003).

Petersons. *Writing Skills for the GRE and GMAT Tests.* (Princeton, NJ: Petersons, 2002).

▶ GRE Quantitative Test

Petersons. *Peterson's Math Review for the GRE, GMAT, and MCAT.* (Princeton, NJ: Peterson's, 2000).

Kaplan. *Math Power: Score higher on the SAT, GRE, and Other Standardized Tests.* (New York: Kaplan, 2003).

Stuart, David. *GRE and GMAT Exams: Math Workbook.* (New York: Kaplan, 2002).

Lighthouse Review. *The Ultimate Math Refresher for the GRE, GMAT, and SAT.* (Austin, TX: Lighthouse Review, Inc., 1999).

▶ Test-Taking and Study Skills

Barkin, Carol, Carol James, and Elizabeth James. *How to be School Smart: Super Study Skills.* (New York: Beech Tree Books, 1998).

Gilbert, Sara D. *How to Do Your Best on Tests.* (New York: Beech Tree Books, 1998).

Luckie, William R., and Wood Smethurst. *Study Power: Study Skills to Improve Your Learning and Your Grades.* (Newton Upper Falls, MA: Brookline Books, 1997).

Meyers, Judith. *The Secrets of Taking Any Test, 2nd edition.* (New York: LearningExpress, 2000).

Rozakis, Laurie. *Super Study Skills.* (New York: Scholastic, 2002).

Alexander-Travis, Pauline. *The Very Best Coaching and Study Course for the New GRE.* (Piscataway, NJ: REA, 2002).

Wood, Gail. *How to Study, 2nd edition.* (New York: LearningExpress, 2000).

▶ Helpful Websites

www.GRE.org—The official GRE test site. Information on test dates, registration, content, and practice questions from the official test.

www.ets.org—The official site of the Educational Testing Service, the organization that administers the GRE test.

www.syvum.com/gre—Free practice exercises for the quantitative and verbal sections. Includes answer explanations, hints, and vocabulary lists.

www.number2.com—Free companion tutorial and vocabulary builder for the GRE verbal section.

http://www.west.net/~stewart/gre—Free practice questions with detailed answer explanations. Also offers test-taking tips and strategies.